ISSUES IN WAR AND PEACE

Philosophical Inquiries

Edited by

Joseph C. Kunkel

and

Kenneth H. Klein

Longwood Academic
Wolfeboro, New Hampshire

© 1989 Joseph Charles Kunkel and Kenneth Henry Klein

All rights reserved—no part of this book may be reproduced in any form without permission in writing from the publisher, except by a reviewer who wishes to quote brief passages in connection with a review in a magazine or newspaper.

Published in 1989 by Longwood Academic, a division of Longwood Publishing Group, Inc., Wolfeboro, N.H., 03894-2069, U.S.A.

ISBN: 0-89341-561-8 (cloth)
       0-89341-566-9 (paper)

Library of Congress Cataloging in Publication Data:

Issues in war and peace : philosophical inquiries / edited by Joseph Kunkel and Kenneth Klein.

    p.   cm.

    Bibliography: p.

    ISBN 0-89341-561-8   ISBN 0-89341-566-9 (pbk.)

    1. Nuclear warfare--Moral and ethical aspects. I. Kunkel, Joseph, 1936- . II. Klein, Kenneth, 1930-.

U263.I79   1989

172'.422--dc20

          89-32578
          CIP

Dedicated to

Stephen Anderson and David Weinberger

Cofounders of
Concerned Philosophers for Peace

ACKNOWLEDGMENTS

The editors wish to thank the Department of Philosophy and the Rector's Council at the University of Dayton for contributing the funds for inviting Concerned Philosophers for Peace to their first national conference, held at the Bergamo Center in October 1987.

Prior to publication we received the generous cooperation of each of the authors. Valparaiso University provided computer facilities which considerably eased the production of the manuscripts. The Department of Philosophy at the University of Dayton provided travel funds for two trips that allowed the editors to collaborate at timely intervals. In addition, we were aided by the skilled editorial assistance of Marcia Wroblewski of Valparaiso University and Linda McKinley of the University of Dayton. Wyatt Benner of Longwood Publishing Group contributed his many talents to all phases of text preparation. We especially thank our wives, who accepted our absences and steadied our efforts in this project.

Finally, we wish to thank the publishers mentioned below for their gracious permission to publish the following materials contained in this book:

W.W. Norton & Co. for permission to reprint the quotations from Robert Kennedy's *Thirteen Days* contained in John Somerville's paper. Reprinted from *Thirteen Days: A Memoir of the Cuban Missile Crisis*, by Robert F. Kennedy, by permission of W.W. Norton & Company, Inc., Copyright © 1971, 1969 by W.W. Norton & Co., Inc. Copyright © 1968 by McCall Corporation.

Harvard University Press for permission to reprint the quotations from Edward Wilson's *On Human Nature* contained in Jonathan Schonsheck's paper.

Farrar, Straus & Giroux, Inc. for permission to reprint the quotations from Peter Singer's *The Expanding Circle: Ethics and Sociobiology* contained in Jonathan Schonsheck's paper. Excerpts from *The Expanding Circle, Ethics and Sociology* by Peter Singer. Copyright © 1981 by Peter Singer. Reprinted by permission of Farrar, Straus and Giroux, Inc.

The Edwin Mellen Press for permission to reprint portions of Jonathan Schonsheck's article "Constraints on *The Expanding Circle:* A Critique of Singer," in *Inquiry into Values: The Inaugural Session of the International Society for Value Inquiry* (The Edwin Mellen Press, 1988).

The Monist for permission to print a shorter version of Richard Werner's "Nuclear Deterrence and the Limits of Moral Theory." Copyright © 1987, *The Monist*, LaSalle, IL., 61301. Reprinted by permission.

Public Affairs Quarterly, Nicholas Rescher, editor, for permission to print a later version of James Sterba's "Legitimate Defense and Strategic Defense," *Public Affairs Quarterly* 2.4 (1988).

Temple University Press for permission to publish Duane Cady's article, "Exposing Warism," a larger version of which appears in his book, *From Warism to Pacifism: A Moral Continuum* (Temple University Press, 1989). Copyright © by Temple University. Reprinted by permission of Temple University Press.

Dialectics and Humanism, Janusz Kuczynski, editor, for permission to reprint John Howie's "Our War Problem and the Peacemaker Attitude," *Dialectics and Humanism* 13.4 (1986).

JCK & KHK

CONTENTS

Dedication   v
Acknowledgments   vii
What Does Philosophy Add to Nuclear Discussions? An
 Introductory Essay—*Joseph Kunkel and Kenneth Klein*......1

I. Examining the Ideologies of the United States and
    the Soviet Union................................11
   Foreword to Section I............................13
   1. War, Omnicide, and Sanity: The Lesson of the
       Cuban Missile Crisis—*John Somerville*........... 21
   2. Understanding the Cuban Missile Crisis: A
       Dialectical Approach—*Ron Hirschbein*............ 35
   3. Marxism and Nuclear Deterrence—*George
       Hampsch*..................................... 49
   4. On the Implications of Sociobiology for Nuclear
       Weapons Policy—*Jonathan Schonsheck*........... 55
   5. The Arms-Race Implications of Libertarian
       Capitalism—*Joseph Kunkel*.................... 69
   6. If Peace Were at Hand, How Would We Know
       It?—*Ernest Partridge*........................ 83

II. Evaluating Justifications for Preparing for Nuclear
     War.. 95
   Foreword to Section II............................97
   7. Skepticism and International Affairs: Toward a
       New Realism—*Leo Groarke*....................103
   8. Terrorism and Violence: A Moral Perspective
       —*Robert Holmes*.............................115
   9. Nuclear Deterrence and the Limits of Moral
       Theory—*Richard Werner*......................129
   10. Conservative and Radical Critiques of Nuclear
       Policy—*Robert Litke*.........................139
   11. Legitimate Defense and Strategic Defense
       —*James Sterba*..............................147
   12. The Man in the Teflon Suit: A Flaw in the
       Argument for Strategic Defense—*David
       Hoekema*.....................................159

III. Criticizing Modern War and Promoting Peace.........171
    Foreword to Section III.........................173
   13. Experiencing the Death of Humanity—*Robert*
      Ginsberg 179
   14. From Nuclear Winter to Hiroshima: Nuclear
      Weapons and the Environment—*William Gay*......189
   15. Exposing Warism—*Duane L. Cady*.............207
   16. Our War Problem and the Peacemaker
      Attitude—*John Howie*.........................217
   17. Nuclearism and Sexism: Overcoming Their
      Shared Metaphysical Basis—*Paula Smithka*.......229
   18. Democracy and the Threat of Nuclear
      Weapons—*R. Paul Churchill*...................255
   19. On Stories, Peacemaking, and Philosophical
      Method: Toward a Pluralistic Account of
      Non-Violence—*Laurence Bove*.................267

General Bibliography on Cited and Selected Works........279

Philosophical Bibliography on War and Peace in the
   Nuclear Age—*William Gay*.......................299

Index 319

What Does Philosophy Add to Nuclear Discussions?
An Introductory Essay

Joseph Kunkel and Kenneth Klein

Discussions on nuclear topics are of increasing public interest. News interviews, talk shows, and an avalanche of books and articles are featuring comments and presentations from a host of personalities. Philosophy too has focused on this area. A recent survey, for instance, shows that fifty percent of the philosophy articles on nuclear topics written between 1940 and 1985 appeared in the first half of the 1980s. But why philosophy? Does philosophy have anything to contribute that has not already been said by political commentators, peace activists, historians, and weapons experts?

One area that stands out as the domain of philosophy relevant for contemporary nuclear debate is ethics and values. In spite of President Reagan's famous or infamous statement about the "evil empire" in the Soviet Union, public discussion veers away from what makes one's nation good or evil in a nuclear age. Religious leaders, who also contribute to the moral climate of nations, appear more at home discussing sexual matters, doctrinal disparities, and totalitarian dangers of communism than social justice and nuclear ethics. A major exception, of course, was 1983, when the American Catholic Bishops made the cover of *Time Magazine* for their forthright pastoral letter on war and peace. Other denominations followed with their own statements, but the splash is over and subsequent discussions stir but a ripple in the reigning religious orthodoxies. Philosophy is capable of cutting through the multiplicity of denominational traditions to focus on ethical issues without dogmatic underpinnings.

This is not to imply that philosophy itself does not have its traditions. Although one need not be in a tradition in order to appreciate the argumentation, philosophic traditions do confine to some extent. For example, the analytic tradition that dominates the American philosophic scene is sufficiently different from Marxist philosophy that most American philosophers inadequately understand Marxist positions. In 1981, to offset this confinement and to concentrate on nuclear related issues, two young philosophers, graduates of the University of Toronto, began an organization in North America that today is known as Concerned Philosophers for Peace. This organization publishes a semiannual newsletter, contributes to various national and international symposia, and has grown to 450 members. In October 1987, Concerned Philosophers for Peace met in Dayton, Ohio, for its first national conference. The papers in this volume were read and debated at that conference.

What is philosophy? As this volume attests, philosophy is more than an examination of values. Philosophy has three major functions, each of which bears upon nuclear issues. The three functions are the critical, the synthetic, and the moral. The critical function was first seen in the person of Socrates. Indeed, Socrates was probably put to death for his open criticism of Athenian democracy. Part of this critical function is rooted in philosophic scepticism, which can be healthy in small doses and morbid in the extreme. On the positive side, critical thinking connotes argumentation and logic. Logic is a tool for right thinking. Not all right thinking is conspicuous for logic, but logic aids in clarifying one's thinking. Clarification of terms and evaluation of arguments is what critical philosophers do best.

Synthetic thinking is the building-block phase of philosophy. After critical thinking has swept the ground clean, synthetic thinking builds the new edifice. With synthetic thinking, philosophers take positions and project theories. Some of these theories involve specific claims; for example, that humans are free (or determined), that humans are naturally aggressive (or caring), that God exists (or does not exist), that the world is created (or evolving), that evil predominates (or can be overcome by good). Other theories are broader, more comprehensive and metaphysical, encompassing interconnected sets of specific claims. Examples of metaphysical theories are theism, humanism, existentialism, Marxism, idealism, positivism, realism, pragmatism, and libertarianism. Each comprehensive synthesis represents a dominant worldview.

Moral thinking, too, is somewhat synthetic. However, since morality reaches across diverse synthetic theories in performing such a humanly important function as evaluating human actions, morals (or ethics) stands alone as a third function of philosophy. Morals deals with human values and with various defenses that have been offered for holding them. With values as guidelines, humans evaluate their own actions and the actions of others. Values, however, are not themselves set in stone. Philosophers give different accounts of what makes something valuable, what values we should have, and how, if at all, we can rationally defend them against those who have different values. There are pluralistic approaches to values too. These methodologies are the synthetic aspects which can be critiqued, as all three functions of philosophy interweave.

Philosophy is a way of life. Each of us possesses a critical, synthetic, and ethical aspect for our thinking and personality. We may try to ignore some aspects, but ignorance, in this case, is not bliss. Ignoring these aspects allows our upbringing and our culture to control our lives. A more common response is willfully to constrict the parts of life we open up for evaluation. Within that narrow circle we evaluate and criticize freely. Beyond that circle we shut off debate and conform. One such question, normally placed outside our critical circles, is whether nuclear weapons could be used *morally*, particularly on the scale they are likely to be used, if they are used at all, in a present-day military conflict? We claim to be a moral nation, but on an issue as threatening as this, we seem by and large secure in letting the "experts" decide.

Concerned philosophers are bringing the field of nuclear weapons—this includes the political and ideological values which impel nations to accumulate nuclear weapons in their military arsenals—under the light of critical scrutiny. The greatest underlying national fear centers on the political and ideological conflict between the United States and the Soviet Union. Yet, ideologies come under synthetic thinking, and examining such thinking is part of the task of philosophy. Accordingly, philosophers are adding their voices to the international debate over such ideologies. Similar involvement occurred earlier in the nuclear period. After World War II, the two leading French existentialists, Albert Camus and Jean-Paul Sartre, split up over extending the reach of freedom and liberation. Camus and Sartre had fought together in the Resistance during the war. Afterwards, Sartre wanted to continue resisting until full liberation in a communist revolution was achieved, while Camus chose to halt the violence because killing was killing, irrespective of cause. Again, in the mid-fifties, Karl Jaspers, a German existentialist, spoke in a series of radio addresses of the horrors of the atomic bomb, but of the even greater horror of the lack of full human freedom under communism;

he opted for the former in face of the latter. Yet again, in 1958, Sidney Hook, an American pragmatist, debated Bertrand Russell, the renowned British pacifist, on whether being dead was better than being red.

Superpower ideologies continue to influence nuclear policies. Knowing the implications of these ideologies is therefore a first step in understanding nuclear reality. We shall begin with brief remarks on the Marxist ideology. Marxism claims to stand for full liberation, but is accused, by its critics, of curtailing liberty. "Liberation" and "liberty" are two terms that denote freedom. The dilemma stems from Marxism's view of liberation as coming at the end of the human evolutionary cycle: we are thus moving toward full freedom. Too much freedom early on, in the sense of license, is viewed as inhibiting the full liberation of humans. Joseph Stalin, for example, stressing the determinism of Marxist evolution, ruled the Soviet Union with an iron fist from the 1920s until his death in 1953. In the process, many think, he did more harm than good. Mikhail Gorbachev, on the other hand, with his glasnost and perestroika, stresses a developing freedom as an essential part of the liberating experience. Where the people of the Soviet Union stand will come out as the process unfolds. But surely there is nothing in Marxism that precludes Gorbachev's interpretation from becoming standard. We ought to know the possibilities as well as the pitfalls of Marxism, while observing the development. In this regard, philosophers are equipped to aid in asking the right questions.

American or Western ideology is scarcely more sanguine on the issue of freedom versus determinism as related to political liberation. Our roots can be traced to the seventeenth-century thinker Thomas Hobbes. Hobbes, like Marx, is a determinist, but, unlike Marx, who stresses human evolution as a species, centers on the self-interested individual. Being on an equal footing with one another, individuals are naturally in conflict over self-interests. Moreover, unless there is some rational hope for genuine peaceful relations, Hobbes counsels preparations for war. What is true of individuals is also true for self-seeking nations. The devastating part of the doctrine comes in the form of Hobbes's view that in wartime there is no morality and no injustice. Thus, for Hobbes, "anything goes" in wartime.

A modification of Hobbes is found in those who subscribe to freedom over determinism. The freedom, however, is the individual

4

freedom or liberty, which is opposed to liberation developed by a class or nation. Hence, whereas Marxism favors liberation over liberty, Western libertarianism favors liberty over liberation. Libertarians follow Hobbes in supporting self-interest and in preparing for war in self-defense of their own views. The battle lines that are drawn are thus deeply embedded in conflicting ideologies.

The first section of this anthology explores these superpower ideologies. We begin with the Cuban Missile Crisis of 1962. A number of times since 1945, leaders have seriously considered using nuclear weapons, but the Cuban Missile Crisis was the most grave and the most clearly documented. As such, this event serves as an ever-present reminder of what is at stake when the ideologies are supported by large nuclear arsenals. Two interpretations (by Somerville and Hirschbein) of the Cuban Missile Crisis are given. These are followed by three in-depth discussions of the ideologies as they impinge on the nuclear questions. The first (by Hampsch) inquires into the consistency of Marxists advocating wars of liberation while downplaying the nuclear gamble. The second (by Schonsheck) maintains that group or nation cohesion can only be maintained by violence, including perhaps nuclear violence. The third (by Kunkel) shows the nuclear implications of a libertarian capitalistic doctrine that would rather fight than switch. The section concludes with an article (by Partridge) that contrasts the ideological makeup of peace overtures with empirical facts. Can we ever achieve a pragmatic peace by clinging to ideologies?

From its inception, the arms race has generated its own momentum. What could be built has been built. The atomic bomb was followed by the hydrogen bomb. The B-36, the first intercontinental nuclear bomber, was followed by the B-52, then the B-1, and, yet to come, the Stealth Bomber. Intercontinental missiles made their appearance in the late fifties, were MIRVed with multiple warheads in the seventies, and are now in the process of being made mobile. They have already been adapted to submarines with steadily improving distance, power, and accuracy. Cruise missiles have been added in multiple varieties. Smaller tactical weapons have been built for shorter battlefield distances, including sea battles. Satellites have been put up and refined for surveillance, communications, and probably, some day, for defensive capabilities.

Why do we have these weapons? What purpose do they serve?

After World War II nuclear weapons served the makeshift purpose of containing the forces of the Soviet Union. Massive numbers of nuclear weapons were not needed for such a task against what was then a nonnuclear nation. After the Soviets acquired nuclear weapons, followed by an intercontinental delivery system with missiles, the American purpose shifted to deterring Soviet usage via a capacity for massive retaliation. As the Soviets began catching up in large numbers of deliverable weapons, the nuclear purpose shifted in both nations to Mutual Assured Destruction, or "MAD." MAD meant that there had to be a large enough second-strike force in both arsenals in case either nation should strike first. The implication was that a first strike would be suicidal, albeit indirectly so, because of the opponent's residual, retaliatory, second strike. As the technology developed for the invention of smaller and intermediate weapons, and the development of more accurate intercontinental strategic weapons, MAD was theoretically supplemented with what was called a more "flexible response"—the capacity of fighting and winning smaller, "limited" nuclear wars while deterring "all-out" nuclear war. "Nuclear deterrence" can refer to any of these purposes, but surely entails the serious intent, under certain circumstances, to *use* nuclear weapons, not just to strut and deter with them.

Formulating a national or international purpose for nuclear weapons ought to include a moral evaluation of having and of using these weapons. Bringing moral constraints to bear on nuclear policies is the function of the second section of this anthology. The standard moral analysis of war usually begins with a contrast of political realism and pacifism. Political realism, the viewpoint of Hobbes, posits no morality in war, or "anything goes," while pacifism contends that war itself is immoral. The first article (by Groarke) in this section advocates political realism, but with a subjective morality substituted for no morality. The second article (by Holmes) sides with pacifism after giving terrorism as a counterexample to subjective morality. If ethics is subjective, then both the arguments for terrorism and against terrorism are equally valid.

Many philosophers have advocated moral positions intermediate to political realism and pacifism. Intermediate positions distinguish ﹔ that may be "justified" or "unjustified" according to ions. The most notable of such approaches to war are the deontological, the just war, and the consequentialist arguments. Marxism too, which we discussed under ideologies, could be construed as an inbetween method.

The deontological approach looks at intentions. The thrust is to take an intended moral rule and try, in a kind of thought experiment, to universalize the maxim. If the maxim can be universalized for all human beings, then the maxim becomes a moral duty. "Deontological" means the study of duties or *deontos*. The kind of action *threatened* by nuclear deterrence *may not even be threatened* if that action itself cannot be morally performed. The main stumbling block in approving nuclear deterrence from a deontological perspective is the potential killing of innocent human beings, such as children. Killing innocent children can not be universalized into a moral duty.

Just-war doctrine has its roots in natural law ethics and the principle of double effect. War morality seeks to condone the killing of others, the evil effect, while preserving the life of the community, the good effect. War is justified by just-war principles if there is a right intention, if there is a just cause, if innocent lives are not killed, and if there is a proportionately grave reason for so acting. The third clause entails the same concerns as those enunciated under the deontological view, and the fourth clause is sometimes interpreted in a consequentialist manner. As this doctrine, too, is normally interpreted, nuclear deterrence can only be morally *threatened* if nuclear weapons can be morally *used*.

The consequentialist viewpoint focuses on results, calculating the good and bad effects of a projected action. If the good effects outweigh the bad effects, then an action is called good. The calculus is more complicated in that alternate means of obtaining the same results must be compared in the calculation. Since this method is result oriented, nuclear deterrence may be distinguished from nuclear use. In other words, under consequentialism, *threatening* nuclear war for the result of *not engaging* in such a war could possibly be more beneficial than maleficent; hence nuclear deterrence could be justified as a strategy for avoiding a war that would be unjustified if fought.

These three types of argumentation have been discussed at length in the philosophical literature on nuclear war and deterrence. Two articles in this anthology probe deeper. The first (by Werner) shows how one's ideological commitment influences the application of these ethical approaches. The second (by Litke) contends that war justifiers argue on one level, while those opposed to war argue on another. The final two articles (by Sterba and Hoekema) in this second section apply moral principles to the Strategic Defense Initiative (SDI).

While we await a national or international consensus on an ethical purpose for nuclear weapons, treaty discussions and agreements have tended to focus on the nonessential. The Antarctic Treaty prohibits nuclear use of the South Pole; all current nuclear powers, however, are located in the Northern Hemisphere. The Seabed Treaty bans placing stationary nuclear weapons on the ocean floors, but submarines are excluded. The Partial Test Ban Treaty bans nuclear testing in the atmosphere, outer space, and underwater; yet testing goes on underground. SALT I is an interim agreement, and SALT II has never been ratified. The three most promising treaties have been the Non-Proliferation Treaty, the Anti-Ballistic Missile (ABM) Treaty, and the recently concluded INF Treaty. The Non-Proliferation Treaty does little to diminish the nuclear arsenals of the United States, the Soviet Union, Great Britain, France, and China. Rather, the emphasis is upon keeping other nations from getting nuclear weapons. While other nations have subsequently acquired the bomb, the proliferation pace has been slowed. The ABM Treaty has so far stopped a race for defensive missiles to complement offensive arsenals. The value of this treaty, however, is presently being challenged by advocates of the Strategic Defense Initiative. The INF Treaty rids Europe of all tactical U.S. and U.S.S.R. missiles with a range of 500 to 5500 kilometers. While bombs and missiles of shorter and longer ranges can hit the same targets, removing these intermediate-range missiles is a step in the right direction. Proposals have been made for more substantive treaties, such as the comprehensive test ban, START reductions, an antisatellite treaty, European nuclear-free zones, a nuclear freeze, and so on. Verification poses a problem for such treaties, but the problem is not insuperable. When there is a will, we will find a way.

We began this essay on philosophy's contributions to the nuclear debate by noting three functions of philosophy: the synthetic, the moral, and the critical. These functions serve all humanity, as well as individual human beings. As individual human beings become more adept at using these human tools, they become more open to living a truly human life. In the first section of this anthology, we stress the synthetic or ideological function as we examine Marxism, the natural violence inherent in political realism, and libertarianism. In the second section we evaluate the justifications given through various ethical methodologies for preparing for possible nuclear war. The third section, which we are presently going to describe, develops the critical function. Obviously we have been using our critical faculty all along. What makes the third section distinct, however, is that the concepts criticized pervade the reigning superpower ideologies and the war systems ethically and ideologically justified. Accordingly, these essays can be said to promote peace in a very fundamental sense.

The first essay (by Ginsberg) centers existentially on death. The question asked is whether we will face nuclear death squarely or excuse our involvement in the manner of human addicts. The second article (by Gay) examines the potential environmental damage from nuclear destruction and argues that environmental philosophers have a more restrictive, better balanced view than nuclear theorists about what is morally unacceptable damage to the environment. The third essay (by Cady) goes a step further, questioning whether the universal principle of war as justifiable is not itself the problem. An article (by Howie) follows with specific suggestions on how to implement the peacemaker approach. Then an article (by Smithka) examines how gender differences have affected the way humans have conceptualized war and peace. The penultimate essay (by Churchill) decries the loss of democracy in the nuclear decision-making process. And lastly, an article (by Bove) emphasizes narration and personal stories in a more genuine ethical decision-making process.

The papers in this anthology are all written by philosophers. We believe philosophers bring special skills and sensitivities to the analysis of nuclear issues. Their background is no less important than the expertise offered by historians, economists, military strategists, statesmen, and sociologists. In particular, philosophers are trained in evaluating ideologies, advancing moral claims, and clarifying arguments.

This anthology is seminal in its offerings. The essays can be read privately by individuals, but group discussion would be more advantageous. Hearing how others interpret the essays enhances one's own reading. At our conference in Dayton, the authors learned from one another, and hope now to share their learning with you, the reader.

9

As help in getting started, the editors have provided forewords for each of the three sections. These forewords summarize the main arguments and can be read before settling into a reading of the individual papers. Two bibliographies have been included at the end; one (by the editors) on works cited and selected, and a second (by William Gay) on philosophical sources on war and peace in the nuclear age. We have also provided an index.

Section I

Examining the Ideologies of the United States and the Soviet Union

Ideologies are devised, pursued, and transmitted by *people*. What this means for the relations between the United States and the Soviet Union is that the ideologies that inform the U.S. and the U.S.S.R. are implemented, in different times and places, by groups of human beings who hold positions of enormous political power. Hence, their actions, which are binding upon the politically powerless, are shaped by both the ideological and the human factors. The authors of the papers gathered in this section probe how the fostering of the ideologies of the superpowers by their leaders has contributed to hostility, to political insularity, and, in an age of increasingly fecund nuclear and electronic technology, to the growing nuclear peril.

John Somerville and Ron Hirschbein draw some unsettling conclusions from reflecting back upon the Cuban Missile Crisis of the '60s. In "War, Omnicide, and Sanity: The Lesson of the Cuban Missile Crisis," and "Understanding the Cuban Missile Crisis: A Dialectical Approach," both authors see cause for concern in the *motives* that shaped President Kennedy's thinking in the darkest hours of that crisis, and in the fact that Kennedy's behavior toward the Soviet Union appears to have been accepted as a political model by his successors. Kennedy's handling of the Cuban Missile Crisis, on their view, was not at all the carefully calibrated combination of accommodation, moderation, and restraint in the interests of peace that it is commonly thought to have been. It was, instead, something far more worrisome.

Hirschbein argues that Kennedy's behavior evidenced a deep conflict between contradictory impulses, impulses that pulled him in opposite directions. There was, on the one hand, a willingness to be "realistic"—modest in aspiration, pragmatic, melioristic, empirically oriented—in responding to the discovery of Soviet missile sites being constructed in Cuba. Kennedy rejected his initial impulse to attack the missile sites outright. He rejected his own pledge to the military to retaliate for the shooting down of a U-2 over Cuba. On the other hand, Kennedy seems to have endorsed a kind of secular, atomic millenarian way of thinking about history. This millenarian impulse, Hirschbein argues, would have used the newest technology available—nuclear bombs—to force one or the other of two alternatives: either bring about, in one climactic action, certain needful utopian changes in human history, or obliterate that history itself. Kennedy's ambivalent behavior, in Hirschbein's words, reflects the unresolved, sharpening contradiction between the prudent, instrumental realism, and the secular, millenarian enthusiasm that Hirschbein thinks characteristic of the American political heritage.

Somerville is distressed by Kennedy's open-eyed willingness to "risk all" on a limited American political objective. Kennedy's decision that the Soviet Union must immediately remove their missiles from Cuba—or else we would do it for them—was, in Somerville's view, unwise and reckless. No circumstance, he says, gives any government the moral right to bring its people, and possibly all people, under the shadow of nuclear destruction. "This was the first time in human history," Somerville writes, "that a group of men who possessed the physical power to end the human world deliberately took a decision which they consciously expected would have that very result . . ." In his insistence that the Soviet Union give evidence *within twenty-four hours* of its intent to remove the missiles, Kennedy's behavior, Somerville says, shows the exacerbating effect of certain human factors which when combined with his ideological commitments put us all in peril. These human factors were: intimidation, anger, wounded pride, accommodation to public pressure, a sense of urgency, and self-interest. Most worrisome of all, Somerville and Hirschbein agree, was Kennedy's resolute readiness to risk the destruction of everything he cherished if the Soviet Union did not immediately remove the missiles. Robert Kennedy's memoir shows clearly, on Somerville's reading, that John Kennedy *hoped, but did not expect,* that the Soviets would back down. What he expected, instead, was war—nuclear war—with all its horrendous consequences. "In sending the ultimatum, he and all the rest had chosen to risk ending the world and even expected it to end."

What gives cause for continued concern, according to both Somerville and Hirshbein, is that Kennedy's reckless behavior has profoundly influenced his successors. His willingness to risk nuclear war in pursuit of the goals of American ideology has become an inspiration, rather than a source of shame. A Cuban Missile Crisis syndrome, Hirshbein observes, has clouded the judgment of Kennedy's successors. The apparently successful application of the "gradual escalation policy" has convinced them that the resolute, carefully reasoned application of superior force can send adversaries into retreat. This policy guided American strategy in Indochina and continues to inform American nuclear strategy.

The ideologies of the U.S. and the U.S.S.R are themselves composites of a number of philosophical hypotheses about nature, man, government, history, the universe, and God. Some of the disparate elements involved in these contrasting ideologies include the following: theism, atheism, democracy, libertarian capitalism, economic determinism, dialectical materialism, and epistemological empiricism. The remaining papers in this section examine some of these themes.

George Hampsch suggests, in "Marxism and Nuclear Deterrence," that the policy of nuclear deterrence to which the Soviet Union is committed stands in contradiction to the Marxist understanding of the ultimate meaning of reality. Hampsch's reasoning goes as follows: (1) The effectiveness of the strategy of deterrence requires not only the intention to *threaten* to use nuclear weapons in retaliation against an enemy's use, but the resolute will to *use* them if necessary. (2) Theoretically, "total war" is less likely now than it has been in the past, since there have been technological advances in nuclear field weapons, delivery systems, missile targeting accuracy, and durability of communication channels between adversaries. Nevertheless, the hope of keeping a modern war "limited," where that war is also of sufficient magnitude to threaten the vital security interests of the major ideological blocks, is highly improbable. (3) Yet, in the total war of a World War III, no possible Marxist goals could be accomplished by an act of massive retaliation. Such an act by a socialist state would violate the conditions for its basic values being realized, and would have to be considered irrational from the viewpoint of Marxism, whatever the circumstances.

Is the moral dilemma that Hampsch points out any less of a dilemma for noncommunist countries than for communist countries? Do not our own democratic values involve us in the same moral conundrum, though on different ideological grounds? For instance, does not the U.S., too, maintain and threaten to use its nuclear weapons with the full, clear expectation that some day we may in fact use them? Yet, in light of the second-strike capacity of our adversaries, how could the military use of nuclear weapons avoid violating the very values which the United States, as well as the Soviet Union, offers as its reason for deploying such weapons? These questions ought to be kept in mind as we explore, in the following essays, two disparate aspects of Western ideology, namely, violence as natural and necessary for human cohesion, and economic freedom as devoid of any governmental control.

Before moving on to these essays, however, we want to raise one other issue. Those who endorse the American and Western European ideology commonly hold theistic beliefs forsworn by those who endorse a communist worldview. That will make a difference in the importance we attach to history, to living in this world. The deeper theological question involved here, which is implicit, too, in Hirschbein's reasoning about American millenarianism, must be asked: how does belief in God affect the thinking of those who have the power to end human history? Do Christians, Jews, and Muslims have less commitment to being good stewards of the resources necessary for life on earth than our nontheistic counterparts in communist countries? Surely not. Yet, the worry emerges: would the religious belief of our Western political leaders, which is by and large Christian, and commonly driven by certain eschatological expectations—individual survival, post-mortem punishment for wrongdoing, a paradise after death for the faithful—make us *more* reluctant or *less* reluctant to use nuclear weapons, even on a massive scale, in a big-stakes threat to the survival of our Western ideological system?

In "On the Implications of Sociobiology for Nuclear Weapons Policy," Jonathan Schonsheck contends that some form of deterrence is the optimal nuclear weapons policy. He supports this claim, on the one hand, by what he takes to be certain unavoidable technological and strategic limitations connected with nuclear warfighting and, on the other hand, by appeal to a sociobiological hypothesis about the disposition of human beings toward one another.

On the former point, too much would have to go right with limited nuclear warfighting, he claims, for nuclear conflict, once initiated, to remain limited. And no instantiation of the Strategic Defense Initiative, he believes, will ever prove sufficiently reliable rationally to shift the United States from a policy of preclusion (deterrence) to a policy of interception (defense). Accordingly, he concludes that, on technological and strategic grounds alone, there is no superior alternative to nuclear deterrence as a nuclear weapons policy.

On the latter point, Schonsheck's views are rooted in a particular theory of human nature and evolution. The geopolitical scene, he claims, *irremediably* consists of mutually suspicious and hostile groups, and this fact can best be explained sociobiologically. Drawing upon the work of Shaw and Wong, and Wilson, Schonsheck argues that group selection pressures dispose human beings not only to in-group amity, but also to out-group enmity. Intergroup conflict/warfare, the argument continues, has been positively functional in humanity's evolution; hence, an important factor in unifying and energizing human loyalty groups is opposition to other loyalty groups. Accordingly, Schonsheck contends that mutually suspicious and antagonistic loyalty groups, incarnated as nation-states and alliances of nation-states, are, and are likely to be, a permanent feature of the geopolitical landscape. The conclusion he draws is that neither unilateral disarmament nor mutual disarmament will be viable nuclear-weapons options for national loyalty groups.

Anticipating the rejoinder that human beings are at least capable of forming an amity-seeking global loyalty group, Schonsheck thinks that, though theoretically possible, this will not in fact ever happen. In opposition to Peter Singer, Schonsheck argues that membership in loyalty groups is too fluid and transient to justify Singer's sanguine judgment that the power of ethical reasoning may eventually induce individuals to "expand the circle" that encloses the members of their own moral community. There is no evidence, Schonsheck claims, to support even a serious hope that disparate ethnic and national groups will coalesce into a single moral community. Hence, he concludes, political leaders will not propose—nor would citizens tolerate it if they did—a perceived relative reduction in military strength of one's loyalty group. So long as nuclear weapons are conceived as augmenting the strength of a nation, neither unilateral nor mutual nuclear disarmament will be viable options. Hence, some species of nuclear deterrence will always be the optimal nuclear weapons policy.

In "The Arms-Race Implications of Libertarian Capitalism", Joseph Kunkel probes the implications of libertarian capitalism, 1) for the problem of world hunger; 2) for world governance—the endeavor to bring peoples of diverse ideologies into structures which permit them mutually to inhabit the earth; and 3) for the nuclear arms race. Drawing upon the work of three of its defenders—Robert Nozick, Ayn Rand, and Milton Friedman—Kunkel isolates the main tenets of libertarian capitalism as espoused by these thinkers and isolates several injurious implications which the view they hold in common has for the three areas mentioned.

The principles fundamental to libertarian capitalism, according to Kunkel, are 1) a separation of governance from the economy, with the market place deciding all economic issues, and 2) a role for government restricted to not interfering with citizen activity except to prevent harm or to rectify unjust economic gains. With respect to world governance, Kunkel argues that the libertarian framework of Nozick is ideologically biased. Nozick insists that the world governance be along libertarian lines in order to preserve freedom and to prevent any one ideology-based community from exerting interference with or domination over other such communities. However, in so stipulating a libertarian framework, Nozick is ensuring the domination in world governance of that ideology over, for example, a socialist perspective. With respect to the problem of nuclear weapons, Kunkel argues, against Nozick, that insofar as states are conceived as essentially group mutual-protection agencies, building up such states, through competition, will lead naturally to the proliferation of nuclear weapons.

Against Rand he argues that it is both tendentious and naive for her to place the blame for war exclusively on "statism," as though two different kinds of human beings are involved in doing business and in governing. It is not accidental to libertarian theory that although libertarians claim that they do not want government interference in the economy, they are forced, by their strong commitment to self-defense against communist statism, to accept government's interference in an economy dominated by huge defense budgets. Most worrisome, Kunkel argues, is that libertarian capitalism, in its rejection of government aid, in its ready recourse to *defense* in a world that is divided over ideology and devoid of global governance, and in its conception of governments as group protective agencies, will aid economies preponderantly through military means. Kunkel calls the latter a "guns-instead-of-butter approach to international relations." Thus, while saying they are for peace, libertarians are really preparing for war.

A problem of a different sort is uncovered by Ernest Partridge in his "If Peace Were at Hand, How Would We Know It?" What would it take to convince us, he asks, that our claims about those on "the other side" are false? Partridge suggests that we might apply a "falsification rule" to our ideologies in order to expose what might turn out to be mere political prejudices that we hold about our adversaries. In other words, if an ideology is never subject to falsification, how can anyone know that that ideology is true?

The point Partridge is making, if he is correct, would apply to those on both sides of ideological fences. Those convinced, for example, that the Soviet Union is the "evil empire," or that "it's all propaganda" (i.e., whatever comes from the Soviets that looks irenic) or that, with respect to atomic testing, the Soviets "are cheating," might ask themselves this question: what might the General Secretary do, consistent with keeping his office, that would convince us that the Soviet Union is significantly less of a threat to world peace and freedom than we have supposed, and thus worthy of a renewed attempt at disarmament, accommodation, and friendship? Partridge argues that the policies and rhetoric of recent U.S. administrations—the Reagan administration, for example—may have been dominated, at least sometimes, by *a priori* doctrinal beliefs about the Soviet Union which are detached from any conceivable disconfirming data. If the falsifiability question were candidly addressed by hard-line conservatives, Partridge suggests, they might find that what they require of the Soviets is inconsistent with the national pride and practical politics of the Soviet Union, its leaders and people, and thus practically impossible to attain. And the same conclusion would emerge, of course, if the question were asked, in reverse, by the Soviets about the United States.

If we are to give peace a chance, he argues, our political policies and their supporting ideologies must be alertly responsive to changes in relations among the great powers, falsifiable by empirical data and scientific fact, and sensitive to the effects of closed-mindedness that may arise from our commitment to our ideologies. Otherwise, we may not recognize real opportunities for peace and we may wind up, instead, vainly chasing peace through expensive and eventually unworkable technological fixes. By not seeing past our own political ideologies, or by looking for impossible changes, we close off real opportunities for significant accommodation among the great powers.

John Somerville

Dean Rusk, as Secretary of State during the Cuban Missile Crisis of
1962, was of course one of President Kennedy's top advisers, though
not the chief one. That role seems to have been played by the
President's brother Robert, then United States Attorney General, who
appears to have shared his every thought. It was Robert Kennedy who
was selected by the President to negotiate with Dobrynin, the Soviet
Ambassador, and to deliver the final decisive ultimatum to the Soviets.
Fortunately, Robert wrote a detailed account of how every decision
was made in the crisis, and he certainly had no motive to make anything
look worse than it actually was. He was in the middle of it, and he told
the whole ghastly truth about it. He evidently felt he owed this to future
generations, and that feeling must have been mixed with anguish, for
he could not bring himself to publish his memoir while he was alive.
This was done by Ted Sorensen, Presidential Counsel and friend of the
Kennedys, who was also in the group of top advisers. The first printing
of the memoir, *Thirteen Days,* had the entirely accurate subtitle, "How
the World Almost Ended."[1]

The painful, almost unbelievable facts revealed by Robert Kennedy
show clearly that the secret Mr. Rusk is now sharing with the world, a
secret which he terms a "post- script" to the crisis, is essentially wishful
thinking, a grasping at mere straws in an understandable but vain
attempt to establish a moral justification for the decisions our side
actually made. Since this secret, if it had really had any operative
significance in the crisis, would have put things in a better moral light
for us, it is hard to understand why Mr. Rusk did not make it public
long ago. In any case it is a strangely convoluted secret.

Mr. Rusk chose to divulge it in a letter to a conference of experts on
the Cuban Missile Crisis. He did so in these words, as quoted by *The.
New York Times:*

> President Kennedy instructed me to telephone the late Andrew Cordier
> (a former U.N. official), then at Columbia University, and dictate to

him a statement which would be made by U Thant, the Secretary General of the United Nations, proposing the removal both of the Jupiters (U.S. missiles in Turkey) and the (Soviet) missiles in Cuba. Mr. Cordier was to put that statement in the hands of U Thant only after a further signal from us. That step was never taken and the statement I furnished to Mr. Cordier has never seen the light of day. So far as I know, President Kennedy, Andrew Cordier, and I are the only ones who knew of this particular step.[2]

Mr. Rusk adds, "It was clear to me that President Kennedy would not let the Jupiters in Turkey become an obstacle to the removal of the missile sites in Cuba because the Jupiters were coming out in any event."[3] *The Times* quotes Mr. Rusk further as saying that the statement given to Cordier "was simply an option that would have been available to President Kennedy had he wanted to use it."[4]

It is self-evident that all this intricate, covert maneuvering has to do only with the manner in which the peaceful option of a reciprocal removal of missile bases would have been accepted by our side if, as Mr. Rusk himself emphasizes, President Kennedy could still decide to use it, and really wanted to use it. The only significance it has is procedural, not substantive. It simply would have created the appearance that the President was accepting the peaceful option not because it had been proposed by the Soviets but because it had been proposed by the United Nations. Mr. Rusk offered no evidence at all that President Kennedy in his actual decisions kept that option open and available. However, the media have widely interpreted the secret to mean that President Kennedy did keep the option open and available in such a way that, whenever he became convinced that any other course of action would lead to war, he would indeed accept the peaceful and reciprocal removal of missile bases. If Mr. Rusk agrees with that interpretation, then he is really contending that everything Robert Kennedy said about this utterly central point in his memoir was wrong. I doubt he would want to do that, but I must admit that my own correspondence with Mr. Rusk might suggest such a possibility.

In 1976 I wrote my docu-drama about the Cuban missile problem, *The Crisis: True Story About How the World Almost Ended*, which was directly based on Robert Kennedy's memoir.[5] In the process I typed a letter to Mr. Rusk asking him about this central question. I pointed out that Robert Kennedy in his memoir was emphasizing that the final decision of the President and his advisers was to send the military ultimatum to the Soviets, threatening them with war if they did not remove their missiles from Cuba immediately and unilaterally. I also stated Robert Kennedy was emphasizing that the President did not expect the Soviets to obey the ultimatum, and did expect the war to follow, acknowledging at the same time that such a war would end mankind. My question was, how could all that be justified? Mr. Rusk replied only with the general statement that not all of those involved shared Robert Kennedy's views. In any case, let us turn to what Robert Kennedy specifically reported.

Recounting his conversation as he delivered the American ultimatum to the Soviets, Robert Kennedy reports that he said to the Soviet Ambassador:

> We had to have a commitment by tomorrow that these bases would be removed. I was not giving him an ultimatum but a statement of fact. He should understand that if they did not remove those bases we would remove them. President Kennedy had great respect for the Ambassador's country and the courage of its people. Perhaps his country might feel it necessary to take retaliatory action, but before that was over there would be not only dead Americans but dead Russians as well. . . . He raised the question of our removing the missiles from Turkey. I told him there could be no quid pro quo or any arrangement made under this kind of threat or pressure. . . . Time was running out. We had only a few more hours—we needed an answer immediately from the Soviet side. I said we must have it the next day.

> I returned to the White House. The President was not optimistic, nor was I. He ordered twenty-four troop carrier squadrons of the Air Force Reserve to active duty. They would be necessary for an invasion. He had not abandoned hope, but what hope there was now rested with Khrushchev's revising his course within the next few hours. It was a hope, not an expectation. The expectation was a military confrontation by Tuesday and possibly tomorrow. . . .[6]

If Robert Kennedy is right that all this was said, done and expected, it is clear that President Kennedy had already completely cancelled out any possibility of using the peaceful trade-off alternative specified in the secret statement now brought forth by Mr. Rusk. The President and his advisers not only deliberately chose the military ultimatum but expected the war and its inevitable consequences.

Most important of all from the moral standpoint are the consequences that were anticipated from this expected war. Robert Kennedy states them in a sentence that must certainly be the most poignant ever to appear in a government memoir. Speaking of the President, he writes:

> The thought that disturbed him the most, and that made the prospect of war much more fearful than it would otherwise have been, was the specter of the death of the children of this country and all the world--the young people who had no role, who had no say, who knew nothing even of the confrontation, but whose lives would be snuffed out like everyone else's.[7]

Nothing less than that was expected—the annihilation of the whole human race. That was what weighed so heavily on Robert Kennedy's conscience.

This was the first time in human history that a group of men who possessed the physical power to end the human world deliberately took a decision which they consciously expected would have that very result. Robert Kennedy acknowledged the enormity of what was thus involved at the very outset of his memoir where he says,

> This was the beginning of the Cuban Missile Crisis—a confrontation between the two giant atomic nations, the U.S. and the U.S.S.R., which brought the world to the abyss of nuclear destruction and the end of mankind.[8]

That the world did not end on that occasion is, in view of the facts, something for which our side can hardly claim any moral or physical credit. It was a surprise to us, as Mr. Rusk concedes, but he still wants to take the credit for it.

At the conclusion of Robert Kennedy's memoir, his friend Theodore Sorensen, who put it into print, appends the following "Note" that all of us ought to ponder.

> It was Senator Kennedy's intention to add a discussion of the basic ethical questions involved: what, if any, circumstance or justification gives this government or any government the moral right to bring its people and possibly all people under the shadow of nuclear destruction? He wrote this book in the summer and fall of 1967 on the basis of his personal diaries and recollections, but never had an

opportunity to rewrite or complete it.[9]

Robert Kennedy agonized over that question, but, not surprisingly, did not find an answer, and was honest enough not to pretend there was any sane answer.

The question that also necessarily arises in this particular case is, why did our decision makers feel compelled to reject the peaceful alternative of reciprocal removal of the respective missile bases? For it was acknowledged that under international law the U.S.S.R. had as much right to accept Cuba's invitation to put missile bases in Cuba as we had to accept Turkey's invitation to put missile bases in Turkey, which is even closer to the U.S.S.R. than Cuba is to us. In fact, this seemed so obvious to Adlai Stevenson, our Ambassador to the U.N. at the time, who was also a member of the President's "Ex Comm" (the group of top advisers: Executive Committee of the National Security Council), that he persistently argued for that settlement, maintaining also that it would not materially affect the balance of power between our country and the U.S.S.R.

However, there was little or no support given this view for reasons brought out by Kennedy. Kennedy reports what happened when Ambassador Stevenson

.... strongly advocated. ... that we make it clear to the Soviet Union that if it withdrew its missiles from Cuba, we would be willing to withdraw our missiles from Turkey and Italy, and give up our naval base at Guantanamo Bay.

There was an extremely strong reaction from some of the participants to his suggestion, and several sharp exchanges followed. The President, although he rejected Stevenson's suggestion, pointed out that he had for a long period held reservations about the value of Jupiter missiles in Turkey and Italy, and some time ago had asked the State Department to conduct negotiations for their removal, but now, he said, was not the time to suggest the action, and we could not abandon Guantanamo Bay under threat from the Russians.[10]

Again Kennedy writes:

The fact was that the proposal the Russians made was not unreasonable and did not amount to a loss to the U.S. or to our NATO allies. On several occasions over the period of the past eighteen months, the

President had asked the State Department to reach an agreement with Turkey for the withdrawal of Jupiter missiles in that country. They were clearly obsolete, and our Polaris submarines in the Mediterranean would give Turkey far greater protection.

At the President's suggestion Secretary Rusk had raised the question with the representatives of Turkey following a NATO meeting in the spring of 1962. The Turks objected, and the matter was permitted to drop. In the summer of 1962, when Rusk was in Europe, President Kennedy raised the question again. He was told by the State Department that they felt it unwise to press the matter with Turkey. But the President disagreed. He wanted the missiles removed. . . . The State Department representatives discussed it again with the Turks and finding they still objected, did not press the issue.

The President believed he was President and that, his wishes having been made clear, they would be followed and the missiles removed.

He was angry. He obviously did not wish to order the removal of the missiles from Turkey under threat from the Soviet Union. On the other hand he did not want to involve the U.S. and mankind in a catastrophic war over missile sites in Turkey that were antiquated and useless. He pointed out to the State Department and the others that to reasonable people, a trade of this kind might look like a very fair suggestion, that our position had become extremely vulnerable, and that it was our own fault.[11]

But still it was decided that the ultimatum had to be sent. And it was sent.

Anger as a factor contributing to the final decision to send the ultimatum arose also from the widespread indignation over the sudden news that our side had been deceived by the Soviets after they had assured us they were not placing offensive weapons in Cuba. Of course the Soviet reply was that the weapons were not offensive weapons but defensive, and that Cuba needed them for self-defense since she had but recently been invaded at the Bay of Pigs by forces trained, equipped and financed by the U.S. government. However, the memoir shows that there was no disposition in the Ex Comm to consider any mitigating factors like the Bay of Pigs invasion, or the fact that our side had, before that invasion, given out false public assurances that we were not organizing, training and financing any such invasion, nor to our equally false public assurances that we had no spy planes flying over Soviet territory (from our bases in Turkey) until the Gary Powers spy plane was shot down. The fact that in political and diplomatic history it is taken for granted that all governments will normally lie about military secrets, did not lessen the very strong feelings that were instantly aroused by the discovery of the Soviet bases in Cuba-- feelings not only in the public at large, but in Congress and the executive branch as well. Waves of pressure arose for instant military action against the bases. Even as unlikely a figure as Senator Fulbright joined in the pressure that was being brought to bear on the President, as recorded by Robert Kennedy in his memoir.[12]

Kennedy also took note of an additional factor that powerfully increased the degree of this pressure. He writes:

> It was election time. The autumn days of September and October were filled with charges and countercharges. Republicans 'viewing with alarm' were claiming the U.S. was not taking the necessary steps to protect our security. Some, such as Senator Homer E. Capehart of Indiana, were suggesting that we take military action against Cuba.[13]

It is always emphasized by those who defend the decision our government took in the Cuban Missile Crisis, that President Kennedy resisted (at first) these pressures that were so insistent for immediate military action to remove the bases by a "surgical strike," as it was usually termed, "before the missile bases become operative." Because John Kennedy refused to yield to these pressures immediately, the conclusion has often been drawn that his policy in the crisis as a whole was one of restraint and moderation in the interest of peace.

But this would be to forget what the final decision actually was—a military ultimatum—and what the expectation regarding it was—that it would not be obeyed, and war would follow. Nevertheless, the political beauty of the ultimatum was that while it seemed restrained, since it did not rush precipitately into armed action, it nevertheless chose the path of armed action, and reinforced the stance and image everyone seemed to want. That is, the stance that says to the other side: we are stronger than you, and must be recognized as such; and we do not have to give you equal rights; we do not have to permit you to do to us what we permit ourselves to do to you. You must therefore comply with our demand, or we will go to war against you. Equal rights might be good international law but it would be a very bad precedent for our "national interests." That is what became the bottom line.

It is not too much to say that in the Ex Comm it was felt that to abandon this stance, to give up this double standard, would be political suicide, in the careerist sense. This is reflected in the passage where Robert Kennedy recounts a portion of a conversation he had with the President on the subject of military action, beginning with our naval blockade of Cuba or "quarantine," as it was then called. He wrote:

> 'I just don't think there was any choice,' I said, 'and not only that; if you hadn't acted, you would have been impeached.' The President thought for a moment, and said, 'That's what I think, I would have been impeached.'[14]

These facts, reported by the President's brother and steadfast partner, indicate some of the powerful causes that led to the final decision to send the military ultimatum which risked the end of the world, and even "expected" it. However unwise, imprudent and reckless that decision objectively was, the fact that the Soviets (contrary to our own expectations) obeyed the ultimatum made it look like a magic wand, a gift from a fairy godmother. It not only seduced any number of people into thinking that the policy must have been one of even-handed justice in the interest of peace; it also became an irresistible model for later administrations to follow in dealing with the Soviets. That is, just threaten to begin the war that will blow up the world, and they will back down. "Firmness" is the word that became attached to this omnicidal paradigm—Kennedy's "policy of firmness" in the Cuban Missile Crisis.

But in actual, documented fact, it thoroughly frightened Robert Kennedy, as it ought to frighten anyone who is not inclined to believe in magic wands and fairy godmothers. To realize that you can actually end the whole human world by nuclear incineration and radioactive poisoning which would necessitate perhaps five years of indescribable suffering and agony before the five billion souls who comprise the human family are all dead and unburied, "including all the children," is something everyone tries not to think about. The trouble is we soften the blow for ourselves by calling this war and thinking of it as such, with all the old familiar connotations of war such as courage and patriotism, and human survival, because that too, always went with war, however bad and sad the war might have been.

Robert Kennedy saw through this, although he did not have the word that helps to make the reality clear in its qualitative difference from war—the word "omnicide," which signifies the killing of all humans, including the killers themselves. This word forces us to face the reality: when we talk about nuclear conflict we are no longer talking about war. We are talking about omnicide, the crime so enormous that it could be committed only once, the sin so unspeakable it never even had a name, until now. Robert Kennedy rightly sensed all this and kept it in the center of his thought, where it certainly belonged. It bothered him that in sending the ultimatum he and the rest had chosen to risk ending the world, and even expected it to end. He kept thinking that he might be able to write that final chapter of *Thirteen Days* which would deal with the ethical question of what would justify their actual decision, but he could not find anything that would.

Now, after all this, Mr. Rusk's secret is being presented to us as the happy, long-lost justification of the whole thing: John Kennedy allegedly would have prevented the catastrophic war as soon as he ascertained the Soviets were not going to obey the ultimatum. That is the way the media have played the secret up—"Kennedy Secretly a Dove" was the headline of the *Washington Post*.[15] "Secret Fallback Plan" was the headline that *The New York Times* [16] August 28, 1987, gave to long, comforting articles. Could this possibly be anything but the same magic wand of the same fairy godmother?

Let us take it seriously and see Rusk's whole case rests on the assumption that our President can send an ultimatum that says to the Soviets: You must remove your missiles from Cuba within twenty-four hours, and if you do not, we will bomb them and thus start war against you. And at the same time the President is actually acknowledging to his brother (unless Robert Kennedy is lying) that he does not really expect the Soviets to obey the ultimatum, and does expect the war, with all its horrendous consequences. He "hopes" the Soviets will obey; he does not "expect" them to. But, in any case, the President feels compelled to send the ultimatum because of the immense public and Congressional pressure for some kind of military action to deal with the Soviet missile bases, about which the Soviets had unforgivably tried to deceive us. And finally, if he does not take that kind of military approach, he will be impeached.

Common sense and sober fact tell us that once you have, for reasons of that kind, delivered a military ultimatum to the U.S.S.R., limited to twenty-four hours, an ultimatum that must necessarily become known to the entire world, you have crossed your Rubicon. There can be no turning back. But Mr. Rusk's secret is being presented to us as meaning that, after having delivered such an ultimatum, it still was possible for the President, if and when he ascertained that the Soviets were not going to obey it, to take it all back. He would then announce that he was now prepared to accept the alternative proposal of a peaceful and reciprocal removal of the missile bases because that had now been proposed also by the United Nations.

But, in the first place, how would the President ascertain that the Soviets were not going to obey the ultimatum? Would he be satisfied if he simply received a written statement from the Soviets: "We are not going to obey your ultimatum." Would he then agree to the reciprocal removal of bases, which is just what the Soviets had been proposing, and which would be recognized as such, no matter who else would propose it? Would he be content thus to expose himself to the American electorate, to Congress, and to the whole world as one who first sent such an ultimatum to the Soviets, and then ignominiously backed down and retracted it just as soon as he learned that the Soviets were not going to obey it? Would that not be an unthinkable negation of the very reasons for having delivered the ultimatum? What kind of "fallback plan" is that? It would have doubly invited impeachment.

Of course, there would still be two other ways of ascertaining that the Soviets were not going to obey the ultimatum. One of these is that the Soviets might simply do nothing; they would let the twenty-four hours go by, and wait for us to drop the first bomb. If we did not drop it, but said we were now ready to accept the peaceful alternative of reciprocal removal of the bases, it would be the same case as our President publicly backing down after having taken a strong stand, the very image that the President admitted he could never politically afford. The remaining way he would know that the Soviets were not going to obey the ultimatum would of course be for them to bomb first, before the twenty-four hours had elapsed. Then, also, it would be too late for the President to implement the secret statement, to transform himself from the proud, threatening eagle of the ultimatum to the peaceful, gentle dove of the Rusk letter. That would have been an unthinkable public capitulation under fire. The secret statement thus turns out to be a sad case of what someone once called "the murder of a beautiful theory by a gang of brutal facts."

Operatively, objectively and substantively, the secret statement never could have meant anything once the ultimatum had been delivered. John Kennedy himself realized that better than anyone else. If he still dictated the secret statement, one can only conclude that he meant it as a kind of confession that what he was saying in the statement represented the decision he had wanted to make, that he recognized it as ethically the only right decision. But at the same time he considered himself compelled to make a very different decision for political reasons. These were reasons that preferred ending the human world to granting the Soviets equal rights, that represented the ultimate variant of "better dead than red"—better no world at all than a world with the Soviets as our equals.

The President was thus wrestling with the same problem that so troubled his brother Robert. It raised the same question that Robert was never able to answer in terms of ethical principle. But John Kennedy answered it in terms of immediate political practice; and, under the pressures upon him, he chose the path of military action even though he admittedly expected it to lead to war and the end of the world. The only reason the world did not end then was that the Soviets unexpectedly chose to have it continue even though this cost them a temporary political defeat.

Years later Theodore Sorensen wrote an op-ed article in *The New York Times* in which he warned President Nixon not to try to use in Vietnam the same tactics that John Kennedy had used in the Cuban Missile Crisis because they were far too dangerous; the fact that they succeeded then, he admitted, was only luck. As for the beautiful but unworkable theories that are murdered by gangs of brutal facts, the awful truth is that some of them will not stay dead. In politics they are like fairy tales that have a life of their own in the mythologies that play an all-too-real role in our practical political life and death. President Reagan's administration certainly resurrected the "strong" (Rambo) stance of Kennedy's policy as his model of how to deal with the Soviets. Can we rely on blind luck? Or have we devised a really workable fallback plan by which some secret statement could actually play the role of saving the world at the last minute in case we again decide to send some kind of military ultimatum to the Soviets? It would be well indeed to have such a plan, as it is now universal doctrine in the U.S.S.R. that Kennedy's policy in the Cuban Missile Crisis was really nuclear blackmail, and they are firmly resolved never to give in to it again.

Wishful thinking always presupposes some very strong wish, and it is fair to say that the documentation in *Thirteen Days* indicates the understandably strong reasons Mr. Rusk has for wishing to think that "President Kennedy would not let the Jupiters in Turkey become an obstacle to the removal of the missile sites in Cuba because the Jupiters were coming out in any event," as he expressed it to *The New York Times* in revealing his secret. The documentation shows that President Kennedy was thoroughly angry that Mr. Rusk had not carried out his repeated instructions to remove those very missiles from Turkey months before the crisis. The President was angry precisely because he felt, as did the others, that it was now impossible to remove them as a way of settling the crisis because that would mean publicly giving in to "Soviet threat and pressure." Mr. Rusk now apparently wants to believe that President Kennedy would have and could have accepted that peaceful alternative even after sending the military ultimatum to the Soviets. But the brutal facts revealed by Robert Kennedy (and strangely ignored by Mr. Rusk) show why that would have been utterly impossible.

The hard truth is that there is no way we can find any comfort at all in the policy we actually followed in the Cuban Missile Crisis. The only lesson we can derive from it is that this policy must be rejected because it fails to pass the simple test of sanity. Whatever our differences may be, let us all insist that our policies must recognize that nuclear conflict—omnicide—is the supreme enemy of everything human, an enemy all-inclusive, all consuming, irreversibly final, and therefore it can never be an acceptable option in the foreign policy of the United States.

City University of New York

Notes

[1] Robert F. Kennedy, *Thirteen Days: A Memoir of the Cuban Missile Crisis* (New York: W. W. Norton & Co., 1969).

[2] *The New York Times,* August 28, 1987.

[3] *Times.*

[4] *Times.*

[5] Author Press, 1426 Merritt Drive, El Cajon, California 92020.

[6] Kennedy, 108-9.

[7] Kennedy, 106.

[8] Kennedy, 23.

[9] Kennedy, 128.

[10] Kennedy, 49.

[11] Kennedy 94.

[12] Kennedy 54.

[13] Kennedy, 25.

[14] Kennedy, 67.

[15] *Washington Post*, August 29, 1987.

[16] *Times,* August 28, 1987.

2 Understanding The Cuban Missile Crisis: A Dialectical Approach

Ron Hirschbein

> I felt we were on a precipice with no way off. . . . .President Kennedy
> had initiated a course of events, but he no longer had control over them.
>
> —Robert Kennedy[1]

More than a quarter of a century has elapsed since U-2 reconnaissance revealed a telltale, trapezoidal configuration of missile sites in remote areas of Cuba: the Soviets were installing medium-range ballistic missiles. President Kennedy's resolution of the ensuing crisis raises important and intriguing questions for philosophers.

1. In retrospect, there is little dispute about what occurred. In response to the discovery of the missiles, the President convened a group of advisors (the Ex-Comm)[2] and debated various alternatives. He decided that the missiles must be removed, but he rejected the advice of both the hawks and the doves.[3] Rather than relying upon immediate military action or negotiation, he pursued a policy of gradual escalation; he wanted to give Khrushchev the time and the inclination to back down. Accordingly, he instituted a naval blockade, but when this action failed to convince his adversary to remove the missiles, he considered other options.

The Kremlin communicated two rather inconsistent proposals for resolving the crisis. The President cleverly responded to the more congenial proposal and ignored the other. However, before the Soviets could reply, Kennedy quickly escalated the situation by instructing his brother to deliver an ultimatum to the Soviet Ambassador: remove the missiles within twenty-four hours or the U.S. would destroy them and invade Cuba. The Kennedy brothers expected that the ultimatum would precipitate World War III, but the next day Khrushchev unexpectedly agreed to remove the missiles if Kennedy promised not to invade Cuba again. He promised, and the missiles were removed. The Crisis was thereby resolved to Kennedy's satisfaction.[4] It is also widely recognized that Kennedy's daring resolution of the crisis profoundly influenced his successors. His willingness to risk everything is an inspiration, not a source of shame. Just as Neville Chamberlain proved once and for all that negotiation and compromise invariably produce humiliation and defeat, John Kennedy demonstrated, to those with a will to believe, that the resolute application of U.S. technological supremacy can work wonders in history. Even Kennedy's most fervent supporters warn that this influence is less than salutary. In 1966, Theodore Sorensen (a Kennedy confidant and Ex-Comm advisor) warned that a "Cuban Missile Crisis syndrome" was clouding the judgment of Kennedy's successors: the apparently successful application of the new gradual escalation policy convinced them that the resolute, but carefully calibrated application of superior force could rout adversaries and send them into retreat.[5] It appears that this policy guided American strategy in Indochina, and more disturbing still, it continues to inform American nuclear strategy.[6]

2. Unfortunately, the facts do not speak for themselves; there is no consensus about how to interpret the data. For example, Graham Allison, former Dean of the Kennedy School of Government at Harvard, claims that Kennedy's resolution of the crisis was ". . .one of the finest examples of diplomatic prudence and perhaps the finest hour of John F. Kennedy's presidency."[7] But, farther down Massachusetts Avenue at M.I.T., Noam Chomsky refers to Kennedy's actions as "the lowest point in human history".[8]

The Cuban Missile Crisis raises perennial philosophic problems because the experts agree on the facts but cannot agree upon how to interpret the data. This problem invites the application of a venerable philosophic method termed "dialectics." This method rejects the popular and convenient notion that social reality is a coherent, seamless whole. It presupposes that the political process is shaped by the interplay of evolving, contradictory forces. The apparent contradiction between Allison and Chomsky does not necessarily reflect deficiencies in their thinking; it reflects the radically contradictory nature of Kennedy's crisis management.

In order to demonstrate the plausibility of this claim, I hazard the following hypothesis: Kennedy's behavior reflects the unresolved, sharpening contradiction between the prudent instrumental realism and the secular, millenarian enthusiasm that characterizes the American political heritage. After defining these terms, I attempt to show that these opposing forces literally pulled Kennedy in opposite directions.

I. Definitions

> Western European political discourse [is] dominated by, two warring sets of ideas: . . . a commitment to incremental change and a recognition of ineradicable human imperfections; the other, a utopianism which sought the final and ultimate attainment, by force if necessary, of a totally harmonious human society.
>
> —Jacob Talmon[9]

Any definition of realism must begin with a caveat: the concept of realism can be put to ideological uses. As Marcuse recognized, in the name of realism, the universe of real, historical possibilities can be constricted to the perpetuation of the status quo. Such one-dimensional realism insists that existing social arrangements are rational if not inevitable; the possibility, if not the inevitability, of social transformation is dismissed *a priori*.[10] For example, the strategic literature abounds with the pronouncements of "unsentimental realists" who claim that, like the poor, nuclear weapons will always be with us.[11]

The concept of realism, however, can be used less tendentiously to refer to the capacity of decision makers to relate means and ends by accurately testing reality. In psychoanalytic terms, such realism is a product of the ego. Unlike the unconscious, the ego resigns itself to making the best of a bad situation; the world does not permit the gratification of our fondest aspirations. The realist resigns himself to modest but attainable goals. Rather than relying upon preconceived notions for attaining goals, he utilizes data obtained from observation and experiment. Recognizing his fallibility, he merely purports to derive a tentative, probabilistic understanding of the social world. In a phrase, realists are modest in aspiration, empirically oriented and meliorative in their approach to adversaries.[12]

Kennedy was sufficiently rational, for example, to run a successful campaign. Both he and his advisors accurately assessed political reality and acted accordingly. However, after his election, he frequently failed to appreciate the limits of presidential power. In the words of historian Barbara Tuchman:

> Government remains the paramount area of folly because it is there

that men seek power over others—only to lose it over themselves.[13]

While it is widely recognized that Kennedy succumbed to irrational impulses in orchestrating the Bay of Pigs invasion and in escalating the Indochina War, it is difficult for mainstream political analysts to consider the possibility that the same impulses clouded Kennedy's judgment during the Missile Crisis. However, as we shall see, Kennedy's realism was not durable. Indeed, if elites restricted their beliefs, values and hopes to what can be validly deduced from observation and experiment, they would renounce cherished certitudes, recognize the cultural bias inherent in their values, and acknowledge that human progress is, at best, grudging and incremental. Critical thinking and reality-testing produce the last thing most people want: a sobering, realistic assessment of the world.

The widely celebrated pragmatism of the men who control the American nuclear arsenal is not as robust as many believe. There is reason to fear that millenarian enthusiasm can overwhelm the usual restraints that inhibit strategic decision makers. There is nothing new about such apprehension. Alarmed by the realization that apocalyptic visions were guiding his colleagues, David Lilienthal, the first chairman of the Atomic Energy Commission, resigned his post. Later, he explained that both he and his colleagues had been enchanted by a chiliastic vision of the atom, a vision of a nuclear messiah that would either usher in a golden age for the elect or destroy the planet:

> The Atom has had us bewitched. It was so gigantic, so terrible, so beyond the power of imagination to embrace, that it seemed to be the ultimate fact. It would either destroy us or it would bring about the millennium. . . . Our obsession with the Atom led us to assign to it a separate and unique status in the world. So greatly did it seem to transcend the ordinary affairs of men that we shut it out of those affairs altogether; or rather, tried to create a separate world, a world of the Atom.[14]

The atomic millenarian possesses the newest weapons, but he is possessed by the oldest psychology, namely, the unconscious. If Freud's ruminations about the instincts are correct, humans have a strong, persistent, unconscious desire to free themselves from tension. The tension-free state—a double entendre is intended—is the millennial dream of an enduring epoch of unprecedented tranquility for the elect: a halcyon time in which foreign enemies are vanquished and the usual vicissitudes of terrestrial existence are overcome.[15] As political theorist Michael Walzer explains, secular millenarianism invests adherents with a new and far-reaching sense of purpose; it invites the faithful to reach the glorious end of days through sheer political willfulness.[16]

In the popular mind, millenarianism is restricted to Protestant Fundamentalists who believe that Jesus will return after the apocalypse to preside over a new order. However, Fundamentalism is but one variety of millenarian aspiration. As the influence of traditional millenarianism faded, a new faith in this-worldly redemption arose: the Enlightenment faith in progress and perfectibility through scientific discovery, technological inventiveness and national destiny. Unlike their religious counterparts, secular millenarians do not passively await divine intervention in history; they attempt to use their newfound, technological prowess to work wonders in history.

In essence, millenarianism is an eschatological philosophy of history, but not necessarily a religious one. Millenarians deny that history is a random collection of events. It is believed that through divine or human intervention, history ascends in majestic steps toward this-worldly redemption; the best is yet to come. It is enthusiastically and uncritically believed that the difficulties of the past will be surmounted and the world will be transformed to suit the aspirations of the elect.[17]

In a phrase, millenarians embrace unrealizable aspirations. However, they are not merely overoptimistic utopians. When it appears that their aspirations are quixotic, they sometimes strive for the ultimate state of tension-free existence, death. Millenarians cannot live without hope.

Unfortunately, there is reason for apprehensiveness. Episodes such as Jonestown reveal the death wish endemic to millenarianism. This phenomenon, however, is not limited to the margins of society. Millenarianism in high places produces leaders who are both victims and executioners. From Masada to Beirut, Western civilization is strewn with the bodies of millenarian zealots and their victims. As Camus warned, today's millenarian zealot seems to embrace the source of his destruction as his salvation because he, ". . .lives in a world of abstractions, of bureaus and machines, of absolute ideals and crude messianism."[18]

This dialectic between bureaucratized realism and political messianism has long been at the center of great events. The literature highlights some of the following examples:

a. Initially, prelates and monarchs fomented the Crusades for self-serving reasons. But ironically, many of these leaders succumbed to the millenarian fervor they unleashed. The hapless Templars immolated themselves in Palestine when they failed to usher in a new Jerusalem.[19]

b. The chiliastic vision that inspired Cromwell's Glorious Revolution inspired both American and French revolutionaries in the next century. Americans seemed particularly prone to the delusion that they were destined to bring forth the new Zion. Hamilton ridiculed such visions of a Golden Age, and urged his countrymen to reconcile themselves to the imperfections of human existence. However, Hamilton's admonition was ignored by those who put their faith in the manifest destiny of the new republic.[20]

c. The tension between realism and millenarianism was acutely felt in the tormented life of President Wilson. He entered office as a consummate realist and "managed to keep us out of war." But, like so many others, he succumbed to the enticing promises of the millenarian faith as he fought the "war to end all wars". When he failed to convince the Senate that the League of Nations would fulfill the ancient millenarian dream of peace on earth, he left office a disheartened and broken man.[21]

This brief excursion into Western history is hardly definitive. It is merely designed to show that there is reason to suspect that contradictory, irreconcilable impulses have perennially shaped world-historical events. It would have been surprising if Kennedy and the "best and the brightest" could have escaped this dialectical interplay of opposing forces.

II. Kennedy's Remarkable Ambivalence

> The essence of ultimate decision remains impenetrable to the observer—often, indeed, to the decider himself. . . .There will always be dark and tangled stretches in the decision-making process—mysterious even to those who may be most intimately involved.
>
> —President Kennedy's recollection of the crisis.[22]

A dialectical approach to the Crisis reveals that both Kennedy and his advisors were beset by contradictory impulses. Curiously, most of the literature recognizes that the Ex-Comm offered conflicting advice: Stevenson was realistic enough to urge negotiation and compromise; Acheson and the Joint Chiefs seemed to advocate an apocalyptic battle that would settle scores with the Soviets; and McNamara tried to synthesize these contradictory recommendations into the widely-celebrated gradual escalation policy.[23]

However, the literature seldom gives appropriate emphasis to the President's personal ambivalence. Many analysts, regardless of their persuasion, reduce Kennedy to a one dimensional caricature. Sympathetic historians such as Arthur Schlesinger, Jr. insist that his performance was a dazzling, carefully calibrated combination of firmness and restraint.[24] However, critics, such as historian Garry Wills, claim that Kennedy was a victim of macho psychosis: he had to prove his masculinity to Khrushchev and Castro.[25]

With playwright Friedrich Dürrenmatt we must recognize that "he who confronts the paradoxical exposes himself to reality." Not only did Kennedy receive conflicting advice; his own behavior was strikingly paradoxical. Kennedy did not manage the crisis by pulling a coherent, tried-and-true policy off the shelf. It seems that certain forces operated behind the backs and against the wills of the crisis managers; as the remarks cited above suggest, the President himself could not fully understand his motivation.

The President's conduct was baffling. On occasion, he was realistic. He resisted his initial temptation to attack the missile sites, and, in the words of his brother, he thought five or six moves ahead and concluded that a confrontation with the Soviets would likely escalate into a nuclear war that would profit no one. Unlike the Reagan Administration, he had no delusions about "surviving and prevailing."

Many critics contend that Kennedy abandoned such prudence as the crisis deepened; this is not entirely true. As the recently declassified Minutes of the October 27 Ex-Comm meeting suggests, the crisis brought out the best, and the worst, in the President.[26]

That fateful day, he confronted two rather inconsistent offers from the Kremlin. The first suggested that the Soviets would remove the missiles if the Americans pledged not to invade Cuba once again. The second insisted that, in addition, America would have to remove its missiles from Turkey *quid pro quo*. It appears that, initially, Kennedy entertained making such a trade. However, when he encountered strident opposition, he ignored the unacceptable proposal and responded to the one he found more congenial. Moreover, the same day, a U-2 was shot down over Cuba. Attempting to avoid escalation, the President broke his pledge to the military and refused to retaliate.

These decisions suggest that, in part, Kennedy was realistic enough to avoid a nuclear confrontation. If we restrict our attention to Kennedy's restraint, Allison's accolade seems appropriate. Unhappily, however, Chomsky's indictment is not baseless: Kennedy was also driven by reckless impulses that defy the usual accounts of elite behavior.

Those who commend Kennedy's "firmness" (i.e. his willingness to risk a nuclear holocaust) explain that such risks were necessary due to the gravity of the situation: the Cuban missiles supposedly increased the threat to the Western Hemisphere. While Kennedy articulated this view in his public pronouncements, his private assessment of the Soviet threat was markedly different. The Ex-Comm Minutes reveal that, in the President's view, the Cuban missiles did not alter the strategic balance. During the October 16 meeting he quipped, "What difference does it make; they have enough missiles [within their borders] to blow us up anyway." The Secretary of Defense shared this assessment. McNamara declared, "a missile is a missile"; its origins are less important than its destination.[27]

Even though the Cuban missiles did not heighten the threat to hemispheric security, President Kennedy rejected all proposals for negotiation, and he refused to endorse what he and his brother deemed a rational offer: dismantling the obsolete Jupiter missiles in Turkey *quid pro quo*.[28] Despite, or perhaps because of, the perceived risk, the President committed an act of war and blockaded Cuba.[29] The Soviets did not run the blockade, but neither did they remove the missiles.

Despite Kennedy's bravado, even certain critics are reluctant to abandon the reassuring belief the President was motivated solely by political realism.[30] To be sure, there is some truth to the claim Kennedy's recklessness was politically motivated. U.S. relations with Cuba were a pivotal issue in the 1962 elections. After the Bay of Pigs fiasco, Kennedy felt compelled to come to the aid of his party by publicly confronting Khrushchev and by acting quickly and decisively.

His refusal to negotiate and his insistence upon resolving the crisis quickly, before the impending election, lend credence to this analysis. Indeed, on more than one occasion, Kennedy declared that he would be impeached (and that he *should* be impeached) if he failed to remove the missiles. The blockade, according to this view, was intended to send the right message to the Kremlin and to Kennedy's domestic constituency.

However, as historians such as Ronald Steele suggest, Kennedy's recklessness may also have been generated by his faith in American omnipotence.[31] Kennedy believed that America was destined to play an uncontested, premier role in the world, and that the nation could fulfill its destiny if its leaders had the intelligence and the resolve to exploit American technological advantage. From this perspective, the blockade was not entirely a political act designed to sway the forthcoming election. It was a doctrinal reaffirmation of faith in the power of American technology wedded to national resolve. It was recognized that the blockade per se could not remove the missiles that were already in place, but it was believed that this display of American courage and might would give Khrushchev second thoughts about keeping the missiles in Cuba.

In any event, Khrushchev did not receive the right "signal" and the crisis veered out of control. Nevertheless, the President moved closer to the brink. Robert Kennedy reveals that the President decided to convey an ultimatum to the Soviet Ambassador: remove the missiles within 24 hours or face an American attack. McNamara reveals the depth of his pessimism when he indicates that after he left the Saturday Ex-Comm meeting, he paused to watch a particularly beautiful sunset; he thought it would be his last.[32]

As McNamara paused and ruminated, the families of American officials were being prepared for evacuation, and the Soviets were shredding documents in their Embassy. President Kennedy continued to hope for the best, but, according to his brother, he expected the worst:

> The president was not optimistic, nor was I. . . . The expectation was a military confrontation by Tuesday and possibly tomorrow.

The President was not insensitive to the probable results of his actions. His brother sensitively depicts his anguish:

43

> The thought that disturbed him the most, and that made the prospect of war much more fearful than it would otherwise have been, was the specter of the death of the children of this country and the world. . . .[33]

In retrospect, the principal players in this nuclear drama reiterated this grim assessment. The President indicated that the chances of nuclear war were between one out of three and even; and Chairman Khrushchev allowed that "the smell of burning was in the air".[34]

Despite this evidence, those who champion Kennedy's actions still insist that, in the final analysis, Kennedy acted prudently. At the recent Harvard commemoration of the crisis, Dean Rusk claimed that the President secretly authorized him to resolve the crisis peacefully if the ultimatum failed: the Turkish missiles would be removed under the auspices of the United Nations as the more strident Kremlin proposal demanded.[35]

However, as John Somerville has argued:

1) Should not more credence be given to the less sanguine revelations of the President's brother? 2) Was it reasonable to expect a communique from Khrushchev, let alone the beginning of negotiations to commence, after issuing an ultimatum? 3) Was it implausible to expect that the ultimatum would give the Soviets incentive to launch a pre-emptive first strike?[36] 4) Even if Rusk is correct, the Kennedy Administration was playing with fire, or, rather, thermonuclear fusion. On more than one occasion, the crisis escalated out of control due to breakdowns in the chain of command. For example, General Thomas Powers (the SAC commander) disobeyed his superiors and allowed the Soviets to intercept his orders to ready B-52s for a nuclear strike.[37]

More recently, members of the Harvard group have argued that the recently declassified minutes of the October 27 Ex-Comm meeting indicate that JFK entertained the possibility of trading the missiles in Turkey. They conclude that this indicates that the President was unwilling to risk war with the Soviets.[38] This conclusion does not fit the facts. Kennedy's ruminations suggest that he considered acting in a manner that was meliorative and pragmatic. But his actions—namely, issuing the ultimatum—indicate that he willingly risked the destruction of himself and everything he cherished.

Apparently the Soviet leader had trampled upon the President's faith in the power of his military technology and unflinching courage. This faith had infused the President's life with meaning, direction and hope. Khrushchev's humiliating deployment of the missiles and his failure to respond properly to the blockade had sullied the President's image once too often. As Kennedy told a reporter prior to the crisis, "if Khrushchev wants to rub my nose in the dirt, it's all over."[39]

Millenarians, be they religious or secular, cannot live without hope. When it appeared that the President's millenarian dreams betrayed him, he risked plunging the world into a nuclear nightmare. No wonder Daniel Ellsberg, a high level advisor during the crisis, warns:

> We all live in Guyana now, and there is no place to run to. From Utah to Norway to east of the Urals, we must take our stand where we live, and act to protect our home and our family: the earth and all living beings.[40]

California State University, Chico

Notes

[1] Robert Kennedy, *Thirteen Days: A Memoir of the Cuban Missile Crisis* (New York: W. W. Norton, 1969), pp. 70-71.

[2] This term is an abbreviation for the Executive Committee of the National Security Council. However, certain Ex-Comm members were not on the NSC.

[3] These terms were first used during the crisis to describe factions within the Ex-Comm.

[4] This narrative was developed twenty years ago by Robert Kennedy in his *Thirteen Days*. It is corroborated, by and large, in the recently declassified *Minutes* of the Ex-Comm; see "October 27, 1962: Transcripts of the Meetings of the ExComm" in *International Security* 12 (1987-88): Winter. This version of the Transcript is edited. I wish to thank Barton Bernstein of Stanford University for sending the unedited version.

[5] Theodore Sorenson, "Kennedy Vindicated," *The Cuban Missile Crisis,* ed. Robert Divine (Chicago: Quadrangle Books, 1971) 208.

[6] This argument is made by Fred Kaplan in *The Wizards of Armageddon* (New York: Simon & Schuster, 1983) chapter 23.

Kaplan's analysis was corroborated by Daniel Ellsberg, an architect of this policy, during his lecture at California State University, Chico, on March 17, 1988.

[7] Graham Allison, *Essence of Decision* (Boston: Little, Brown & Co., 1979) 39.

[8] Noam Chomsky, "Strategic Arms, the Cold War & the Third World" *Exterminism & Cold War,* eds. New Left Review (London: Thetford Press, Ltd., 1983) 223.

[9] Cited by Michael Barkun in *Disaster and the Millennium* (New Haven: Yale University Press, 1974) 28-29.

[10] Herbert Marcuse, *One-Dimensional Man* (Boston: Beacon Press, l964) chapter 6.

[11] See, for example, Albert Carnesdale, Paul Doty, Stanley Hoffman et. al., *Living With Nuclear Weapons* (Toronto: Bantam Books, l983).

[12] The contrast between political realism and political millenarianism is made explicit in Richard Hofstader's essay, "The Paranoid Style in American Politics," in the volume of the same title (New York: Alfred A. Knopf, 1966).

[13] Barbara Tuchman, *The March of Folly* (New York: Alfred A. Knopf, 1984) 382.

[14] David Lilienthal, *Change, Hope and the Bomb* (Princeton: Princeton University Press, l963) 20.

[15] The literature on the role of secular millenarianism in political life is becoming more extensive. Representative works include, Normal Cohn, *The Pursuit of the Millennium* (Fairlawn: Essential Books, Inc., 1957); Ernest Tuveson, *Redeemer Nation* (Chicago: University of Chicago Press, 1968); Henry May, *The Enlightenment in America* (New York: Oxford University Press, 1976); and Jacob Talmon, *Political Messianism* (New York: Fredrick Prager, Inc., l960).

[16] Michael Walzer, *The Revolution of Saints: A Study in the Origins of Radical Politics* (Cambridge: Harvard University Press, l965) 29.

[17] See, for example, Theodore Olson, *Millenarianism, Utopianism,*

and Progress (Toronto: University of Toronto Press, 1982).

[18] Albert Camus, "Neither Victims nor Executioners" *War and Christian Conscience,* ed., Albert Marrin (Chicago: Henry Regnery, 1971) 462.

[19] See Cohn's discussion in *The Pursuit of the Millennium.*

[20] See Tuveson's discussion in *Redeemer Nation.*

[21] See Tuchman's discussion in *Practicing History* (New York: Ballantine Books, 1982) 141-152.

[22] Quoted in Allison, frontispiece.

[23] This account is given by Robert Kennedy.

[24] Arthur Schlesinger, Jr., *A Thousand Days: John F. Kennedy in the White House* (Boston, 1965).

[25] Garry Wills, *The Kennedy Imprisonment* (Boston: Little, Brown and Co., 1981) 278-279.

[26] "Transcripts" in *International Security.*

[27] Cited by Richard Betts, *Nuclear Blackmail & Nuclear Balance* (Washington: The Brookings Institution, 1987) 116.

[28] Robert Kennedy 98; and "Transcripts" 36-44.

[29] The blockade was euphemistically called a "quarantine"; apparently this was done to minimize domestic and foreign apprehensiveness.

[30] See, for example, I. F. Stone's "What Price Prestige?" in Divine.

[31] Ronald Steele, "Lessons on the Cuban Missile Crisis" in Divine.

[32] Sloan Foundation Video Tapes, "1982 Interviews with Surviving Ex-Comm Members"; I wish to thank Mr. Art Singer, Vice President of the Foundation, for these tapes.

[33] Robert Kennedy 106-09. Also see Barton Bernstein's "The Cuban Missile Crisis" *Reflections on the Cold War,* eds., Lynn Miller and Ronald Pruessen (Philadelphia: Temple University Press, 1974) 122-124.

[34] Nikita Khrushchev, *Khrushchev Remembers,* trans. S. Talto (Boston: Little, Brown and Co., 1974).

[35] J. Anthony Lukas, "Class Reunion," *The New York Times,* 30 Aug. 1987.

[36]John Somerville, "The Cuban Missiles and Rusk's Secret," (unpublished) October 1987.

[37] David Welch and James Blight, "An Introduction to the Ex-Comm Transcripts," *International Security.*

[38] See Lucas.

[39] Quoted by Stone 157

[40] Daniel Ellsberg, "A Call to Mutiny," *Protest and Survive* (New York and London: Monthly Review Press, 1982) xix.

3 Marxism and Nuclear Deterrence

George Hampsch

Significant changes in global attitudes toward the frightful dangers of nuclear war and toward the need for disarmament are finally starting to take place. Serious negotiations are in progress between the USA and the USSR wherein the concern for global security is taking precedent over concerns for short-term national or ideological advantage. Areas of cooperation between states with different social systems are expanding. Ideologues of both sides who advocate increasing tensions, provocations and confrontations between these states are in the process of becoming politically isolated. A new spirit is manifesting itself, and energies in the struggle for world peace appear renewed among the peoples of the earth.

In light of these changes, it is important that philosophers and social theorists of all orientations engage in the search for viable solutions to those social conditions and problems which create attitudes hostile to peace. To do so, in fact, has become a moral imperative. Who will deny that the most serious and overriding obligation facing humans collectively is the avoidance of any conflict which may lead to a nuclear holocaust? An integral part of that obligation is to strive to overcome attitudes and situations which engender policies of deliberate state-to-state confrontations. It is in this area particularly that philosophers and other scholars in the humanities and the sciences may best fulfill their obligation to struggle for world peace. Naturally this includes scholars in the socialist states. They too must face the perplexing problems which arise from seeking peace in a nuclear world. Let us consider in particular the difficulties which originate from a policy of nuclear deterrence.

There are many problems facing contemporary Marxism. Some problems are theoretical; many more are of a practical nature. One problem which encompasses both aspects—a problem which has received scant attention, at least from the theoretical side—is the existence of a moral dilemma which results from the socialist states maintaining a permanent policy of nuclear deterrence.

Marxist scholars must undertake a more serious attempt to confront this moral dilemma beginning now and continuing into the 1990s. The policy of nuclear deterrence stands in seeming contradiction to Marxist social goals, to the Marxist philosophy of history, and to the Marxist understanding of the ultimate meaning of reality.

I sense, on the part of some scholars in socialist states, a reluctance to address this problem because these efforts may clash with the current foreign policy of the socialist states, and because public criticism concerning the morality of a policy of nuclear deterrence may damage the vital security interests of those states professing Marxist principles. This reluctance, however, cannot deter the efforts to resolve the moral dilemma of nuclear deterrence.

The difficulty is this: the prevention of nuclear war can be assured only if its prevention is confronted as part of the larger problem of preventing all war between nation-states, especially between the two major ideological blocs. Prevention of conflict in turn hinges on changes in the very nature of state-to-state relationships. Given the current competing set of worldviews and the subsequent character of the ideological struggle, however, the probability of changing qualitatively the relationships between these contending states to ones which are predominantly non-adversarial, is remote within the foreseeable future.

This is not to imply that steps cannot immediately be taken to lessen the dangers of nuclear war, by such measures as a nuclear freeze, arms limitations, arms reductions, and no-first-use policies or consequently nuclear pacifism. But failure to place the nuclear weapons question clearly within the larger context of reaching world peace through resolving the ideological conflict, leads necessarily to a subsequent difficulty, which indeed constitutes a thorny moral paradox for Marxists.

This paradox centers on the distinction between nuclear pacifism (advocated by the socialist states) and nuclear deterrence (also advocated by the socialist states). A commitment to nuclear pacifism does not preclude a simultaneous commitment to nuclear deterrence. Every state possessing nuclear weapons and an adequate delivery system, in fact, does have a stated policy of nuclear deterrence.

It should be recognized, however, that a policy of nuclear deterrence cannot be based on bluff, but must rest on an actual threat with the intention to use nuclear weapons in whatever measure is deemed necessary to assure that the deterrent effect prevails. Of course, several authors have made the distinction between a mere *threat* and *the intention to carry out the threat.*[1] This distinction may be valid in the case of parents threatening their children with punishment, or even in the situation of a criminal threatening his/her victim during an armed robbery. However, it is unfortunately the case that no nuclear nation-state can be expected to refrain from the use of nuclear weapons if it perceives its national or ideological vital interests to be at severe risk, and that the use of these weapons gives hope that those interests would be safeguarded thereby, or at worst, that its adversary would also suffer the loss of its vital interests in the war.

The reasons which initiate a policy of nuclear deterrence require that the threat to retaliate be intended, at least in those instances when the state is forced to preserve its national and ideological vital interests. As long as the ultimate obligation of political leaders is seen to be the protection of national security and the ideological vital interests of the nation-state, nuclear deterrence must be based on a sincere intention to carry out the threat, whenever the national or ideological security of the state or that of its allies is perceived to be in jeopardy.

Socialist leaders, however, in effect have condemned the use of nuclear weapons; yet they maintain that to threaten even massive retaliation in order to achieve deterrence is morally justified, at least for the present. This position, however, appears to lead to the rejection of the intuitively plausible principle of justified threatening, namely, "threatening is only morally justified if carrying out the threat is morally justified."

Marxist scholars, generally, have not confronted or even directly admitted the moral paradox involved in nuclear deterrence. This paradox can be avoided, I suggest, only by accepting a Kantian deontological ethical stance which rejects outright the moral justification of deterrence under any circumstances, or by retreating to the other end of the ethical spectrum to accept an act-utilitarianism which sees no problem with the principle of justified threatening, because the utility arising from deterrence outweighs the harm incurred from the risk of nuclear genocide, or even from the risk of humanicide or omnicide. Marxists, however, accept neither of these ethical stances, and hence are left in a moral quandary, which is admitted only rarely.

No possible Marxist goals can be accomplished, except perhaps accidentally, by an act of massive retaliation. Such an act by a socialist state would violate its basic values, and would have to be considered irrational and absurd from the viewpoint of Marxism, whatever the circumstances.

Issuing a threat to retaliate with the intention to possibly end human history, to destroy all life on this planet, and to remove all meaning from reality is in conflict with the deepest values of Marxist-Leninists. As mentioned previously, it stands in contradiction with Marxist social goals of perfecting human society, with the Marxist philosophy of history, and with the Marxist understanding of the ultimate meaning of reality as centered on intelligent life. Yet the policy of nuclear deterrence still appears quite rational, and indeed necessary for the socialist states. Hence, Marxist scholars face a profound moral dilemma.

This dilemma must be resolved in the practical realm by moving beyond the perceived need for nuclear deterrence as quickly as possible. I suggest that those Marxists who insist that the need for nuclear deterrence is a permanent one, must be willing to live permanently with a moral dilemma as well.

The moral issue arising from nuclear deterrence cannot be sidestepped by arguing that a military confrontation between the ideological blocs can remain limited even with the existence of nuclear arsenals. This kind of reasoning, I submit, is faulty and dangerous.

Leaders in socialist states, of course, do recognize the differences between massive retaliation and flexible response, between countervalue—that is, countercity strategy—and counterforce strategy, between mutual assured destruction (MAD) and the countervailing and prevailing nuclear utilization targeting strategies. They recognize that a limited nuclear war, limited to battlefield weapons, or to intermediate-range theater weapons, or even to a minimal exchange of strategic weapons, is possible *in the abstract*, because of technological advances in graduated throw-weight capacities, in targeting accuracy, and in the increased durability of communication channels between the adversaries even after a nuclear exchange. *In practice*, however, the notion of a limited war between the major ideological blocs is highly improbable because it violates a basic principle of Clausewitz regarding the utmost use of force.[2]

For Clausewitz the purpose of every state in war is to break the will of the enemy to resist. Any state must exert whatever amount of force is necessary to break the will of the adversary to resist. If the perceived national (and now also must be added the ideological) vital interests of the adversary state are at risk, the utmost use of force ordinarily is required. If the perceived national and ideological vital interests of both sides are at risk, total war results.

In total war neither side can allow the other to win, that is, to set the terms for peace. Intra-war deterrent limits, therefore, will not hold if one side begins to lose, that is, begins to perceive its vital interests to be in jeopardy because of the imposed limits. At that moment the only limitations on the means used are determined by strategy, economics, technical abilities, that which Clausewitz calls "the moral quality" of the armed forces, and the temper of the populace.

It is obvious that World War III would be such a total war. Hence the probabilities that a conventional war would remain nonnuclear, or that a nuclear war would remain limited, are practically nonexistent. World War III must not come to pass. In a world of nuclear armaments, this war would entail at best an act of genocide (i.e., the systematic extermination of a nation or a people for social or political purposes) by the winning side, but humanicide or omnicide would be the more likely result.

Because of this clear realization, socialist leaders have urged not only freezes, no-first-use policies, arms reductions and eventual disarmament, but they have issued a challenge to change our understanding of the very nature of peace, and the nature of the vital interest of states as well.[3] All persons of good will must accept this challenge and strive toward these goals.

Since world peace obviously is of mutual benefit in the ideological conflict of the contending blocs, the recognition by each side that policies of nuclear deterrence create a moral dilemma not only for itself but for the other side as well, should propel both towards its resolution through practical measures. Practical resolution of the dilemma requires the continual reduction of nuclear arsenals while maintaining strategic military balance and stability. At the same time, each side must expect its antagonist to maintain and advance its ideological principles.

Gradual elimination of the need for nuclear deterrence, and, eventually, of the need for conventional deterrence as well through confidence-building measures, should be the final goal of all state-to-state relations between the contending blocs.

Important as this is, it does not resolve the immediate moral dilemma of nuclear deterrence facing Marxists. Marxist scholars must commit themselves more resolutely to this problem. Joint creative effort on their part must be forthcoming now and into the 1990s. A commitment to Marxism requires a commitment to resolve this moral dilemma of nuclear deterrence through providing viable policy alternatives for the socialist states. These efforts cannot shun risk or await a favorable attitude by the other side. Merely to blame the other side for the dilemma is no longer sufficient. Marxism must be true to itself and its principles, on its own terms. The fate of humanity must be its *ultimate* concern, whatever the risks.

There are strong indications that recent nuclear arms proposals by the socialist states reflect awareness of this dilemma and the urgency to resolve it. It is not clear, however, that major risks are yet being contemplated to achieve this goal. In any case, the work remains for Marxist scholars and indeed for non-Marxists who are willing to face up to the dilemma of nuclear deterrence.

Holy Cross College

Notes

[1] Perhaps the best known presentation of the distinction is that of Gregory S. Kavka, "Some Paradoxes of Deterrence," *The Journal of Philosophy* 75 (1978) 285-302.

[2] Carl von Clausewitz, *On War,* eds. and trans. Michael Howard and Peter Paret (Princeton, N.J.: Princeton University Press, 1976) 77. See also, Bernard Brodie's introductory essay to this edition of *On War* 53-54, and W.B. Gallie, *Philosophers of Peace and War* (Cambridge: Cambridge University Press, 1978) chapter 3. For an opposite view on escalation, see Herman Kahn, *On Escalation* (New York: Frederick A. Praeger, 1965), or his *On Thermonuclear War* (Princeton, N.J.: Princeton University Press, 1960) chapter 3.

[3] Statement by Mikhail Gorbachev, General Secretary of the CPSU Central Committee, January 15, 1986 (Moscow: Novosti Press Agency Publishing House, 1986).

On the Implications of Sociobiology
for Nuclear Weapons Policy

Jonathan Schonsheck

I. Introduction to the Issues

This paper is a fragment of a much larger project whose central thesis
is that (some variant of) nuclear deterrence is the optimal nuclear
weapons strategy for the United States.[1] Not only is it a fragment; it is
a *programmatic* fragment. The various sections are not intended to
conclusively argue their respective claims; such would take
considerably more space than can be devoted here. Rather, this paper
is a sketch of its portion of the overall argument, intended to show the
direction, and the sorts of evidence and argumentation, that will appear
in a substantially longer version.[2]

I am not enamored with nuclear deterrence *ab initio*; rather, after
considerable research and reflection, I have come to the conclusion
that there is no superior alternative, on either strategic or on moral
grounds.

Elsewhere I have argued that limited nuclear warfighting ought to
be rejected, because too much would have to "go right" for such a
conflict to remain limited.[3] I reject "defense" as an alternative, because
it is not credible that any incarnation of the Strategic "Defense"
Initiative could prove so reliable that it would be rational for the United
States to shift from a policy of preclusion (deterrence) to a policy of
interception (defense). Incarnations of SDI that are *more* credible
technologically are not in fact strategies of "defense" but variants of
deterrence; as such, they must be considered along with other weapons
systems which are designed to enhance, and not replace, deterrence.[4]
Not incidentally, as *variants* of deterrence, the various incarnations of
SDI are burdened with all the moral liabilities that philosophers have
attributed to deterrence.

Philosophical rejections of nuclear deterrence typically have the
format of detailing, in pristine isolation, the moral debits of deterrence,
that is, without looking to the moral credits that accrue to deterrence,
and without any assessment of the moral debits (and of course credits)
of alternative nuclear weapons policies. But every nuclear weapons

policy—*including the policy of having no nuclear weapons*—has moral consequences, has both moral credits and moral debits. It is both philosophically and politically irresponsible to urge the rejection of current public policy unless one, in conjunction, argues for the moral superiority of some *alternative* policy.[5]

In this paper I argue that the geopolitical scene *irremediably* consists of mutually suspicious and hostile groups, and that this fact can best be explained sociobiologically. If this is correct, it has profound implications for the selection of a nuclear weapons strategy.

II. Evolutionary Biology and Sociobiology[6]

In *The Fate of the Earth,* Jonathan Schell refers to "the old truth that all men are brothers."[7] Schell couldn't be more wrong; it simply is not the case that "all men are brothers" (or, eschewing sexism, that "all people are siblings"). Despite the attractiveness of the old saying, it is a mere metaphor; taken as an empirical claim, it is obviously false on genetic grounds. What is of interest, however, is not its falsity *per se,* but the *reason* that it is false, and the *implications* of its falsity. It is *because* "the human family" is a metaphor only, and that the genetic reality is that the globe's population is divided into groups with biologically distinct ancestries, that sociobiology is so relevant to the issues of nuclear weapons policies.

Although the offspring of (sexually reproducing) parents closely resemble their parents, there are genetic differences amongst the offspring (except in the case of monozygotic multiples), and these genetic differences—usually through various sorts of interactions with the environment—result in differing traits amongst the offspring. No environment can long support the geometric rate of reproduction of which species are (theoretically) capable; some individuals will survive and reproduce; other individuals will not survive. In general, those which survive have in fact survived in virtue of a trait or traits which, in their particular environment, gave them a differential advantage in the struggle for survival. Over time, the characteristics of a species change; the pressures of natural selection assure that species will evolve to resemble their more successful members. *Individual selection*—that selection pressures bear on individual organisms, and that individuals are (broadly) selected for or against in virtue of their individual traits—is the core of evolutionary biology.

Refinements must be made, however, if certain phenomena are to be explained. Consider first the social insects. Individual worker bees will defend their hives by stinging intruders, even though the defending bee dies in the attack. Similarly, individual ants will launch suicidal attacks in defense of their respective colonies. Now no one seriously maintains that this is "learned" behavior; it must be genetically based.[8] So long as one is confined to *individual* selection, one cannot explain this behavior. Dead defenders do not reproduce; the genetic endowment for such behavior, it would seem, would be selected against. How is it that the genetic endowment for suicidal defense in honeybees, for example, has been selected for? The worker bees of a given hive are sisters; all have descended from the hive's queen. In sacrificing herself in defense of the hive, a worker does not pass on her genes, and in particular, the genetic endowment for suicidal defense. However, that genetic endowment is *shared* by the survivors, and of course was passed down to them by their mother, the queen, who will pass it on, in turn, to the future queen, via the successfully defended queen. The genetic endowment for traits which are *individually* destructive, but which contribute to the survival of other individuals of very similar genetic make-up—for example, that individual's relatives—will be preserved, and will be passed down through collateral lines of descent. Thus, selection pressures bear not only on individuals, but on families; in the struggle for survival amongst families, those families with self-sacrificing members would prosper at the expense of those families without self-sacrificing members. And the genetic endowment contributing to that behavior would be preserved in the surviving members of those prospering families. This explanation is known as "kin selection," or alternatively as "inclusive fitness."[9]

Selection pressures bear not only on individuals and on families, but on *groups* of individuals. Thus, it sometimes happens that the struggle for survival—as when the struggle is for control of some essential resource—is not between two (or more) individuals per se, nor two (or more) families (qua families), but between two or more *collections* of individuals—between tribes, for example. Very broadly speaking, we would expect those groups whose members were unified, energized, and motivated to sacrifice for the group, to prevail over competing groups whose members were less cohesive, less energized, and less motivated.

No one (rationally) claims that contemporary human behavior is wholly determined by genetic endowment. However, it would be foolish to deny the evolutionary history of homo sapiens, or to hold that contemporary human behavior is unaffected by the selection pressures that bore on our ancestors for the vast majority of the species' history. So, what are (some of) the consequences of individual selection, kin selection, and group selection on homo sapiens?

III. Some Implications of Sociobiology

The way I have selected to investigate the implications of sociobiology is to consider the implications discussed by Peter Singer in his early work on these issues, *The Expanding Circle: Ethics and Sociobiology*, and then to offer a critique of significant portions of Singer's position.

Singer claims, correctly, I believe, that the pressures of individual, kin and group selection favors groups whose individual members carry a genetic endowment predisposing them towards *sociability*—e.g., cooperation, reciprocity, sacrifice for the group. Social life requires that each member of the group observe a certain line of conduct towards the other members of the group. What line of conduct? That which could be justified by "impartial" reasons. Singer rightly claims, as regards the justification of one's actions, that "a barefaced appeal to self-interest will not do."[10] To what ought one appeal? Singer's central notion is "universal impartiality," or "disinterestedness." He writes,

> That one's own interests are one among many sets of interests, no more important than the similar interests of others, is a conclusion that, in principle, any rational being can come to see.[11]

Singer continues,

> In making ethical decisions I am trying to make decisions which can be defended to *others*. This requires me to take a perspective from which my own interests count no more, simply because they are my own, than the similar interests of *others*.[12]

To *which* "others" must I justify my actions? The interests of *which* "others" must I count as much as I count my own? Singer acknowledges that, at least at first, the "others" include only members of one's own tribe.

> . . . Ethics involves justifying one's conduct to one's tribal group or society. . . .Obviously there are actions one can defend in a manner that is acceptable within one's own society, but unacceptable to members of other societies. Tribal moralities often take exactly this form.[13]

According to Singer, it is *moral reasoning* itself which will compel people to acknowledge an ever-expanding moral community to which one's actions must be justified.

> The idea of a disinterested defense of one's conduct emerges because of the social nature of humans and the requirements of group living, but in the thought of reasoning beings, it takes on a logic of its own which leads to its extension beyond the bounds of the group.[14]

How far will it expand?

> If I have seen that from an ethical point of view I am just one person among the many in my society, and my interests are no more important, from the point of view of the whole, than the similar interests of others within my society, I am ready to see that, from a still larger point of view, my society is just one among other societies, and the interests of members of my society are no more important, from the larger perspective, than the similar interests of members of other societies. Ethical reasoning, once begun, pushes against our initially limited ethical horizons, leading us always toward a more universal point of view. . . .The circle of altruism has broadened from the family and tribe to the nation and race, and we are beginning to recognize that our obligations extend to all human beings. . . .The only justifiable stopping place for the expansion of altruism is the point at which all whose welfare can be affected by our actions are included within the circle of altruism. This means that all beings with the capacity to feel pleasure or pain should be included . . . .

> The expansion of the moral circle should therefore be pushed out until it includes most animals.[15]

Singer claims that selection pressures conjoined with the power of ethical reasoning itself are forcing individuals to "expand the circle" that encloses the members of one's moral community; soon, all humans will consider all other humans (and some animals too) as members of a single, global moral community. As such, each will see oneself morally bound to regard all others as moral equals, and will be prepared to justify one's conduct, with impartial reasons, towards all other humans.

Are the various selection pressures, conjoined with the power of ethical reasoning itself, pushing people into this philosophical position? I think not; Singer has neglected some important consequences of these selection pressures. When these neglected consequences are incorporated into the implications of sociobiology, the outlook for homo sapiens is decidedly less cheerful.

IV. The Critique: No "In-Group" *Amity* Without "Out-Group" *Enmity*

I begin my critique of Singer by invoking the wonderful words of David Hume:

> But would these reasoners look abroad into the world, they would meet
> with nothing that in the least corresponds with their ideas, or can
> warrant so refined and philosophical a system.[16]

Let us set aside the difficult issues of "animal rights," and focus on the sufficiently difficult issues of human actions towards other humans. When Singer claims that "the circle of altruism has broadened from the family and tribe to the nation and race, and we are beginning to recognize that our obligations extend to all human beings," to whom does the "we" refer? The "expansion of the circle" described by Singer, the counting of all humans as moral beings, moral equals, quite simply and obviously does not obtain. Singer is mistaken in the one example that he provides, and in a wide array of examples that he does not consider. For example, he says:

> Romans looked on barbarians as beings who could be captured like
> animals for use as slaves or made to entertain the crowds by killing
> each other in the Coliseum. *In modern times Europeans have stopped,
> treating each other in this way.*[17]

Grotesque cultural chauvinism aside, Singer seems to have forgotten the array of atrocities known collectively as the Holocaust—atrocities not dissimilar to the ones mentioned (except that they occurred on a far greater scale), perpetrated by Europeans, and hardly ancient history. Consider now the numerous instances of ongoing ethnic violence that dot the globe. The "we" who consider all other humans as moral equals surely does not refer to the Tamils as regards the Sinhalese (and conversely). Nor can it refer to the Tibetans as regards the Chinese (and conversely), nor to the Palestinians as regards the Israelis (and conversely), nor to the Muslim Afghans as regards the Marxist Soviets. Closer to home, it is hardly applicable to Irish Catholics as regards Irish Protestants (and conversely); moving to the cradle of civilization, it is inapplicable to the Armenians as regards the Turks (and conversely). Of course this list is but a minute sample of the extant sectarian, tribal, ethnocentric violence that is the most striking feature of the current geopolitical scene. Perhaps Singer and a few other vegetarian philosophers are included in the "we" whose circle of altruism has expanded to include all sentient beings, but as anything like a characterization of the world's population, it is ludicrous. It is not just that members of competing groups do not acknowledge the interests of the members of opposing groups as not equivalent to the interests of the members of one's own group. It is that doing certain harmful things to the members of the "out-group" merit "in-group" honor and praise.

How has it come about that the most accurate political characterization of the globe is that it contains indefinitely many mutually suspicious and hostile groups? It is because selection pressures, especially the pressures of *group* selection, predispose not only "in-group" amity, but also "out-group" *enmity.*

Membership in, and identification with, a group of closely related individuals (what researchers R. Paul Shaw and Yuwa Wong call "nucleus ethnicity"[18]) was, for most of the species' history, essential for survival. For

> . . .in the past million years or so an increasing proportion of man's "hostile environment" has been other nucleus ethnic groups engaged in resource competition. While the *unit* of selection remains that of the gene and their individual carriers, intergroup conflict has rendered groups of ever-expanding size and internal structure effective *forces* of selection.[19]

In the struggle for survival—most importantly, a struggle between groups of humans for control of important resources—groups which were highly unified and energized would have fared better than those which were less unified or less motivated. "In early homonid evolution, it is likely that membership in an expanded group would have increased each individual's access to scarce resources and ability to manage others."[20] Shaw and Wong conclude

> . . .that individuals have evolved not only to be egoistic, but to be nepotistically altruistic; that individuals, and individuals in nucleus ethnic groups, are predisposed to mobilize for resource competition in ways that will enhance inclusive fitness and reproductive potential; and that a link exists between ethnic mobilization for competition over scarce resources and the idea that intergroup conflict/warfare has been positively functional in humanity's evolution.[21]

That predisposition is made manifest through "learning rules," as described by sociobiologist E. O. Wilson:

> The learning potential of each species appears to be fully programmed by the structure of its brain, the sequence of release of its hormones, and, ultimately, its genes. Each animal species is "prepared" to learn certain stimuli, barred from learning others, and neutral with respect to still others.[22]

Elsewhere, Wilson speaks of "innate censors and motivators" which powerfully affect our behavior, prerational "pushes" and "pulls" which make certain lines of conduct more likely, and other lines of conduct less likely.[23]

Human beings are, by nature, *bifurcators:* we divide the world into "in-group" and "out-group," into "us" and "them." Wilson writes,

> In all periods of life there is [a] . . . powerful urge to dichotomize, to classify other human beings into two artificially sharpened categories. We seem able to be fully comfortable only when the remainder of humanity can be labeled as members versus nonmembers, kin versus nonkin, friend versus foe.[24]

We are predisposed, then, by "innate censors and motivators," to be egoistic (or selfish) as a result of individual selection, but *also* to be "nepotistically altruistic" as a result of kin selection. And group selection would favor those "nucleus ethnic" groups which are the most cohesive, and, in times of resource scarcity, the most aggressive. Bifurcating the world, dividing it into "us" and "them," provides one with one's identity. Additionally, to a very large extent what is permissible and impermissible conduct towards others is determined by this classification:

> In general, primitive men divide the world into two tangible parts, the near environment of homes, local villages, kin, friends, tame animals, and witches, and the more distant universe of neighboring villages, intertribal allies, enemies, wild animals and ghosts. This elemental topography makes easier the distinction between enemies who can be attacked and killed and friends who cannot. This contrast is heightened by reducing enemies to frightful and even sub-human status.[25]

Indeed,

> Human beings are strongly predisposed to respond with unreasoning hatred to external threats and to escalate their hostility sufficiently to overwhelm the source of the threat by a respectably wide margin of safety. Our brains do appear to be programmed to the following extent: we are inclined to partition other people into friends and aliens, in the same sense that birds are inclined to learn territorial songs and to navigate by the polar constellations. We tend to fear deeply the actions of strangers and to solve conflict by aggression. These learning rules are most likely to have evolved during the past hundreds of thousands of years of human evolution and, thus, to have conferred a biological advantage on those who conformed to them with the greatest fidelity.[26]

Succinctly stated, and invoking the terms of Shaw and Wong, human beings are innately, that is, biologically, predisposed towards *both* "in-group amity" and "out-group enmity."[27]

Are contemporary human beings "tribal" in this way? Yes and no. In some societies, where mobility is limited,

> . . .the political behavior of nations remains partially, if not largely, in the service of dominant ethnic groups and . . .this helps clarify how vestiges of in-group amity and out-group enmity have been carried over from band to tribe to community to nation.[28]

Given the mobility of contemporary industrial societies, however, it is not plausible to maintain that one receives one's identity solely from, feels one's loyalties solely to, some group to the members of which one is genetically related. Humans *remain*, however, bifurcators. Given the ability to recognize individuals, and to remember their past behavior, *reciprocity* is possible. Individuals can develop relationships in which the assistance of a person at one time can be reciprocated at some later time. Those who can be relied upon to discharge their obligations will participate in more such mutually advantageous arrangements, enhancing genetic fitness; those who cannot be relied upon will tend to be excluded from such arrangements.

In contemporary societies, humans become members of a wide array of distinguishable groups, groups within which one finds more or less specified sets of permissions, obligations, and prohibitions: what I shall call "loyalty groups."[29] These include, but are by no means limited to: families, neighborhoods, cities, nation-states, professional societies, fraternities, fraternal organizations, high schools, colleges and universities, alumni associations, corporations and industries, churches and religions. Often the specific prohibitions, obligations and permissions of such loyalty groups are disparate, operating on separable portions of one's life; sometimes they conflict, engendering the most serious sorts of individual moral dilemmas.

I assert the following: (i) that in *different contexts* we conceive of ourselves as members of different loyalty groups; (ii) that our membership in various loyalty groups differs as regards duration, depth of allegiance, and so on, (iii) that a person can choose to join or leave (the influence of) the various loyalty groups of which one considers oneself a member, but that, very importantly, (iv) we derive our identity from loyalty groups, and rarely conceive of ourselves other than as a member of some loyalty group or another. We bifurcate the world in many different ways, depending upon the context, but almost always as the member of some loyalty group. Finally, and most importantly, (v) a significant *factor* in unifying and energizing loyalty groups is opposition to (from friendly rivalry to mortal hostility) another, or other, loyalty groups of the relevant context.

Singer is correct in his claim that selection pressures favor sociability, including the observing of a certain line of conduct towards the other members of one's group, a line of conduct that can be justified by invoking "impartial" reasons. He is correct in claiming that we are often required to provide such justifications, *in fact* regarding the interests of "others" as equal to one's own. But Singer is mistaken in his claim that the power of moral reasoning will compel individuals to regard the interests of all other human beings as equal to one's own.

Granted, individuals conceive themselves as members of many different loyalty groups. But membership in such groups is fluid and transient; Singer's optimism requires something far more rigid and stable: a *universal* moral community. There is no empirical evidence that supports such a coalescing of disparate ethnic and national groups into a single moral community; indeed, of late there has been a rise in ethnocentrism and sectarian violence.[30] And this is predictable, when one takes the measure of kin selection and group selection on thousands of generations of our ancestors.

A globe populated by mutually suspicious and hostile groups is a political reality which we all—philosophers, politicians, statesmen—must acknowledge, a reality which constrains work both practical and theoretical.

V. Implications for Nuclear Weapons Policies

If mutually suspicious and antagonistic loyalty groups, incarnated as nation-states and alliances of nation-states, are an irremediable feature of the geopolitical landscape, there are important consequences for the selection of a nation's nuclear weapons policy. So long as nuclear weapons are conceived as augmenting the strength of a nation, unilateral nuclear disarmament will not be a viable option. Political leaders will not propose, and citizens will not tolerate, a perceived relative reduction in military strength. The prospects for mutual nuclear disarmament are not much brighter. The citizens of the competing nations are "bifurcators"; they divide the world, each group perceiving itself as trustworthy and peace-loving, but the opposition as dishonest, scheming warmongers. The complex issues of "verification" of arms reduction treaties are but a veneer of civility overlaying this hostility. In consequence, and since "defense" is not a technologically plausible option, as I have argued, some species of nuclear deterrence is the optimal nuclear weapons policy.

Nothing I have said, however, precludes the possibility of (somewhat) reduced levels of nuclear weapons. (The disinclination of the general public to see, despite the scientific evidence, that a significant portion of the existing stockpile of nuclear weapons is superfluous, is explicable in sociobiological terms.) Additionally, measures can be taken to *stabilize* deterrence, and to *restore* stability should deterrence fail. It is to these issues that philosophical attention can most profitably be turned.

LeMoyne College

Notes

[1] An earlier version of this paper, under the title "Sociobiology and Nuclear Weapons Policy," was read at the First National Conference of Concerned Philosophers for Peace meeting at the University of Dayton, Ohio, October 15-17, 1987. I benefited greatly from the heated discussion which ensued.

[2] In Defense of Nuclear Deterrence, unpublished ms.

[3] Jonathan Schonsheck and J. Barron Boyd, Jr., "The Rationality of M.A.D.ness," unpublished ms.

[4] Jonathan Schonsheck, "Confusion and False Advertising of the Strategic 'Defense' Initiatives," *International Journal on World Peace*, V.3 (1988) 69-107. See, too, Jonathan Schonsheck, "Philosophical Scrutiny of the Strategic 'Defense' Initiatives," *Journal of Applied Philosophy*, 3.2 (1986) 151-166, excerpted in *Ethics and Strategic Defense: American Philosophers Debate Star Wars and the Future of Nuclear Deterrence*, ed. Douglas P. Lackey (Belmont, CA: Wadsworth Publishing Co., 1989.)

[5] Jonathan Schonsheck, "Wrongful Threats, Wrongful Intentions and Moral Judgements about Nuclear Weapons Policies," *The Monist* 70 (1987) 330-356.

[6] Portions of this and the following section have been extracted and modified to become an independent paper, "Constraints on *The Expanding Circle*: A Critique of Singer," *Inquiries into Values: The Inaugural Session of the International Society for Value Inquiry*, ed. Sander H. Lee (Lewiston, NY: Edwin Mellen Press) 695-707.

[7] Jonathan Schell, *The Fate of the Earth* (New York: Alfred A. Knopf, 1982) 185.

[8] I do not here embrace the "nature/nurture dichotomy," that every trait is due exclusively to nature or exclusively to nurture. I am a proponent of gene-environment interactionism. However, the "brain" size of the social insects is too limited for the environment to contribute *learning* to the defensive behavior (though, of course, it contributes the triggering stimulus).

[9] R. Paul Shaw and Yuwa Wong, "Ethnic Mobilization and the Seeds of Warfare: An Evolutionary Perspective," *International Studies Quarterly* 31 (1987) 4.

[10] Peter Singer, *The Expanding Circle: Ethics and Sociology* (New York: New American Library, 1981) 93.

[11] Singer 106.

[12] Singer 106 (emphasis added).

[13] Singer 111.

[14] Singer 114 (emphasis added).

[15] Singer 119-20.

[16] David Hume, "Of the Original Contract, *Hume's Moral and Political Philosophy,* ed. Henry D. Aiken (Darien, CT: Hafner Publishing Co., 1979).

[17] Singer 113 (emphasis added).

[18] Shaw and Wong 10.

[19] Shaw and Wong 11.

[20] Shaw and Wong 11.

[21] Shaw and Wong 12.

[22] Edward O. Wilson, *On Human Nature* (New York: Bantam Books, 1978) 67.

[23] Wilson 5.

[24] Wilson 72.

[25] Wilson 114.

[26] Wilson 122-23.

[27] Shaw and Wong 10.

[28] Shaw and Wong 10.

[29] This name was inspired by Andrew Oldenquist, "Loyalties," *The Journal of Philosophy*, LXXIX.4 (1982).

[30] cf. the current turmoil amongst the ethnic Armenians in the Soviet Union's Republic of Azerbaijan.

5

The Arms-Race Implications
   of Libertarian Capitalism

Joseph Kunkel

Three modern proponents of libertarian capitalism, each representing a different approach to underpinning the arguments, are Robert Nozick, Ayn Rand, and Milton Friedman. Robert Nozick argues that respect for rights allows a minimalist government which only protects against individuals infringing on one another. Ayn Rand concentrates on natural virtue, with selfishness or self-interest advanced over altruism. Milton Friedman contends in a consequentialist manner that capitalism alone among economic principles is supportive of freedom. In this essay I propose to examine the effects of these views on the arms race.[1]

The paper is divided into two sections. The first presents the main tenets of libertarian capitalism as espoused by these thinkers, and then offers brief counterarguments to their positions. My intention is to provide an overview by way of introduction, while at the same time balancing the libertarian perspective with contrary, albeit not conclusive, argumentation. The second section, which is the main focus, brings out the implications for the arms race. Such an issue is seldom directly addressed by libertarians. Thus, for example, in Tibor R. Machan's otherwise excellent anthology *The Main Debate*, libertarian authors are contrasted with Marxist authors on many themes, but not on the arms race.[2] In order to ferret out the nuclear implications, at least regarding libertarian capitalism, I propose to examine three issues that relate to the topic. The first is the libertarian view on remedying a principal cause fueling war, namely, world hunger. The second is the libertarian view on world governance as a means for bringing together peoples of diverse ideologies. The third is the libertarian view on war itself, which today for major powers translates into preparing for nuclear conflict.

The Tenets of Libertarian Capitalism

Capitalism affirms that the common good can best be served not by centralized government planning, but by the free flow of the market place. One gets whatever one needs for a price in the market place. Since everyone's needs are different, everyone ought to be allowed to meet her own needs without interference by the state. By not interfering in the economy, the state maximizes the liberty of the citizenry—hence the name libertarianism. Libertarian capitalism thus embodies two principles: a separation of government from the economy, with the market place deciding all economic issues, and, secondly, a role for government restricted to not interfering with citizen activity except to prevent harm or to rectify unjust economic gains.

Nozick calls our original acquisition of holdings our entitlement.[3] We begin life's development with the possessions we have when we are born, and wherever we are born. In this way no one can be held responsible for distributing or redistributing the goods of the earth. As the sole proprietor of my entitled possessions, I am only justified in transferring my own holdings to other persons. For Nozick no one, under justice, is entitled to holdings except by original acquisition or by transfer of holdings. Justice, according to Nozick, also stipulates that any other type of acquiring holdings, such as taxing the rich to feed the poor, is unjust, and in need of rectification.

The reaction to injustice, for Nozick, follows from the principle of self-defense. Traditionally, self-defense entails protection from those who would forcibly violate others' rights. Since rights, however, for Nozick are associated with the entitlement of holdings, he redefines self-defense to stipulate that everyone "may defend himself against unknown or unreliable procedures and may punish those who use or attempt to use such procedures against him."[4] In accord with this principle, individuals form group mutual-protection agencies. These, in turn, through one of several possibilities reduce to single dominant protective agencies for separate geographical areas. These dominant protective agencies spell out the rules for protecting against, compensating for, and punishing harms that are committed against their clients. These agencies thus become *de facto*, not *de jure*, minimal states for their areas. In the process of forming such states, Nozick remains within his narrowly prescribed boundaries of individual self-protection and of our own power to enforce this self-protection. Going beyond these minimal safety needs, Nozick argues, constitutes coercion and therefore is an unwarranted infringement upon individual rights.

Various criticisms have been leveled against Nozick's theory. One of the main criticisms attacks the restrictive meaning of what is said to harm or to limit the freedom of individuals. For instance, what if some people who defend themselves "against unknown or unreliable procedures" are of the socialist persuasion and choose a group mutual protection agency accordingly? What happens if such an agency becomes the *de facto* dominant protective agency for a geographical area? Obviously there is no problem for Nozick if socialists dominate a community in accord with Nozick's principles. But what if they disagree fundamentally with Nozick and lead according to their own principles? The issue concerns the meaning of freedom and what constitutes an infringement on rights, and socialists hold that rights are socially, not individually, based.

In a similar vein, Virginia Held contends that freedom is more than the negative freedom from interference by others:

> . . . .[W]e can be free *from* physical assault as we sit in the park and free *to* eat a lunch while we are there. The former requires that police protection against assault be provided by the society; the latter that the society has provided a park and made it possible for us to acquire food.[5]

Freedom *from* is not more fundamental than freedom *to*, and either aspect of freedom can be infringed upon. A person living in poverty, without medical care or the possibility of a job, and with limited education can be harmed by "unknown or unreliable procedures" functioning in society. Such a person thus has her right to freedom *to*, or to positive freedom, interfered with by societal norms. Should not the dominant protective agencies also protect against societal interference?

Rand approaches the issue by distinguishing selfish activities from altruistic ones. Each person, she says, only survives by looking after his own self-interest. Self-interest is not meant in the Hobbesian sense of warring against all others, but as a "nonsacrificial relationship with others."[6] Individuals ought to "deal with one another as *traders,* giving value for value." Altruism, on the other hand, "holds that man has no right to exist for his own sake, that service to others is the only justification of his existence, and that self-sacrifice is his highest moral duty, virtue, and value." Rand is not hereby denying that individuals in Nozick's sense may choose to transfer some of their own holdings to others. Her point is rather that the underlying orientation of a society is either based on self-interest or altruism, and such an orientation ought to be founded on self-interest. For Rand, governments that push positive freedoms are unethically sacrificing individuals for the sake of others. Altruism maintains death, instead of life, "as its ultimate goal and standard of value." Rand thus polarizes fundamental concepts. An individual or a state is predominantly one quality or its opposite, hot or cold, virtuous or evil. Where, for instance, one would place parents and children, or the sick, starving, and poor in this schema is not clear: are parents, in parenting children, self-interested or self-sacrificing, or some of each? The world seems to be more complicated than Rand's dichotomies allow.

Milton Friedman endorses capitalism because it alone has an economic system that enhances freedom. He says:

> Fundamentally, there are only two ways of co-ordinating the economic activities of millions. One is central direction involving the use of coercion—the technique of the army and of the modern totalitarian state. The other is voluntary co-operation of individuals—the technique of the market place.[7]

In the market place there is no coercion. As Friedman says, "The consumer is protected from coercion by the seller because of the presence of other sellers with whom he can deal. The seller is protected from coercion by the consumer because of other consumers to whom he can sell."[8]

Friedman is not so much arguing out of set principles as looking at results. In this regard he is a consequentialist. But he too tends to dichotomize. Thus, in arguing that the market place is the sole ingredient in economic freedom and that everything else is coercion, Friedman leaves out factors that are inbetween. For example, is there no coercion on the employees inside multi-conglomerate companies as long as their products compete in a free market place? Friedman says, "The employee is protected from coercion by the employer because of other employers for whom he can work. . . ."[9] Is Friedman seriously talking about any employee, with or without family, male or female, black, white, or yellow, at any age—40, 50, or 60, with or without that employee's pension plan? Freedom from, perhaps, but freedom to or for what?

On the role of government, Friedman is a bit more realistic. He does not contend that all government involvement in the economic process is coercive, nor unjust in Nozick's sense, nor nonvirtuous in Rand's sense. Friedman—or actually in this case the Friedmans, Milton and his wife Rose—quoting Adam Smith, accept as part of the positive authority of government "the duty of erecting and maintaining certain public works and certain public institutions, which it can never be for the interest of any individual, or small number of individuals, to erect and maintain."[10] They also add another positive duty of government: "the duty to protect members of the community who cannot be regarded as 'responsible' individuals."[11] Nonlibertarians, of course, would argue to bolster this list of positive duties, while libertarian purists call for its deletion.

Libertarian Capitalism and the Arms Race

Libertarian capitalism, as we have shown, entails two principles: first, a government strictly divorced from the economy with economic issues decided in the market place, and second, the restriction of the role of government to the negative duties of preventing harm or rectifying unjust economic gains. In introducing these principles I have also indicated that their conclusiveness is debatable. In this section I want to go further, to draw out the consequences of these principles for the question of nuclear arms. Accordingly, three issues that bear on the question of international violence will be examined within the libertarian capitalist perspective. These issues are world hunger, a framework for world governance, and war. By examining these issues I believe the adverse implications of libertarian capitalism for the arms race will be made obvious.

In approaching world hunger, Nozick would insist that everyone's rights be respected. The rich cannot be taxed to feed the poor. This position, of course, is countered by the arguments questioning the fundamental meaning of rights, freedom, and so on—arguments we discussed previously. The Friedmans take a different tack; they are consequentialists. They say, "We know of no society that has ever achieved prosperity and freedom unless voluntary exchange has been its dominant principle of organization."[12] Hunger thus can only be alleviated by free trade. In response to the query, "What possessions do the poor have to trade?" the Friedmans point to the poor's labor.

The poor can trade their labor for food and money. The only interference in this process, according to libertarians, is government intervention. Centralized planning, as in India or in the Soviet Union, forces the economy to become sluggish.[13] A free economy, on the other hand, surpasses a centralized planned economy because no one person or group can adequately plan for the ever changing needs of the market place.

The Friedmans are fond of supporting their open-market thesis with the example of Hong Kong. They describe Hong Kong as having no tariffs and no government direction of economic activity, and yet enjoying "one of the highest standards of living in all of Asia."[14] But even if we grant what they say about Hong Kong, a single example does not support a universal principle of open market.

Further supporting evidence for a part of the thesis comes from an unlikely source. Researchers, including Frances Moore Lappé and Joseph Collins, at the liberal Institute for Food and Development Policy, based in San Francisco, have concluded that government aid is an obstacle to alleviating world hunger.[15] Their argument, also consequentialist, is that U.S. government aid goes to countries that support anti-communism, instead of countries that are poor. Similarly, governments of recipient nations tend to funnel such aid to those who support their regimes, not to the poor of their land. In this way government aid on both sides of the exchange entrenches, rather than emancipates, the poor.

Where Lappé and Collins disagree with the Friedmans is in the latter's assumption that left to itself, capitalism would resolve the problem of world hunger. This assumption follows from an idyllic utopianism in libertarianism that sees evil only in government, never in business relations, only in political officers, never in business financiers. Business enterprises are pictured as self-cleansing, perhaps inherently cathartic. By contrast, Lappé points out that five major grain-trading companies "account for an incredible 70 to 80 percent of all U.S. grain trade."[16] These companies are involved in every area of the food industry and are capable of keeping competitors out. As multinationals they are independent of national governments, and have the power virtually to dictate international food policies. To make the same point within the canons of libertarianism we need only recall the two centerpieces of Ayn Rand's novels *The Fountainhead* and *Atlas*

Shrugged.[17] Rand greatly preferred the latter work to the former. The government is the culprit in *Atlas Shrugged,* while playing only a minor role in *The Fountainhead.* At least in *The Fountainhead* we are given a clear picture of business leaders who are capable, on their own, of mischief in the market place. Contrary to many libertarians, I contend that both works carry a message for our time.

A criticism of a different kind can be found in the Friedman's own work. In chapter four the Friedmans propose a negative income tax to benefit the needy of the United States.[18] Such a tax is not proposed as an unworkable government subsidy, but as an improvement over the present package of subsidies. Still, the tax itself is government aid, and as such negates the libertarian credo. Indeed, many strict libertarians criticize the Friedmans for breaking faith with libertarianism on this point. But one could argue that the Friedmans are not so much going against their views as being more practically consequentialist about what will work in the United States. Similarly, government aid cannot be said to be universally wrong if such aid can work in the United States. Perhaps we have only been given an ideal to aim at, instead of a principle written in stone.

To sum up these remarks on alleviating world hunger, libertarians maintain that governments may not aid the needy lest they violate the rights of the rich. For this reason free trade alone is posited as the libertarian approach to attacking world hunger. Admittedly, libertarians generally allow aid through voluntary organizations, as long as the volunteers are self-interestedly altruistic, but such aid runs independent of the kinds of argument being made. The point of this section is not that free trade will not improve the lot of the world's hungry, but that limiting the alleviation of hunger to free trade is unacceptable for several reasons. First, the limitation on government aid brought about because of individual rights views rights, as we saw in the previous section, only from the perspective of "freedom from." Second, the Friedmans' consequentialist approach to the same topic does not prove that free trade alone is beneficial. Third, there is good evidence that free-traders left to their own inclinations will not set about improving the plight of the needy. Lastly, the Friedmans have not shown that government aid is always maleficent; in fact, they have supplied contradictory support for and against their thesis. What we are left with is an idealistic libertarian crusade, and a host of poor human beings standing untouched, outside the circle.

Our second issue is world governance. On this topic Nozick gives the best libertarian presentation. Nozick's approach is utopian, or what he calls a "utopian framework."[19] Our examination will be limited to his framework for the actual world. A crucial difference, however, between our real world and Nozick's actual world is Nozick's limiting his discussion to communities, not nations. In a community, every member "face-to-face" helps shape by unanimity the constraints or restrictions imposed on everyone. On membership in a community, Nozick stipulates that everyone must be allowed to opt out of any community—with certain communal restrictions regarding compensation, etc.—when they so desire, and enter into another community if that community admits them. Within this framework some, or all, communities may decide to model themselves after a communist society with equal sharing, distribution of wealth, and other restrictions. In other words, separate communities need not espouse libertarianism within. However, the overall world governance must be structured along libertarian lines, namely, a limited central authority to prevent some communities from interfering with other communities, to adjudicate intracommunity conflicts, and to enforce some individual rights, perhaps of children, and so on. Nozick is thus willing to allow individual communities to decide "face-to-face" on nonlibertarian forms of government, as long as the world governance is thoroughly libertarian.

This last sentence carries the wide-open appeal of Nozick's utopian framework, while at the same time underscoring the suspicious nature of the proposal. Nozick's framework is tantamount to a Soviet philosopher proposing that the Soviet Union allow pockets of capitalism—with the requisite prior agreement of each of those community members to give up all socialistic subsidies—as long as the overall world government becomes socialistic. In each instance there is a veneer of openness, but no openmindedness in reality. For example, Nozick insists that for a community to vote for a communist distribution of wealth or a limitation on sexual behavior, every citizen must agree to the legal arrangement. Another way of saying the same thing is that any citizen, unless and until she decides to leave a particular community, has a veto on every governmental regulation. Surely under such terms the overwhelming result would be minimalist governments.

Nozick also appears to be arguing that, given the plurality of separate community governments, no ideology should be allowed to dominate others, and therefore a central world authority should be empowered only to protect each community against interference by others. This argument is clever but transparent. If a world government is empowered to act in defense of one or another community in accord with how that world government adjudicates, then it is dominating others. If that world government adjudicates in line with the libertarian ideology, then at least one ideology is in power as the dominant protective agency. Would a communist community really receive an unbiased ruling on social rights and intracommunity conflicts from a libertarian world authority? No. A libertarian world government, which favors freedom *from* over freedom *to*, would be as one-sided as a communist world government, which favors freedom *to* over freedom *from*. Insistence on one worldview over the other exacerbates the ideological divisions within the world.

The third international issue, the one most directly bearing on the arms race, is war. The close relationship has been noted between Nozick's narrow view of entitlements, and the right to defend oneself against any acquisition of holdings other than by birth or by transfer from the original owner. To protect oneself against other individuals, including the poor and hungry who might try to acquire some of our holdings, we form group mutual-protection agencies. These latter groups, although contractually restricted internally in scope, protect with unlimited power, like Hobbes's leviathan, against external encroachments. What Nozick seems oblivious of is that in today's world, building up states through a competitive procedure, like dominant protective agencies, leads naturally to the proliferation of nuclear weapons.

Opposing such an implication, the Friedmans and other libertarians declare the principal cause of war to be the lack of free trade. As evidence, the Friedmans cite the century from 1815 to World War I as a period when free trade flourished under the British Empire, and the world, they say, was "the most peaceful in human history among Western nations. . . ."[20] What a convenient use of hindsight! Why 1815? Because the Napoleonic Wars came to an end in 1815. If the Friedmans had said 1800, as another libertarian dates the peaceful century, they would have had to contend with the numerous casualties of the Napoleonic Wars.[21] Similarly what about the bloody American Civil War in the 1860s? That is dismissed as the fault of slavery, not free trade. What about the 1848-49 attempted revolutions that swept across Europe? They are not mentioned. And why the decline of the peaceful century? Another author lists Britain's Reform Bill of 1867 and the rise of Bismarck in Germany in the 1870s—some years before 1915.[22] Finally we have Michael Novak's American date for the beginning of capitalism as 1776.[23] With such documentation, any date can signify anything.

Nevertheless the Friedmans are obviously echoing a theory put forth in an earlier essay by Rand. In "The Roots of War," Rand places the blame on statism.[24] Statism, Rand contends, has its roots in primordial savages who made the tribe supreme over individual rights. "The degree of statism in a country's political system, is the degree to which it breaks up the country into rival gangs and sets men against one another." "Statism . . .is nothing more than gang rule." Libertarian capitalism, on the other hand, is fundamentally opposed to war. "Trade does not flourish on battlefields, . . .profits do not grow on rubble." Those who temporarily profiteer in war do so for political, not economic reasons. "They are merely political scavengers cashing-in on a public trend."

Contrary to Rand's thesis, if statism is rooted in our primordial savage ideology, is statism not rooted in our subconscious, communicated in our family upbringing, handed down in our traditions? If so, how can Rand so easily single out traders and capitalists as immune from a disease we all carry? How can she put the blame on big government, but exempt big business, including advertising and the media? Are business and government, economics and politics really so divorced, or are they more intertwined? The libertarian response is twofold. Libertarians argue that if government were not statist, business would never be; thus government, not the people, is the prime offender. Rand then supposedly did not write *The Fountainhead*, which reverses the latter relationship. Secondly, they compare the United States with the Soviet Union and declare that a statist government is akin to a socialistic one. While the United States needs to curtail its domestic and international subsidies, all Americans can join forces in opposing the absolute statism existing in communist countries. An alternative response sometimes given by libertarians is to regard the United States as not libertarian in orientation. This allows libertarians to label anything unliked, such as war and violence, as statist, not purely libertarian. Such a view is tantamount to Marxists arguing that Stalin was not a Marxist, and all the evils usually attributed to the socialist systems in China and the Soviet Union as somehow falling outside true communism. Utopian views are hence made immune from factual criticism, and at the same time marked as historically irrelevant.

Let us return to the two principles of libertarian capitalism. On the one hand, libertarians separate economics from government as though a different kind of human being composed each of the two segments of a nation, and on the other hand, they mandate government primarily to be responsible for self-defense. Parenthetically we might inquire why there is such a strong self-defense link in an orientation that touts a century of peace? Or we may ask if Rand's war profiteer is a scavenger when he profits in defense of the libertarian principle? Rather, given the strong anti-communistic leanings of libertarianism, if the sole aim of government is projected as self-defense, then defense is going to become the staple of the national budget. If we use the United States as an example—admittedly utopian libertarians do not allow historical exemplification—we find that, excluding social security and other entitlements, which libertarians generally oppose, military expenditures comprise over fifty percent of the general funds of the federal budget.[25] Hence although libertarians may claim they do not want government interference in the economy, they are forced, by their strong commitment to self-defense against communist statism, to accept the government's interference in the economy through the huge defense budget. The economist Seymour Melman has adequately documented this interference in several studies including *The. Permanent War Economy*.[26]

Today about 35,000 U.S. businesses receive contracts from the Department of Defense.[27] Each of the top ten of Fortune 500 companies is a major weapons or petroleum supplier to the military. Seventy-two military plants which are entirely owned by the government are run by private corporations. Almost one-third of the scientists and engineers of the United States work for the defense establishment. University research is becoming increasingly militarized with about half of the Pentagon's basic research being done by universities. At $185 billion in military sales in 1985, the military industry in the United States, were such an industry a separate national economy, would have ranked as the thirteenth largest economy in the world. The list goes on *ad nauseam*. If libertarians were really against such expenditures, would they not be more vocal in their opposition? Instead, they oppose treaties with socialist, statist nations, and call for continued defense buildups.

In conclusion, libertarian capitalism is committed to an ideology that flounders on nuclear armamentation. What is particularly of concern is the doctrine's rejection of government aid, but ready recourse to defense, within a world that is without global governance and divided over ideology. Free trade is important, but cannot be regarded as the only approach to world hunger, any more than democratic legislatures have allowed a total government hands-off approach to national welfare. We cannot be consistent when we proclaim abroad what we are unable to stomach at home. If libertarians oppose statism to the extreme of disallowing all government aid for the economy, while they support dominant protective agencies, these protective agencies will aid the economy through military means in a guns-instead-of-butter approach to international relations. Libertarians are then accepting in an unhealthy guise the government aid they reject in theory. When international choices turn out to be either free trade or nothing—the latter perhaps in the spirit of Garrett Hardin's life-boats cut adrift—either minimalist dominant protective agencies or no world governance, and either libertarian capitalism or nuclear war, libertarians can say they are for peace, but with such a noncompromising attitude they are really preparing for war. Libertarian capitalism has met its match in nuclear arms, and come up empty-handed.

The University of Dayton

Notes

[1] I am indebted to Fredric C. Young and Jan Narveson, with whom I disagree on significant issues, for their constructive criticisms of an earlier draft.

[2] (New York: Random House, Inc., 1987).

[3] R. Nozick, *Anarchy, State, and Utopia* (New York: Basic Books, Inc., 1974) 150-53.

[4] Nozick 108.

[5] V. Held, *Rights and Goods* (New York: Macmillan, Inc., 1984) 125.

[6] For the quotations in this paragraph cf. A. Rand, *The Virtue of Selfishness* (New York: The New American Library, Inc., 1964) 31-34.

[7] M. Friedman, *Capitalism and Freedom* (Chicago: University of Chicago Press, 1962) 13.

[8] Friedman 14.

[9] Friedman 14-15.

[10] M. and R. Friedman, *Free to Choose* (New York: Harcourt Brace Jovanovich, 1980) 29.

[11] M. and R. Friedman 32.

[12] M. and R. Friedman 11.

[13] See M. and R. Friedman 54-64.

[14] M. and R. Friedman 34ff.

[15] See F. Moore Lappé, J. Collins, and D. Kinley, *Aid As Obstacle* (San Francisco: Institute for Food and Development Policy, 1980).

[16] F. Moore Lappé, *Diet for a Small Planet* (New York: Ballantine Books, rev. 1982) 46.

[17] A. Rand, *The Fountainhead* (New York: The Bobbs-Merrill Co., 1943) and *Atlas Shrugged* (New York: Random House, Inc., 1957).

[18] M. and R. Friedman 119-26.

[19] Nozick 297-334.

[20] M. and R. Friedman 52.

[21] See D. Osterfeld, "The Nature of Modern Warfare," *The Libertarian Alternative,* ed. T. Machan (Chicago: Nelson-Hall Company, 1974) 350-56.

[22] Osterfeld 351.

[23] See M. Novak, *The Spirit of Democratic Capitalism* (New York: Simon and Schuster, 1982) 13-16.

[24] See A. Rand, *Capitalism: The Unknown Ideal* (New York: The New American Library, Inc., 1966) 28-36. The remaining quotes in this paragraph are taken from this article.

[25] See, for instance, the Council on Economic Priorities, R. DeGrasse, Jr. with P. Murphy and W. Ragen "The Costs and Consequences of Reagan's Military Buildup" (New York: The Council on Economic Priorities, 1982) 32-33.

[26] (New York: Simon and Schuster, 1974).

[27] The information in this paragraph is taken from two issues of *The Defense Monitor,* published by the Center for Defense Information in Washington, D. C. The two issues are "Militarism in America" XV. 3 (1986), and "No Business Like War Business" XVI.3 (1987).

6 If Peace Were at Hand,
How Would We Know It?

Ernest Partridge

I

It was a scene that will endure in the history books: with the Statue of Liberty in the background, a smiling Mikhail Gorbachev stood on Governor's Island alongside the President and President-Elect of the United States. Earlier that day, December 7, in an historic address before the United Nations General Assembly, Gorbachev announced a unilateral reduction of 10% of the Soviet armed forces, and a withdrawal of 5,000 tanks and six tank divisions from Eastern Europe. Furthermore, he promised that the remaining forces in Eastern Europe would be re-deployed in a clearly defensive posture.[1]

Despite these bold initiatives, and the warmth, hope and good will of the preceding Washington and Moscow summit meetings, when President Reagan's final budget was released in early January, 1989, it showed yet another increase in military spending. Asked about this apparent inconsistency, retiring Secretary of Defense, Frank Carlucci, observed that the apparent "improvement" in relations between the superpowers occurred because of, rather than despite, the recent military build-up. Surely, he argued, the Soviets would not have made these concessions but for our military readiness. Accordingly, we were well advised to continue our arms build-up.[2] Carlucci reflected the position of President Bush who, during the election campaign, contended that "where we have seen flexibility [on the part of the Soviets], it has come because the price of aggression was too high. . . ."[3] This is an argument often heard from prominent members of Congress, and from members of both the retiring and incoming Administrations.

Recall that, in the early days of the Reagan administration, it was effectively argued that, due to the Soviet military buildup during the Carter Administration, there was an urgent need for a radical increase in our military budgets. We were told that President Carter's restraint in military budgeting and deployment was not reciprocated by the Soviets. In brief, said the critics, when we armed, they armed; and when we cut back, they armed. "You just can't trust those Russians."

And yet today, apparently innocent of historical memory and

without an iota of a sense of irony, we have reversed that sequence. When they build, we build; and when they cut, we continue to build.

Now that Gorbachev has taken the initiative of reducing his forces in Eastern Europe, should we respond in kind? "No," says Les Aspin, Chairman of the House Armed Services Committee:"the proper response. . .would be not to reduce our defense budget, not to match with a unilateral cut of our own."[4]

And is it possible that Gorbachev is moved primarily by a simple concern that a nuclear armed world is inherently a dangerous and therefore undesirable world? General Scowcroft, President Bush's new National Security Advisor, is skeptical. Suspecting darker motives, Scowcroft suggests instead that Gorbachev's peace proposal

> . . .represents a recognition on his part that he badly needs a period of stability, if not improvement in the relationship, so that he can face the awesome problem he has at home of trying to restructure that economy. That's his basic objective. I think also he is interested in making trouble within the western alliance, and. . .believes that the best way to do it is a peace offensive, rather than to bluster the way some of his predecessors have.

Finally, President Bush's first choice for Secretary of Defense, John Tower, appears unready to give Gorbachev the benefit of his doubts. For at his Senate confirmation hearing on January 25, 1989, Mr. Tower warned:

> We must not luxuriate in wishful thinking. And in spite of the progressive moves of Mr. Gorbachev, in spite of the very intense, and I am afraid, all-too effective public diplomacy campaign of his, there is still a formidable threat that confronts the United States and the free world. That threat has not diminished yet, through the era of perestroika and glasnost.[6]

In the face of an apparent massive military buildup by our adversary (as alleged in the early years of the Reagan administration), a reciprocating buildup on our part might have the merit of plausibility. But what, in the face of a stream of dramatic positive concessions and initiatives by the Soviet leader, could justify a continuing expansion of our defense budget? The burden of that $300 billion slice of our national treasury is compounded by our unprecedented budget deficits, the drain of talented scientists and engineers from our civilian economy to military research and development, a neglect of our public schools and universities (the seed-beds of our future technological, economic and cultural human resources), all of which is leading to a decline of our human capital and our global competitiveness. In short, it seems that our preparations to meet an ever-receding military threat are rendering us incapable of addressing an ever-growing economic peril.

II

Aside from these domestic perils, has the Soviet leader in fact given us reason to reconsider our continuing arms build-up? To better contemplate this question, I propose a brief exercise in historic recollection and imagination. Recall the Soviet Union of the Brezhnev era, and before that, the Stalin regime. Try to imagine what it was like, early in the Reagan administration, to think and to *feel* like Ronald Reagan and his supporters.

For a sample of this worldview, consider President Reagan's address, on March 8, 1983, at the 41st annual meeting of the National Association of Evangelists in Disney World. It was on this occasion that Mr. Reagan characterized the Soviet Union as "an evil empire" and "the focus of evil in the World." It was then the policy of the United States, as it is now, to deter this "evil empire" from marching across Western Europe or from launching a massive and coordinated nuclear attack on the United States. Toward this end, we had tens of thousands of strategic nuclear warheads targeted on the Soviet Union. And they, reciprocally, had about as many targeted on us and our allies. Leonid Brezhnev was, at that time, the General Secretary of the Soviet Union.

Suppose, in early 1983, at the time of the "evil empire" speech, someone had asked the President and his advisors what sort of evidence might cause them to alter their opinion of the Soviet Union as the primary threat to world peace and freedom? The question might be asked from a different perspective: suppose a Soviet leader actually wanted to abolish the arms race, and to end all aggressive acts or intentions against us. To do any of this he would, of course, have to remain in office. Consistent with that necessity, what might the President of the United States expect him to do?

85

Would the following suffice?

Concerning *freedom:*

— The Soviet leader might release several hundred political dissidents, and install legal procedures that would promise the release of most of the remainder. Western observers (e.g., from the *New York Times*), would be invited to inspect prison camps in the Siberian Gulag.

— He would introduce multi-candidate elections (albeit, at first, at low level public offices). Among the candidates would be such bonafide dissidents as Andrei Sakharov.

— He would end the jamming of "The Voice of America," "Radio Liberty," and all other foreign broadcasts, and would encourage cultural exchanges to the point, even, of inviting defecting artists to perform in the Soviet Union.

— Foreign publications such as *Time* and *Newsweek* would be available for sale to ordinary citizens, in the streets of Moscow, Leningrad and other major Soviet cities.

— When significant events of international consequence occurred in the Soviet Union, the Soviet leader would display an unprecedented forthrightness and candor, and would invite international inspection.

— In general, he would proclaim and practice a policy of "openness" (glasnost) with regard to public discussion and debate, and "restructuring" (perestroika) with regard to political and economic organization.

Concerning *the arms race:*

— The Soviet leader would unilaterally suspend nuclear testing for a year and a half, despite continuing testing by the United States.

— He would extend an invitation to United States scientists to set up seismological instruments near the Soviet test site to examine the feasibility of monitoring nuclear tests.

— He would propose, then permit, inspection of strategic weapons facilities, radar sites, nuclear weapons tests, and Warsaw Pact maneuvers.

— He would propose, and eventually sign, a treaty to eliminate medium-range nuclear weapons in Europe.

— He would unilaterally reduce Soviet forces in Eastern Europe, and restructure the remaining forces into a defensive posture. In addition, he would reduce the manpower of his armed forces by 10%, and would begin destroying some of the stocks of nuclear weapons, again, unilaterally.

— Responding, at last, to years of international demand, he would agree to withdraw the Soviet troops from Afghanistan.

All this and more has been done or proposed in the intervening time by the new Soviet leader, Mr. Gorbachev. The results have been manifest: even Mr. Reagan's fabled animosities toward communism and the Soviet Union were sufficiently mollified to allow the Soviet and American leadership to agree to an Intermediate Nuclear Forces arms agreement.

Not all are convinced, however. We have noted above, the persisting suspicions of influential members of Congress, and of the new Administration. Such qualms and warnings have been routinely expressed with each significant step toward accommodation between the global rivals. For example, the Washington summit in December, 1987, proved to be too much for a few longtime conservative supporters of Mr. Reagan. At a press conference announcing "The Anti-Appeasement Alliance," these critics vowed to oppose the new INF treaty when it came before the Senate for ratification. Howard Phillips, a co-chairman of the Alliance, called the President "a useful idiot for Soviet propaganda." The other co-chair, Richard Vigeurie, characterized Mr. Reagan as "an apologist for Mikhail Gorbachev."[7] After the Washington summit, suspicions about the Soviets persisted within the administration. Despite the new treaty, there were to be no significant cuts in the defense budget.

To the Anti-Appeasement Alliance, and other unyielding skeptics, the Soviet reforms and proposals were "not enough." We were reminded that there are still political prisoners in the Soviet Union. Opposition parties are not permitted. The Soviet media are still controlled by the Party. The so-called "test moratorium" was nothing but a pause, following extensive tests. The "mutual inspection" proposals are devices to open our industries to industrial espionage. The unilateral cuts in the Warsaw Pact forces, and in the Soviet military, are merely devised to weaken the NATO alliance. Furthermore, Gorbachev's military cutbacks have been forced upon him by a failing domestic economy, and he is simply trying to make a public relations virtue out of an economic necessity. As for the rest, say the critics, it is just so much propaganda, aimed at weakening our resolve. As George Will has repeatedly quipped: "Mr. Gorbachev is Khrushchev with a tailored suit and a thin wife."

Just what might it take to get such "hard line conservatives" to believe otherwise? Notwithstanding a stream of astonishing and courageous initiatives and concessions by the Soviet leader, the critics' complaints and warnings about "the perfidious Russians" are unabated. At length, one might begin to wonder if the conservatives' suspicions of Mr. Gorbachev are susceptible to *any* imaginable refutation. This is a significant question, albeit a question that is rarely posed. This question is the focus of the remainder of this essay.

III

The Falsification Rule: Critical philosophers have long acknowledged that for an assertion to be meaningful, it must have limits and boundaries. Thus, to assert one thing is, by implication, to deny something else. For example, to say that "mermaids do not exist," we must know what it would be like to encounter a mermaid (i.e., to "falsify" the assertion), even though we believe, all along, that there are none to encounter. Similarly, to assert meaningfully that all humans are less than twelve feet tall, we must know what such a nonexistent human being would be like.

Claims which systematically disallow any imaginable refutation have been called, by Garrett Hardin, "leakproof hypotheses." A personal recollection might illustrate this.

As a child, I was brought up amongst religious fundamentalists. When told that the theory of evolution was false, I asked "But what about fossils?" Two contrary answers that I vividly recall were, "They were placed in the ground by the Lord to test our faith," and "They were put there by the Devil to confuse us and to lead us astray." In addition, I was told of "doubting Thomas" and reminded that the greater the temptation that is overcome by faith, the greater one's virtue and reward in heaven. ("Temptation," by this account, means "weight of evidence" and "logical warrant"). Against this array, Darwin didn't stand a chance! No imaginable argument or preponderance of evidence could stand up to the infinite power of the Lord to "test" or of the Devil to "deceive."

Students of philosophy are aware of numerous other "leakproof hypotheses": (1) "The world was created by an omnipotent deity, just fifteen minutes ago, complete with memories and records." (2) "Everything in the universe, including measuring devices within, is doubling in size every hour." (3) "All that exists are minds and their ideas." (4) "All voluntary acts are selfish, in that they are done because the agent desires to do them." Though many such sentences have the appearance of meaning, they have been dismissed from science and philosophy, not because they are demonstrably false, but because they are disengaged from the world of our experience. Because such assertions are unaffected by contingencies and "surprises" in the world of our experience, they cannot effectively guide our conduct.

When such "transcendental beliefs" are entertained during ritualistic or ceremonial occasions, such as "putting one's mind in the Sunday School mode", they may be relatively harmless. A belief in transubstantiation need not affect the way we cut our daily bread. But when these beliefs, detached from reality, also "detach" the believer from the actual world that they appear to describe, the results can be troublesome. And when the "believers" in question hold great political power or influence, these "transcendental beliefs" can have horrendous consequences as they disengage public policy from events in "the real world," and thus disable the capacity to adapt to changes and unique developments.

The following are four of the most prominent assumptions that serve to place defense policies beyond the reach of practical falsification:

— *"It's All Propaganda."* Students of the history of philosophy will recognize this as a variant of "the deceiving devil hypothesis." It is the assumption that all Soviet policies, even domestic policies such as glasnost and perestroika, are merely designed to fool the Western powers, and thus to cause us to lower our guard.

— *The Worst Case Assumption.* The threshold test ban treaty is a case in point. By making all the "worst possible" assumptions about the geological features of the Semipalitinsk nuclear test site, about the theory of seismic wave propagation, and about Soviet "tamping" techniques, it is possible to interpret the relevant seismic data as "evidence" of occasional Soviet cheating. Never mind that virtually no seismologists agree.

— *The Double Standard.* Standards for judging our leaders' words and behavior are very broad, open, generous and forgiving, while just the opposite standards apply to Soviet words and behavior. "They" sponsor "terrorists," while we sponsor "freedom fighters."

— *The Next Move is the Last.* [8] Virtually every new step in the Arms Race has been initiated by the United States, and then reciprocated by the Soviet Union. (The hydrogen bomb, submarine launched missiles, the cruise missile, etc.) Each time, it was confidently believed that the Soviets would "cave in," and thus that the new strategic advantage to "our side" would be enduring. Each time our expectations have been disappointed. Since the "next move" is, by definition, always future-oriented, past experience does not refute. "Next time it will be different."

By a *strict* adherence to the falsification rule, the assertion, "The Soviet Union is an incorrigible threat to world peace and freedom," is perhaps meaningful. We might be able to imagine circumstances that could change the minds and policies of the most determined critics of the Soviets. After all, even Ronald Reagan eventually budged and agreed to a treaty with "The Evil Empire." But what about the qualms, noted earlier, of former Senator Tower, and of the "Anti-Appeasement Alliance?" Is there any *imaginable* initiative from Moscow that might change the attitudes of these uncompromising anti-Soviets? Perhaps a statement of "unconditional surrender," coupled with the public scrapping of Soviet arms and a plea to "please come over and rule us" might convince them. Even then, one can imagine some diehard conservatives saying: "Watch out, it's a trick!".

If the persistent suspicion of Soviet motives is subject to falsification only by "conceivable" *(logically* possible), but practically improbable events, does this mean that the falsification rule is of little use to critics of current defense policies and budgets? Perhaps so. However, a "falsification rule" might prove to be a sharp, critical tool if the requirement of "logical possibility" of refuting data is relaxed to include the looser requirement of "practical possibility." Thus a conceivable, if highly improbable, writ of unconditional surrender from the Soviets might be an unnecessarily restrictive test of the practical significance of the claim that the Soviets are "implacable enemies of freedom and peace." Instead, we might ask the hard liners: "What might Mr. Gorbachev do, *consistent with keeping his office*, or even his life, that would convince you that the Soviet Union is significantly less of a threat to world peace and freedom?" From our hypothetical position of early 1983, what he has done in his four years in power is, to say the least, astonishing. Reflect for a moment: could *you*, at the time, have believed that such a sequence of events would unfold? And yet, despite these astonishing developments, and despite all the smiles at the Summits and the photo opportunity on Governor's Island, the consumption of our national treasury by the defense establishment continues unabated.

Perhaps, then, it is time to ask the hard line critics "Granted, Gorbachev is not exactly following our script. Still, what would he have to do, consistent with remaining in office, which is prerequisite to his doing anything, that would convince you that the Soviet Union is significantly less of a threat to freedom and peace than you have supposed, and thus worthy of a renewed attempt at disarmament, accommodation and even friendship?" I suspect that if this question were candidly addressed and answered by these critics (a futile expectation, I fear), we might find that what they require of the Soviets is inconsistent with the national honor and practical politics of the Soviet Union, its leaders and its people, and thus practically impossible to attain.

IV

Tactical Implications for Peacemakers, and Activist Philosophers:
If we are to "give peace a chance," our policies, and their supporting ideologies and worldviews, must be open and appropriately responsive to changes among the great powers, and elsewhere in the world. They must also be responsive to scientific fact, and to logical coherence and cogency. Philosophers are particularly well-equipped to assess public policy against these requirements.

Accordingly, when a politician, statesman or candidate claims that "we must keep our guard up against the nefarious and perfidious Russians," we are entitled to ask "unless and *until what?*" "Please describe the condition of the world which will allow us to back down from this deadly confrontation." Or again, we might raise this challenge: "You are asking us to pay $300 billion each year, or about $1,200 per capita, for something called "national defense." Please tell us, just what are the objectives of this expenditure? How might we know that we have accomplished these objectives, so that we might reduce or even eliminate this drain on the public treasury?" Then we might ask, "How do we distinguish between genuine peace offers from the Soviets, and 'mere propaganda'?" Finally, "Are you asking for a *coup d'etat* in the Soviet Union, or will 'evolution' to a more benign condition suffice? If the former, how can we realistically ask for and expect cooperation from and accommodation with the present regime? If an 'evolution,' how are we prepared to assist it, or, for that matter, simply to recognize it?"

Complementary questions should also be addressed to the left: "Suppose we follow your suggestion, and attempt to foster reciprocation, communication and trust between the United States and the Soviet Union. At what imaginable point of betrayal and deceit by the other side do we abandon the noble experiment, and dry our nuclear powder once again?" In short, we ask both sides: "Just what is the cash-value and the payoff of your policies and proposals? How do they engage with our practical problems? What imaginable circumstances in the real world of great power conflict are implied, and excluded, by the ideology and world view upon which your policies are based? Just what defines 'success' (or 'victory'), and what identifies 'failure.' How, in short, are you prepared to recognize whether your policies are working or not?"

The Stakes: Throughout eight years of Mr. Reagan's regime of government by public relations, of leader as national pastor and Master of Ceremonies, these questions were not answered, and eventually were less often asked by a delinquent press. The public seemed not to care. Mr. Bush's challenge will be to reestablish commerce between policy and evidence by asking such questions as these. Otherwise, with no realistic concept of falsifiability, which is to say, of "failure," there will be no accountability, and little hope of intelligent accommodation with significant events and circumstances in the real world, much less control of them.

In short, throughout four decades of confrontation between the superpowers, the significance of the falsifiability rule in public affairs has been made vividly clear, through its disregard. We have paid, and will continue to pay, the price of a refusal to be instructed by events and open to change. As the late physicist Richard Feynman remarked at the close of his sharp dissent to the Challenger Report: ". . .reality must take precedence over public relations, for nature cannot be fooled."

The alternative to public and official sensitivity to the falsification rule is dreadful to contemplate. Blinded by self-serving and self-righteous ideology and propaganda, we will continue to refuse to recognize and seize upon opportunities for peace. We will fail, because the ideology denies, a priori, the possibility of such opportunities. Avenues to peace will be denied, because they constitute a falsification of the ideology of "the evil empire, unalterably opposed to freedom and peace," an ideology devised to admit of no falsification. Accordingly, through a persistent quest of "peace through strength," our military-industrial-technological establishment will continue to consume our national resources and treasury until, at last, it either breaks our economy or is found to fail when the missiles arrive. Unconstrained by the falsifiability rule, we will travel down that road to destruction, undeterred by the challenge of practical experience, logical cogency, or scientific and technological fact.

Fortunately, the "practical falsifiability rule" is quite simple, clear, and appealing to common sense. No prior training in logic is required to catch the point of the challenge: "What would it take to convince you that your claim is false?" The logical bite of that challenge can be grasped and appreciated, even by an ordinary Congressman. Thus it is a rule that can and should be put to good use by those who are trying to disengage foreign and defense policies from fantasy, and to reengage these policies with the real and dangerous world of imperfect knowledge, fallible humans, and nuclear weapons.

University of California, Riverside

Notes

[1] *New York Times*, December 87, 1989.

[2] "This Week with David Brinkley," ABC Television, January 15, 1989.

[3] "Different Views of America's Global Role," Andrew Rosenthal, *New York Times*, November 2, 1988.

[4] "This week with David Brinkley," ABC Television, December 11, 1989.

[5] "This week with David Brinkley," ABC Television, January 22, 1989

[6] Transcribed from a tape of Tower's testimony, "Morning Edition," National Public Radio (KVCR San Bernadino), Janary 26, 1989. Mr. Tower was subsequently rejected for reasons unrelated to his adherence to the position stated above.

[7] *Los Angeles Times*, December 6, 1987.

Section II

Evaluating Justification for Preparing
for Nuclear War

Ethical and meta-ethical questions are explored in this section. The focus is on justifications for continuing the arms race. As ought to be expected, philosophers are not of one mind on this issue. In fact, the plurality of orientations and conclusions has itself, as we shall see, become a concern for two of the authors. Two others treat the politically sensitive Strategic Defense Initiative. The discussions presume some knowledge of the major ethical methods currently in vogue. Thus, political realism, pacifism, deontology, consequentialism, and the just-war doctrine are advocated and/or critiqued in the essays that follow. A brief review of these ethical approaches is offered in our introduction to this volume.

The first two essays contrast political realism and pacifism In "Skepticism and International Affairs: Toward a New Realism," Leo Groarke argues for political realism but with a new twist. He contends that states active in international affairs should continue to pursue their own self-interest, as well as their moral and ideological goals, but should do so in a way that recognizes the subjective character of those values. Groarke contends that the moral skepticism brought about by this approach would grease the skids to greater tolerance and openness, and would mitigate the likelihood of armed conflict between countries informed by different moral principles.

Traditionally, skepticism has been a powerful force in a number of philosophical domains: epistemology, metaphysics, religion, and ethics. Groarke, advocating skepticism in the field of ethics, argues that adoption of moral skepticism could have salutary implications for international relations. How would it do that?

Urging the subjectivity of our outlook generally, the skeptic contends that there are competing moral principles which are equally defensible. No one set of moral standards, not even our own, can be established as universally guiding. Accordingly, we should regard moral standards as having a subjective character, not an objective character. Our moral standards, in other words, proceed not from a truth-oriented frame of reference but from a preference-oriented frame, or so the skeptic says.

The key implication is this: skepticism touches less the particular moral and ideological convictions that we hold—these convictions are a function of the customs and conventions of our society—and more the way we hold them. The concession that there are no objective moral truths, Groarke says, does not carry the corollary that we should not be committed to living by our subjective moral standards. But knowing there are no objective standards does alter the character of our commitment to our subjective standards. It makes us more willing to compromise on what we see as 'the moral truth,' and thus defuses the moral fanaticism that sometimes accompanies patriotism.

In "Terrorism and Violence: A Moral Perspective," Robert Holmes questions the generally held view that conventional warfare which includes a large number of civilian fatalities can be viewed as morally acceptable while terrorist activities are condemned as immoral. Holmes defines terrorism as violence done or threatened often against innocent persons for social, political, or moral ends. When terrorism is so understood, states, in their domestic and international affairs, are on a par with roving groups of fanatics in being involved in terroristic activities. Terrorism by groups is hence not less rational nor moral than many of the conventionally accepted modes of violence. Among the examples of state authorized terrorism that Holmes cites are Hiroshima, Nagasaki, South Africa, the American supported centers in Nicaragua, the Soviet supported forces in Afghanistan, Vietnam, and Israeli and Arab attacks in the Middle East. Terrorism is thus terrorism, regardless of who is behind it and irrespective of the lofty goals that motivate those who engage in it.

In challenging the accepted view separating war from violence, Holmes is also opposing the position of Groarke, who must maintain that forms of violence are moral whenever nations or groups within nations are subjectively convinced of their own morality, and even though innocent civilians will bear the brunt of the fighting. If terrorism and warfare both involve the organized and willful use of violence against citizens for the achievement of political goals, then the violence of the one is morally no worse than the violence of the other. Either both are morally acceptable or neither is. Groarke, if consistent, needs to say that both are morally acceptable, while Holmes's sentiments lie with the contention that neither position is morally acceptable. Holmes thus favors forms of nonviolence fashioned in accord with the pacifist persuasion.

Richard Werner looks at deontological and consequentialist

arguments in "Nuclear Deterrence and the Limits of Moral Theory." In the process of examining these arguments, Werner contends that such paradigmatic moral theories are useless for guiding action on complex moral issues as deterrence, because one and the same theory can legitimately yield conclusions both for and against deterrence and other issues. Werner is not suggesting that moral theories are barren for applying to individual or social policy. Far from it.Rather, he maintains the moral theories generate their policy conclusions only *after* the ideological persuasion of the ethicist has been taken into account. If the ethicist is conservative she will conclude conservatively; if liberal, liberally. And as the description of the facts is not assumptionless, the ethical application will not be value-neutral. Moral theory thus does not imbue ethical decisions, but is informed by those decisions. Moral theory, says Werner, enters discourse only as a means of rationalizing what one has already decided to do or as a means of deceiving oneself about the supposed ethical certitude of one's decisions.

Moral choice, accordingly, belongs to some other mode of deliberation than applying theory to case. Werner recommends a more experiential approach to ethics which relies on human judgments and conversation instead of moral theory and lengthy reasoning. The reader at this point may want to compare Werner with Groarke. Is Werner, too, siding with subjectivism and skepticism, or is there an objectifiable difference between the views of Werner and Groarke? Both take opposite positions on deterrence, but such differences may rest upon varying ideological persuasions.

Robert Litke, too, is concerned to press a point about ethical reasoning that dovetails with the point made by Werner. In "Conservative and Radical Critiques of Nuclear Policy," Litke argues that ethical reasoning can prescribe two quite different kinds of change in nuclear policy, conservative change and radical change. Conservative ethical reasoning prescribes change *within* the framework, change which preserves established frameworks and urges gradual rather than abrupt modifications. Radical ethical reasoning prescribes change *of* the framework, thorough and fundamental change.

The conservative argues for change within the framework of the war system, calling for clarification of the morally acceptable ("just war") limits of war fighting and for clear thinking about whether atomic weapons would violate those conditions. The radical argues for change of the war-framework itself on the grounds that nuclear weapons have so altered the war system that the traditional ethical framework must be abandoned as a means for settling conflicts of national interest.

The contemporary scene is manifestly split between radical and conservative ethical thinking about what nuclear weapons have done to warfare. Radicals, convinced that a nuclearized war system is itself immoral, are vexed with conservatives whose traditional moral theorizing, they think, amounts to moral justification for certain varieties of nuclear warfighting. Conservatives, having done their best to offer arguments prescribing moral limits on the conduct of war, are vexed with radicals who are unable to articulate viable alternatives to the war system for settling serious international conflicts. Although advocates of each use of moral theory tend to call into question the moral seriousness of the other, Litke argues that both uses have their place. Conservative moral theory addresses short-term problems; radical moral theory, long-term problems. While each stands under judgment of the other, Litke claims that both are needed to render a full-bodied critique of the contemporary nuclear scene.

At this point in Section II discussion shifts from theory to application. The last two authors explore some of the moral implications of the Strategic Defense Initiative. In following the arguments, the reader may wish to see for herself whether Werner's claim is persuasive, that arguments only convince the convinced.

James Sterba mounts powerful arguments against the Strategic Defense Initiative on both technological and moral grounds. On technological grounds, Sterba points out that SDI is vulnerable to three kinds of difficulties: SDI defends only against long-range ballistic missiles; it is subject to numerous design and operational difficulties; and its effectiveness can be reduced, if not cancelled, by a variety of easily accomplished countermeasures. On moral grounds, Sterba finds SDI unacceptable. Placing himself within the framework of "just war" tradition, Sterba contends that a legitimate defense must meet the requirements of just war theory, both with respect to the "just-cause" and the "just-means" components. Evaluating each of six proposed justifications for SDI, Sterba alleges that none of the justifications satisfies the just-means component *unless* the program were combined with a radical cut-back in the development and deployment of offensive nuclear weapons. "If Strategic Defense is not combined with deep cuts in the development and deployment of offensive nuclear weapons, then it would most likely serve as a stimulus not to arms control but to an arms race possibly on a scale previously unknown."

Current American weapons policy appears to envision no significant reduction in offensive weapons capabilities. Therefore, Sterba concludes that SDI is morally unjustifiable for imposing an added threat on the Soviet Union. No nation should have to endure the threat of a first strike from another nation, Sterba claims, when that threat is not necessary for maintaining the other nation's national security. Since the Soviet Union's nuclear strategy, like our own, is oriented to deterrence, and since SDI would add a defensive component to our already large offensive capabilities, the net effect of SDI is to enlarge, not to lessen, the danger of nuclear conflict.

In "The Man in the Teflon Suit," David Hoekema also opposes SDI, but with different reasoning. For purposes of argument Hoekema bypasses the technological controversy, setting aside issues of feasibility and cost. He focuses instead on the moral issue. His main concern is whether the premise is true that having the intention and the capacity to defend against attack is morally preferable to having the intention and the capacity to retaliate against an attacker. Hoekema argues that such a premise is false unless a proviso is added. Using the example of Jesse James armed with offensive weapons *as well as* a defensive Teflon suit, Hoekema shows that defense is only morally preferable *provided* the defense does not protect or augment offensive capacity. When a person or nation augments an offensive capacity with an effective defensive capability, the danger to others is thereby increased, not decreased, and the morality of that defense is lessened. We are thus left with an unusual situation. Were the superpowers significantly to reduce their offensive land-based ballistic missiles so as to increase the morality of their acquiring a defensive capability, the need for such a defensive system to protect against fewer and fewer missiles would correspondingly diminish. What is particularly worrisome, as pointed out by both Hoekema and Sterba, is that military and political leaders in the United States frequently defend the Strategic Defense Initiative as a supplement to our offensive nuclear forces. In attempting to gain an edge, the United States may be destabilizing the nuclear balance.

Leo Groarke

A skeptic is a doubter. Philosophical skeptics raise questions about our ability to establish any truth. Many philosophers see their arguments as a fundamental obstacle to knowledge and it is in light of this that philosophers have been preoccupied with the problem of skepticism throughout the history of philosophy. In recent discussions of international affairs, this preoccupation manifests itself in philosophical attacks on the skeptical claim that there are no objective moral principles that can or should be applied to actions in the international arena. Such skepticism is usually paired with political "realism," the view that power is or should be the determiner of what is right in international affairs. Traditionally, such a view is found in Hobbes. In more contemporary discussion, it is associated with political thinkers like Aron, Kennan, Morgenthau, and Niebuhr. In answer to thinkers who have taken issue with such outlooks (for instance, Walzer, Brunk and Cohen), I shall argue that skepticism and realism can provide a basis for a promising attempt to achieve and sustain international peace. There are problems with realism as it is usually construed, but they call for amendment rather than rejection. The key to the amendments I propose is a richer notion of skepticism, one which can be distilled from the history of philosophy.

1. Problems with Realism

The essence of realism is a moral and an empirical hypothesis. The empirical hypothesis is that international affairs is a competitive struggle between rational states which pursue their own self-interest through the use of force. The development of the international situation is, on this account, something like a chess match which progresses by cold, calculated *Realpolitik.* Though they are not realists in the strict sense, many commentators construe the arms race as the inevitable result of a rational need for military power in a world governed by power politics. It is in view of such analyses that Gauthier and many others see the "Prisoner's Dilemma" as the fundamental problem in the arms race.

It is perhaps inevitable that this model of international affairs is attractive to many intellectuals, both because it reduces the complexities of international relations to two elements—rationality and self-interest—and because it emphasizes the rational side of international decisions. Be this as it may, such a model fundamentally distorts what actually occurs in international affairs.

One of the problems with such a view is the rationality it accords to states, rationality which should surprise anyone familiar with the strategic, military and technological developments that tend to characterize the arms race. I have discussed elsewhere the irrationality of these developments, and shall confine my discussion here to some general reasons why it is naive to see rationality as the major determinant of the way that states or people act.

The pervasiveness of nonrational elements in our outlook guiding people's actions is seen in the claims of Kuhn, Feyerabend, and a host of other commentators who have argued that the development of science is profoundly influenced by social, psychological, emotional, religious, cultural and ethical concerns. One may debate the extent and importance of this influence, but it can hardly be surprising that scientists are influenced by the religious, cultural, psychological, social and ideological commitments that color their whole outlook on the world, especially as observation and experience leave open (as Kuhn points out) the possibility of alternative points of view. It is in view of this that one must take seriously the common claim that science has been unduly influenced by male assumptions (see, Easlea, for example, or Smithka in this collection) or class domination (as in Heilbronner).

This being said, science encompasses a relatively rigorous process for testing theories and decisions. In contrast, the decisions of states and their leaders are determined by various political processes. In authoritarian regimes, political leadership is the result of internal power politics rather than rational deliberation. In democratic countries, officials are elected for a variety of reasons which transcend the question whether their policies are rational. In contemporary Western politics, this is seen in the role that charisma, personality, religion, patriotism, and ideological commitment play in the electoral process—a role which is enhanced by the public's lack of detailed knowledge on specific issues.

The nuclear debate provides one example of the way in which national debates do not proceed according to the principles of rationality. Extensive media coverage has convinced the public that they are threatened with nuclear annihilation and that this would be an unimaginable catastrophe. Very few people, however, have the detailed information which is needed to make rational decisions about specific arms control proposals or specific weapons systems (e.g., Trident, the Cruise, the Pershing 2, the MX, or the Strategic Defense Initiative). Competing concerns, apathy, inability and traditional prejudices, however outmoded, prevent many from even attempting to understand such issues, while those that try are hampered by public discussion and vested interests which regularly distort the actual situation. Among the most serious problems are one-sided reporting which instills irrational fear and indignation rather than reflection, the manipulation of statistics, and language which conceals an implicit bias (see, e.g., Cockburn, Gardiner, Hilgartner *et. al.*, Zwicker, and the *Observer* article cited in the bibliography). There is little reason to believe that officials elected in the midst of such influences or advisors they appoint (often for ideological reasons or to satisfy political debts) will be paradigms of rationality.

Rather than *Realpolitik*, national decisions thus reflect the kinds of distortions enumerated in psychological analyses of the arms race (see Bronfenbrenner, Caldicott, Fisher, Fox, Lifton and Falk, and White). In general, they suggest that political decision makers cling to outmoded and simplistic ways of approaching problems, black-and-white conceptions of good and bad, and gross caricatures of the views and aims of their opponents. It is in keeping with this that they simply ignore evidence that does not fit with their assumptions. Given that this is the atmosphere in which international affairs actually develops, we can have little hope of understanding it if we cling to the rational actor model of international affairs proposed by standard realism.

A second problem with the realist model of international affairs just outlined is the notion of self-interest upon which it relies—a notion which is extremely narrow and usually understood as the ability to achieve egoistic ends. Certainly such ends are important and often underestimated. Long-term foreign aid is as much an attempt to deal with national problems of surplus commodities, unemployment, and a need for new markets and allies as it is an attempt to help those in need. This being said, not all actions in the international sphere are predicated on narrow egoistic interests, and there are clear cases where states are motivated by other kinds of concerns. Emergency foreign aid is usually an expression of genuine sympathy, and an overemphasis on egoism fails to account for the central role that moral, religious and emotional elements play in political and military matters.

That such factors play an important role in international incidents is easily demonstrated in specific cases. The war between Iran and Iraq is a good example, for it is founded on religious conflict. It is a dogmatic commitment to Islamic fundamentalism, not a rational consideration of egoistic self-interest, which made Iran willing to sacrifice so many of its people and so unwilling to compromise its objectives.

There are other factors which account for most of the atrocities of war. The Allied rejection of noncombatant immunity during the saturation bombings of Berlin, Hamburg, Dresden and Tokyo was not, for example, the result of a rational calculation of self-interest, but an expression, however despicable, of the loss of empathy which results when war hardens the hearts and minds of people in the states that it involves. It is fisticuffs, not a calculated attempt to gain self-interest, which is the appropriate analogy if we want to understand such incidents.

It is in view of these kinds of considerations that we might amend the realism with which we began and state its empirical thesis as the claim that:

> States in international affairs pursue what they perceive to be their own self-interests through the use of force.

Here the word "self-interests" is meant to include the satisfaction of religious and political desires. The word "force" is used in a very general way which includes the use of social and economic, as well as military power (the latter is often overemphasized in realism). Finally, we might note that the word "pursue" does not mean "rationally pursue" and that states often act irrationally.

Despite these amendments, realism so construed retains important affinities to the realism with which we began. Most importantly, it is atomistic and sees the attempt of states to satisfy their own subjective goals as the key to an understanding of international affairs. The difference is that our amended realism endorses a broader notion of desire and stresses the fact that states, like people, often act irrationally. Hobbes will object to at least the first change (for he will not grant any moral ideals which are not reducible to self-love), but both aspects of our amended realism are at least discernible in the views of Morgenthau, Niebuhr, Kennan and other contemporary realists. They typically adopt a notion of national interest which, perhaps inconsistently, leaves some room for ideological considerations, and sometimes grant that states may act irrationally. Their fundamental claim is that these aspects of foreign policy should be minimized, and it is in light of this that we may turn to the normative side of realism.

2. Realism and Morality

The normative side of realism, simply put, is the claim that we should accept the situation described in its empirical thesis, and that states should act accordingly. On the usual account, it stresses that we should not see the international arena as a place where moral considerations should apply. It is in view of this that realism has been called international moral skepticism. I shall have a great deal to say about this shortly, though it is enough to begin by noting that realism as I wish to formulate it suggests that ideological goals are appropriate in the international arena, as long as they are mitigated by a more sophisticated skepticism.

The first normative principle associated with realism as I shall defend it can be stated as the principle that:

> 1. States should *attempt* to rationally pursue their interests (and to eliminate the irrationality that often characterizes international affairs).

If this sounds banal and trivial, this is because we mistakenly assume that international affairs are already rational. In fact this is not the case, and such a principle would have enormous consequences in the real world of international politics.

It is this initial principle and the irrational influences we have already noted that shows that philosophers speak too quickly when they attack realism as the key ingredient in the arms race. It is realism *and* the irrational factors we have mentioned that produce the arms race, and it is far from clear that realism is the culprit. On the contrary, it is arguable that the real culprit of our present situation is our failure to understand our opponents; irrational fear; insufficient knowledge of specific weapons systems; inconsistent use of best- and worst-case reasoning; fascination with technological solutions to human problems; the simplistic notion that security is proportional to the size of a nuclear arsenal; confused strategic thinking; rhetorical appeals that cloud the issue; or any combination of the above, but not realism. (See Groarke, Kennan, Lifton and Falk, Scoville and Narveson).

Realism's warning that we must guard against irrationality is particularly poignant in the short term. For though there may be a time when states can transcend realism, fundamental changes in perspective cannot be expected quickly and we need other ways of staving off disaster. The easiest and most effective is by demonstrating the rationality of present policies, and by defending more rational alternatives. The pervasive assumption that policies are rational and that radical alternatives—Sharp's proposals for civilian based defense, for example—need not be taken seriously must, for example, go as soon as we accept the normative side of realism.

The second normative principle in my amended realism is a consequence of the broader notion of the self-interest already proposed in our amended version of the empirical side of realism. It can be put as the claim that:

> 2. States should pursue moral and ideological concerns in international
> affairs in a way that recognizes their subjective nature.

At first glance, this is something that goes against the grain of many realist arguments, promoting as it does, moral and ideological goals over more egocentric aims. There is, however, a great deal of inconsistency in the realists' views in this regard (see, for example, Gellman's discussion of Kennan) and the important point is that the proposed realism emphasizes the subjective nature of such goals. As Morgenthau puts it in his fifth principle, it "refuses to identify the moral aspirations of a nation with the moral laws that govern the universe." It is this that implies the attitude to international disagreement which is the goal of political realism.

We can better understand this amended realism if we note that it encompasses a moral skepticism which is very similar to the views of traditional skeptics. They hold that there are no objective moral truths and that competing moral principles are equally defensible (see Sextus Empiricus and Mackie; Hume and Hobbes, incidentally, are *not* moral skeptics in this sense). This is not the place to elaborate such views in detail, though we should note that it is founded on the difficulties that arise when we attempt to justify our basic criteria for judging good and bad criteria which seem relative to personal moral inclinations, social and cultural forces, socio-economic status and religious points of view. (Thus George Grant can argue that Rawls' theory of justice is founded on American assumptions). It is in view of this that disagreement over fundamental moral principles seems curiously persistent and intractable. The competing goals of individual freedom and responsibility to a collective have, in particular, profoundly influenced history, and proponents on different sides of the debate play a central role in ancient, modern and contemporary thought. In contemporary times, such disagreement underlies much of the tension that characterizes East-West relations. According to moral skepticism, the ideals that entail this conflict are subjective and there is no way to establish either of them as objectively correct.

The standard criticism of moral skepticism is the claim that it makes everything permissible—including of course, the most despicable things imaginable. This claim does not, however, answer the arguments for skepticism, and betrays a fundamental misunderstanding of the skeptics' point of view. Simply put, the skeptics do *not* reject moral standards. In ancient times, the Pyrrhoneans and the Academics (and the *nomos* sophists, who adopted similar views) explicitly accepted the customs and conventions of society. In medieval times, Ghazali and Nicholas of Autrecourt accepted religious faith. In modern times, Montaigne and Bayle adopted a similar point of view. In contemporary philosophy, emotivists propose an appeal to personal moral sentiment as a guide to action. There is much to be said about all these stances, yet we need only note that none of them rejects moral standards. Rather, they propose them on the understanding that they are subjective and cannot be established as objectively correct.

The difference between moral standards viewed as objective or subjective principles is a subtle one, though it is the key to the realism here proposed. The crucial point is that moral skepticism invites a less dogmatic attitude to one's beliefs. One's convictions are still important (as our deepest sentiments—love, for instance—are important), but they cannot be waved as flags which mark universal moral truths that everyone must accept or be guilty of impiety. There will still be times when one's convictions require sacrifices and commitment, but our moral confrontations will be colored by an explicit recognition of the subjectivity of our outlook.

The link between moral skepticism and the tolerance it implies is anticipated in the history of philosophy. It is reflected in the ancient skeptics' claims that the norms of other societies were as valid as their own—a notable departure from the cultural chauvinism that characterized philosophers like Plato and Aristotle. It is in keeping with this that the skeptics' whole outlook is forwarded as an attack on the pride of "dogmatist" philosophers who claim that their views must represent the one and only truth.

In modern philosophy, this aspect of skepticism is crystallized in the explicit call for tolerance one finds in thinkers like Bayle and Montaigne. They are directly influenced by the ancient skeptics and base their tolerance on their conviction that it is impossible to establish what is true. In particular, they argue that the suppression of religious views is unacceptable. The same argument functions as the backbone of Locke's views in his famous "Letter Concerning Toleration" and reappears as one of the major themes which Mill elaborates as a basis for freedom of expression in *On Liberty*.

Taken from this perspective, the tie between the proposed and standard realism should be clear. Thus the prime concern of contemporary realists is the moralistic self-righteousness that tends to characterize international relations—self-righteousness which encourages misperceptions, intolerance, dogmatism and an unwillingness to compromise what one sees as moral truth. As Kennan writes:

> . . . if we were able to refrain from constant attempts at moral appraisal—if, . . . instead of making ourselves slaves of the concepts of international law and morality, we would confine these concepts to the unobtrusive, almost feminine, function of the gentle civilizer of national self-interest in which they find their true value . . . then, I think, posterity might look back upon our efforts with fewer and less troubled questions.[1]

Morgenthau has the same concerns in mind when he writes: "There is a world of difference between the belief that all nations stand under the judgment of God, inscrutable to the human mind, and the blasphemous conviction that God is always on one's side and that what one wills oneself cannot fail to be willed by God also."[2]

The worst examples of such dogmatism are seen in the worst episodes in our history (the Crusades, Naziism, the Inquisition) and it would be a mistake to think that it no longer plays a role in contemporary politics. On the contrary, it contributes a great deal to present tensions in the world and invites an attitude that makes peace very difficult. Suppose, for example, that one believes that liberty is the highest good, and that collectivism is intrinsically wrong—in a word, evil. As Nielsen notes in "Doing the Morally Unthinkable," such convictions could be used to justify nuclear war. It would, of course, entail other moral evils, but one could

> . . . still intelligibly argue that here we are in one of those tragic, almost unthinkable situations in which we have to choose the lesser evil, though here we have to choose between evils of unprecedented magnitude. Children and the noncombatants of neutral nations would be massively struck down. They would be killed though they were in no way responsible for what happened. Still, that is, a "better-dead-than-red" advocate would contend, the price we must pay to avoid enslavement. The survivors, though they may be few and genetically threatened, would at least be free. Better, some would say, the death of a not inconsiderable number of innocents than the whole world should be enslaved.[3]

The same kinds of calculations are, of course, possible from the ideologically opposite point of view. Better, it could be argued, the death of a not inconsiderable number of innocents than the world and most of its people be still more impoverished and exploited for individual economic gain. The sacrifice in either case is terrible, but sacrifices for the highest good are laudatory and martyrs are our moral heroes.

In marked contrast to such attitudes, moral skepticism accepts deep-seated convictions, but suggests that there can be others, well-intentioned and reasonable, who have very different, but equally defensible, convictions. Our differences are not to be resolved by an appeal to some transcendent truth (one which will show *us* correct), but to practical principles which will allow us to resolve or, more probably, live with our subjective differences. Here it is important to emphasize that skepticism does not mean that we must agree with other points of view. On the contrary, we may retain convictions and simply moderate them with the realization that they are subjective. There may still be extreme circumstances in which we cannot tolerate other points of view, but such circumstances must occur much less often. Given that the fundamental moral wrong is intolerance, some perspectives (for example, that which sustains apartheid in South Africa) will be particularly objectionable.

In contrast to such an attitude, the history of international relations is a history of the clashes that result when different peoples meet with conflicting versions of God's truth. Moral duties are, on such accounts, prescribed by higher laws that must be enforced, and those who break these laws are little more than criminals. The end result of such an attitude is an atmosphere which invites ideological confrontation and suspicion, making international cooperation, compromise and negotiation at best strained and at worst impossible. It is an appreciation of this empirical fact which motivates contemporary realism.

The significance of such an outlook is seen in the prevalence of the ideological intolerance which characterizes American and Soviet attempts to propagate their influence elsewhere in the world. In the West, ideological fanaticism is seen most recently in the actions of the Reagan administration, which saw the Soviet Union as "the focus of evil in the modern world" and was committed to the use of military and economic pressure to press for internal changes in Soviet government (see Scheer). The same kind of thinking is used to justify actions like the American decision to reject two World Court decisions (by majorities of 15-0 and 14-1) in support of Nicaragua's complaint against U.S. direction and support of armed attacks against it, decisions on which two American and five allied judges concurred.

It is in view of such considerations that one cannot dismiss realism, as Cohen does, by arguing that it is founded on a simple failure to distinguish moralistic intolerance and genuine morality. On the contrary, the realists have appreciated, however intuitively, a logical and psychological connection that ties together moral subjectivity and tolerance. Given more time, I would argue both that moral objectivism is untenable and that it cannot justify tolerance, but we have already seen that philosophers dismiss realism far too quickly. Rather than be a cause of the arms race and international misconduct, it provides instead a way to critique the intolerance and irrationality on which the arms race depends.

3. Conclusion

The present paper leaves a great deal to be said. In answer to philosophical attacks on realism, it suggests that realism and skepticism are, properly thought through, good medicine for international affairs, particularly in the historical conditions that characterize our present circumstances. Philosophers who treat realism as the cause of present problems reject it much too quickly. And though the perspectives they propose may someday point the way to a better world, their criticisms of realism are misguided. The tragedy is that more attention to it is, at least in the short term, the most realistic route to peace.[4]

Wilfrid Laurier University
Waterloo, Ontario

Notes

[1] George Kennan, *American Diplomacy: 1900-1950* (New York: New American Library, 1951) 66.

[2] Hans Morgenthau, *Politics Among Nations: The Struggle for Power and Peace* (New York: Alfred A. Knopf, 1973) 11.

[3] Kai Nielsen, "Doing the Morally Unthinkable," *Nuclear War,* eds., Fox and Groarke (New York: Peter Lang, 1985) 58.

[4] I am indebted to my colleagues Robert Litke, Renato Crisit and Rocky Jacobsen for comments on an earlier version of this paper.

Robert Holmes

Maurice Merleau-Ponty once wrote that history itself is terror, and that the common assumption of all revolutionaries is that "the contingency of the future and the role of human decisions in history makes political divergences irreducible and cunning, deceit and violence inevitable."[1]

If this should be true, have we no choice but, in Camus's words, to be either victims or executioners? Must we either allow violence to be done to ourselves and those we care about, or resort to it ourselves against those we perceive as threats?

This is perhaps the central dilemma confronting anyone who has an active engagement with social, political and moral problems. It is not altered by the fact that most of us do not use violence ourselves—that is done for us by others—or by the fact we deplore violence at some level of our thinking. Our social life has so institutionalized violence that, despite ourselves, we support and sustain its use through government, taxation, the economy, and even the educational system, which at the highest levels trains officers for the military and profits from military-related research.

Notice that we do not view all violence in the same light. That which helps to maintain the status quo, whether in the way of police or military action, is approved by those who are its beneficiaries; that which threatens it, whether in the way of criminal or revolutionary violence, is condemned. And on the international scene we deplore the growing threat of nuclear war. But we support preparations for conventional war, as though it were somehow a respectable compromise.

But the mode of violence that is almost universally condemned is terrorism. Although terrorism stands at the other end of the scale from nuclear war, it rivals nuclear war in the dread that it inspires. If we are better to understand the nature of violence, we must at some point confront the problem of terrorism.

My aim will be to argue for the need for a better understanding of terrorists themselves, their motives, values and aspirations, and for greater recognition of responsibility on the part of others, like ourselves, to work for constructive resolution of the problems that give rise to terrorist activities in the first place. This, rather than increasingly tough responses, is the only approach that can promise success in the long run.

I

What is terrorism? More and more the term is used almost exclusively emotively, to stand for virtually any use of political violence of which we disapprove. This deprives the term of most of its usefulness by turning it into little more than another weapon in the arsenal of polemical disputes. One and the same person becomes a terrorist or a freedom fighter, depending upon whether we approve or disapprove of what he does.

But terrorism also has an underlying descriptive meaning. In this more basic sense, terrorism is the practice of terrorizing for social, political or moral ends, typically by the use or threat of violence, often against innocent persons. *Who* does the terrorizing does not matter; what counts is what is done and for what reasons. Individuals acting alone can terrorize; but so can governments or armies. And it does not matter what the cause is for which terrorism is undertaken or how much legitimacy it enjoys. What makes a terrorist a terrorist is the means by which his or her ends are pursued, not the ends themselves.

Terrorism presents the greatest challenge when it is undertaken for a cause. For then terrorism represents a rationally chosen means to an end. And however much we deplore terrorism, it is not necessarily a less rational choice, in the sense of being an effective means to one's ends, than many of the conventionally accepted modes of violence. Trotsky perceived this when writing of the Russian revolution. A victorious war, he observed, usually "destroys only an insignificant part of the conquered army, intimidating the remainder and breaking their will. The revolution works in the same way: it kills individuals, and intimidates thousands."[2] Though he was describing what he calls the state terror of the revolutionary class, what he said applies to terrorism of any sort. Terrorism typically kills few people by comparison with warfare. This will change when terrorists eventually come into the possession of nuclear or chemical-biological weapons, but it remains true today. Terrorism seeks to achieve its ends

116

by breaking the will of the thousands who learn of it. That is why publicity is important to its success. Indeed, if we accept the Clausewitzean definition of war as "an act of violence intended to compel our opponent to fulfil our will," terrorism can itself be considered a form of warfare. Terrorism intimidates by instilling terror, whereas conventional war intimidates by inflicting losses.

Conventional war, however, *may* itself be terroristic. Its rationale then is usually military necessity. This was put bluntly by the Kaiser during World War I, when he said:

> My soul is torn, but everything must be put to fire and sword; men, women, and children and old men must be slaughtered and not a tree or house be left standing. With these methods of terrorism, which are alone capable of affecting a people as degenerate as the French, the war will be over in two months, whereas if I admit considerations of humanity it will prolonged for years.[3]

Essentially the same rationale underlay the fire-bombings of Dresden during World War II and the atomic bombings of Hiroshima and Nagasaki. Those, too, were acts of terrorism, employing massive, indiscriminate violence against mostly innocent persons.

Because of the resources at a government's command, state terror is often the most effective kind. When undertaken openly, governments have a vast propaganda apparatus to justify what they do. But state terror can also be used surreptitiously, as Libya, Iran and Syria have been accused of doing, and against a country's own people, as Stalin did in the '30s, and as some Latin American governments do today. But whereas the latter operate through the torture and assassination of death squads, Stalin worked through the Soviet Union's legal institutions. There was no gunfire in the night, no bodies on Moscow's outskirts in the morning. Yet through trial, conviction and execution, perceived enemies were eliminated as effectively as though they had been gunned down, and others were frightened into submission.

II

Terrorism is commonly represented in the U.S. as primarily Arab. When a toy manufacturer recently produced a doll representing a terrorist, the doll was named Nomad, dressed in Arab garb, and, according to the company's description, engaged in "terrorist assaults

117

ιt villages."[4] Political cartoonists depicting terrorists
ow them grizzled and wearing keffiyehs. Admittedly, some
οι the most dramatic acts of terrorism, from the Munich Olympics in
1972 to the 1986 massacre at the Neve Shalom synagogue in Istanbul,
have been by Arabs directed against Jews, notably Israelis. But much
of recent terrorism in this country—we tend to think of terrorism as
something that mostly happens elsewhere, but we have it here as
well—has been *against* Arabs. The October 1985 assassination of
Alex Odeh of the Arab-American Anti-Discrimination Committee was
a terrorist act. Although it occurred within the borders of Ronald
Reagan's home state of California and killed the same number of
Americans as the 1986 bombing of the discotheque in Berlin—a
second person subsequently died of injuries from the latter attack—it
occasioned no comparable outrage. And it was but one of five terrorist
attacks against Arabs in the U.S. that year, prompting then FBI director
William H. Webster to say: "Arab individuals or those supporting of
Arab points of view have come within the zone of danger —targeting
by a group as yet to be fully identified and brought to justice."[5]

It is misleading to represent even Middle East terrorism as
exclusively the work of Arabs. The Jewish underground used terrorism
against the British in Palestine in the 1940s. Both Yitzhak Shamir and
Menachem Begin, who later were to became prime ministers of Israel,
led such groups: Begin led the Irgun; Shamir, the Stern Gang. The
former was responsible for the 1946 bombing of the King David Hotel
in Jerusalem; the latter for the assassinations in 1944 of Lord Moyne,
Britain's Minister of State for the Middle East, and in 1948 of Swedish
Count Folke Bernadotte, the United Nations representative to the
Middle East. More recently, in the 1980s, Jewish settlers resorted to
terrorism against West Bank Palestinians. Iran, which was high on
President Reagan's list of terrorist governments, is not even an Arab
country. Nor is Arab terrorism all the work of Moslems. The
Phalangists who massacred Palestinians in the Sabra and Shatila
refugee camps of Lebanon are Christians. So are George Habash and
Nayef Hawatmeh, leaders, respectively, of the Popular Front for the
Liberation of Palestine, and the Democratic Front for the Liberation of
Palestine, the two main factions of the PLO after Al Fatah, both of
which have been implicated in terroristic activities.Nor is the West the
sole victim of terrorism. The Soviets were victimized when four of

their embassy officials in Beirut were taken hostage and one of them executed. And some of the worst car-bombings outside of Lebanon have taken place against Syria.

Nor, of course, is terrorism by any means confined to the Middle East or those acting in Middle Eastern interests. The Pol Pot regime in Cambodia undertook a campaign of genocidal terror in Cambodia that has been exceeded in recent history only by the Nazis' exterminations of Jews. Long-standing terror has been used by the IRA in Northern Ireland, by the Basques in Spain, and, by some accounts, at least, by the African National Congress in South Africa. The growing practice of "necklacing" of black South Africans by other black South Africans is a particularly ghastly form of terrorism.

The point is that terrorism is misleadingly represented as a struggle between the forces of good and the forces of evil. Any people desperate enough are capable of engaging in it; any government unscrupulous enough, capable of using it.

III

If terrorism is not clearly less rational than the accepted violence of warfare, neither is it less moral. If a band of men slips across a border and plants bombs at the home of the nation's leader and his family, then disappears into the night as the resultant explosions kill his baby daughter and leave his son permanently brain-damaged as well as killing scores of other people, that is terrorism. But if those same men put on uniforms, swoop over the country in the dead of night and bomb those same targets from military aircraft, as the U.S. did against Libya, that is not considered terrorism. But why not? It would take a casuist of exceeding skill to point to a moral difference between the two. The killing of children does not become less reprehensible because done from a plane, by soldiers trained in warfare and acting under orders from a duly elected leader than when done clandestinely by men acting on their own or in concert with a few conspirators.

Terrorism is not in itself any worse than many conventionally accepted forms of violence. True, terrorism is probably directed against civilians more often than is standard warfare. But ordinary warfare can use terror as a tactic. When it does, the proportion of violence may be small in absolute numbers of persons killed, relative to the overall violence of the war effort, but it dwarfs terrorism by comparison. The terror-bombings of Dresden, Hiroshima and Nagasaki undoubtedly killed far more persons than have been killed by all the terrorists throughout the world in all of the years since. Indeed, the majority of the 50-60 million dead in WWII were civilians, and that would probably be the case in any sizable war in the future.

It is unclear why the same logic thought to justify the killing of civilians in wartime—namely, when so doing is thought necessary in the pursuit of military objectives or avoidable but useful or necessary in their pursuit—does not equally justify killing them in terroristic warfare.

Consider the United States. As a democracy, its government presumably represents the people, and the people bear ultimate responsibility for the actions of the government. That government backed rebels fighting to overthrow the government of another country, Nicaragua. The contras began clandestine training in the U.S. with CIA financing years ago. As late as 1988 they were being trained by U.S. military personnel at secret bases in Florida, and this training was openly financed by the government. Contras documentably engaged in terrorist attacks against civilians in Nicaragua. Although the Sandinista government never retaliated against U.S. citizens, one could see a rationale for so doing, if it ever came to that. For it was the citizens of the United States who allowed the assault upon their country to continue. In the Middle East, rather than supporting insurgents, the U.S. supports an established government under assault from insurgents. Most of the Arab states remain in a state of war with Israel. Palestinians are engaged in what they consider a war of national liberation. The U.S., through massive support of Israel, maintains only a fig-leaf of neutrality. Palestinians can understandably reason that through paying taxes and electing administrations that carry on these policies, American citizens make the same sort of contribution to the war effort of one party in the dispute that is regularly thought to justify killing civilians when munitions factories are bombed in a conventional war or when terror-bombing is undertaken to break the will of an enemy. This is not to make any assessment of the merits of the issues at dispute either in Central American or the Middle East; that would take us well beyond the present concerns. It is only to say that an even-handed assessment of terrorism often reveals as much justification for terrorism as for much of the widely accepted killing of civilians.

Nor is the terrorist as a person necessarily any worse than the soldier in uniform. If the one uses unconventional means, that is because such means are all he has at his disposal. Are we to say to terrorists that if they had an army and an air force at their disposal, it would be all right to use them; but as they do not, they may not use the homemade bombs they do have? Indeed, the terrorist may more often be a person of conviction than the ordinary soldier. The soldier does what he does because he is told to. Often as not, he has been involuntarily pressed into service, and has little or no understanding of the issues for which he has been asked to kill. The terrorist typically does what he does voluntarily, knowledgeably, and with conviction of the rightness of his cause. And he often thinks of himself as legitimately involved in a military struggle. When Georges Abdalla was convicted of terrorist activities in France, he asserted that he was a "Palestinian fighter," not a terrorist. When former Jewish terrorists gathered at the King David Hotel in Jersualem in 1981 to reminisce about their 1946 bombing of the hotel that left 91 dead, one of them said, "I am very proud of the operation militarily. I felt myself like a soldier of these Jewish forces."[6] Whatever one thinks of the merits of their respective causes, these are people who freely commit themselves to a cause, and in so doing, undertake the actions they do with conviction. Indeed, it is precisely because their conviction is greater than that of most people, at least as measured by their willingness to sacrifice and kill, that they are willing to perform acts that ordinary persons consider abhorrent.

Men the world over readily become killers if told to by their governments, or, as with terrorists, if they believe strongly enough in their cause. There is not much difference between them. They were recruited and exploited by our own government in the Vietnam War. An officer of a U.S. helicopter unit, who had commented upon the gloomy prospects of success in the operations in the delta area, was asked what the answer was.

> "Terror," he said pleasantly. "The Vietcong have terrorized the peasants to get their cooperation. . . . We must terrorize the villagers even more, so they see that their real self-interest lies with us. We've got to start bombing and strafing the villages that aren't friendly to the Government." He then added, "Of course, we won't do it. That's not our way of doing things. . . . But terror is what it takes."[7]

But it did become our way of doing things. It was reported soon after:

> U.S. and allied forces are adopting a program of destroying homes and crops in areas which feed and shield the communist forces. For years, Americans have refused to participate in "scorched earth" efforts, leaving them to the Vietnamese. Now Americans are directly involved.[8]

Washington Post correspondent John T. Wheeler reported on one such operation on March 30, 1967:

> The Vietnamese woman ignored the crying baby in her arms. She stared in hatred as the American infantrymen with shotguns blasted away at chickens and ducks. Others shot a water buffalo and the family dog.
>
> While her husband, father and young son were led away, the torch was put to the hut that still contained the family belongings. The flames consumed everything—including the shrine to the family ancestors. The GIs didn't have much stomach for the job, but orders were orders . . . ."God, my wife would faint if she could see what I'm doing now," an infantryman said. "Killing . . .[Vietcong] is one thing, but killing puppies and baby ducks and stuff like that—it's something else, man."

The point is that ordinary people can be brought to do such things. Young Russians have done comparable things in Afghanistan, Israelis in the Middle East and Contras in Nicaragua, as have the Mujahadeen, the Palestinians, and the Sandinistas, in varying degrees and with allowance for the means at their disposal.

But if, as I have maintained, the violence of terrorism is no worse morally than much of that of warfare, it is also true that the violence of warfare is no less terrible than that of terrorism. We have so compartmentalized our thinking that we fail to see this, thinking of one as respectable, the other vile.

What is common to the violence of the terrorist and that of the soldier is that they both treat human beings as though they were physical objects to be removed or destroyed when perceived to be obstacles to the attainment of one's ends. Or treat them as instruments by which those ends are to be promoted. Once one accepts the premise that violence is a permissible means by which to pursue ends, and that one may do virtually anything to achieve those ends, one only needs to accustom people to overcome their natural revulsion to killing to turn them to your purposes. The techniques are there. They are not the special province of terrorists. The armies of the world specialize in them. "We're military people," one of the pilots involved in the U.S. strike against Libya said. "We were told what to do and we did it." Asked about the people who were probably killed on the beach, he remarked that that responsibility "is above my pay grade."[9]

It is this feature of violence, whether military or terrorist, that highlights the central fact in its moral assessment. Kant captured the idea in his second formulation of the categorical imperative: "Act so that you treat humanity, whether in your own person or in that of another, always as an end and never as a means only." To allow yourself to be used by others to do their killing is to allow yourself to become a means. To kill others to promote your own ends is to use them as means. We need to rediscover the humanity of all persons, friends and adversaries alike, and to accord them the respect owed them as persons.

But what, it may be asked, are people to do who suffer persecution and injustice? What were European Jews to do who fled the holocaust and sought a homeland in Palestine, only to be turned back by the British? What are Palestinians to do who seek to return to their homeland, only to be turned back by the Israelis? Should the former have folded their hand and waited for the world to offer them security? And should the latter resign themselves to refugee camps until the Israelis invite them back?

Neither I nor anyone else has easy answers to these questions. But I would make two suggestions, one concerning the need for a change in our outlook toward terrorists, the other concerning our own responsibility and that of others like us who are not principals in most of these disputes, for the perpetuation of conditions that lead to terrorism.

The first is to try to understand terrorists, to open communication with them, to listen to their side of the conflicts they are involved in, rather than, as now, refusing to deal with them at all. Terrorism does not exist in the abstract. People do not just decide to become international terrorists and then conspire with others to go about their deadly business. "We are people," one of the women said at the aforementioned gathering at the King David Hotel. "We know how to love, we know how to hate. We know how to kiss. We have all the emotions of everybody else."[10] We need to recognize terrorists as persons like ourselves, taking into their own hands the violence most of us leave to others. They are not subhuman monsters, to be fought with blood and iron and all the righteous fury that civilized people can muster. And part of our responsibility is to understand what it is that can lead them to perform such acts, and what measure of justice their cause may embody.

When the hijackers of the TWA airliner in 1985 reportedly shouted the words "New Jersey" in the aisles of the plane, most Americans, if they heard it at all, would scarcely have been aware that the reference was to the battleship New Jersey. After the bombing of the Marine Barracks, the battleship had turned its 16-inch guns upon Shiite Moslem villages in Lebanon, hurtling 2,000 pound shells into the homes of those who could not possibly have been responsible for the bombing. One of the hijackers, it was reported, lost his wife and daughter in that shelling. It is decent, well-dressed men in Washington—family men, churchgoers, good neighbors and friends—who ultimately bear responsibility for such actions. With the unprecedented military power at their command, they need only issue a command, and a sequence of events is set in motion that results in shells exploding in Arab villages thousands of miles away. Those in the Middle East who burn to avenge such actions, or to redress what they perceive as wrongs wrought by the policies of these men in Washington, have only guns or explosives, and their own strength and wit, with which to work. When they commandeer a plane, or plant a bomb, they are terrorists. But what they do is no different in kind from what others do or have done. If the challenge is to understand better and appreciate the position of the terrorist, or the revolutionary, or the advocate of violent change, the imperative is to find nonviolent ways of dealing with the problems of injustice, poverty and oppression that are typically at the root of their actions. That requires that *others,* who are not desperate in the way in which the oppressed are, and who have the means, power and influence to redirect the course of events, involve themselves cooperatively with all sides in the controversies that lead to violence in an attempt to find creative solutions to them.

Nonviolence, so conceived, must be active, not passive. In a sense, violence—by which I mean reliance upon violence as the ultimate recourse for resolving problems—is more passive than nonviolence.

Violence often waits until situations have deteriorated to the point where there is gross injustice, doing nothing, or worse yet, doing the wrong things, then flaring up and engulfing those it would help as well as those it ᵒ ⁿˢes. Reliance upon the institutionalized violence of modern w ᵗⁱd not prevent Hitler from coming to power. While it ᵇᵃd him at a horrendous cost of mostly civilian ' ⁱtion arguably as bad as that which, follow' ᵉd to World War II, and which today casts ⁿ over the world. The War was begun by tᵗ ᵃve Poland. But nearly 50 years later Po' War was ostensibly begun to secure tᵗ nese people. But today the whole of ᵗates went to war in 1948 to liberate ᵗinians live by the tens of thousands in ᵗelies on military might to preserve itself; ⱼ erodes as its margin of superiority over its ᵤnishes and its domination of Palestinians ⱼ internal crisis.

ᵤquires a commitment to become actively engaged wiᴛ. ᵉms of peace and justice, rather than ignoring such problems ᵃ₃ ᵤong as things remain orderly, and then sending in troops when bloodshed finally becomes inevitable. This is what nonviolence has meant for leaders such as Gandhi and Martin Luther King, Jr.

But can nonviolence "work?" Can it resolve the problems of injustice and oppression? We do not know. But we do know that resort to war and violence for all of recorded history has not worked. It has not brought either peace or justice to the world. The most it has achieved are brief interludes, in which the nations of the world can regroup, catch their breath, and prepare for the next war. Nonviolence worked in India with Gandhi, in the U.S. with King, and in Scandinavia against the Nazis during World War II. More recently, it has worked when Filipinos placed themselves in front of oncoming government ranks, averting what might have been a bloody civil war when the Marcos government sought to confront rebel commanders in their headquarters. It has brought dignity and respect to the Solidarity movement in Poland when violence would almost certainly have brought a crushing Soviet response. Would it work on a larger scale? Who knows? No one can foresee what the results might be if a country like the U.S. were to spend $300 billion a year in research on techniques of nonviolent resistance and on training people in their use.

What is needed here? A new perspective, I suggest, on our interaction with others in the world, a perspective which, in Kantian terms, respects persons as ends in themselves. We need a willingness to cultivate and put into practice an awareness of the humanity in our adversaries, even when they are terrorists, a perspective which approaches conflict in a spirit of seeking the truth in the issues that divide us from our adversaries rather than assuming our own righteousness and trying only to work out the means to our ends. Violence is for the morally infallible, while nonviolence is for those who recognize their own limitations and their adversaries' hold on important parts of the truth. But nonviolence is, I submit, the only approach which holds the remotest hope of resolving the dilemma with which we began. In the nuclear age, we are at the point where we must move on to a new plane, and make of the future what we want it to be. We must not allow it to be shaped by the same forces, including the same outmoded ways of thinking, that have led us into the predicament we face today.

University of Rochester

Notes

[1] Maurice Merleau-Ponty, *Humanism and Terror* (Boston: Beacon Press, 1969) 96.

[2] Leon Trotsky, *Terrorism and Communism* (Ann Arbor: The University of Michigan Press, 1963) 58.

[3] Quoted in *Crimes Of War,* eds., Richard A. Falk, Gabriel Kolka & Robert Jay Lifton (New York: Vintage Books, 1971) 135.

[4] *The Christian Science Monitor,* Dec. 10, 1986.

[5] *The New York Times,* Sept. 26, 1981.

[6] *The New York Times,* Sept. 26, 1981.

[7] Jack Langguth, *The New York Times Magazine,* Sept. 19, 1965.

[8] *Rochester Times-Union,* Jan. 6, 1966.

[9] *The New York Times,* April 16, 1986.

[10] *The New York Times,* Sept. 26, 1981.

Richard Werner

What ought one to do about the practice of nuclear deterrence? My thesis is that philosophical moral theory fails in the crucial task of answering this.[1] *Each* paradigmatic theory, be it teleological or deontological, can legitimately yield the conclusion that deterrence theory should be promoted or the contrary conclusion that it is to be condemned. The paradigmatic moral theories fail to guide our action.

While I cannot develop the extended thesis here, I also hold that moral theory fails to guide our action concerning most complex social issues. It fails for the same reason it fails concerning nuclear deterrence: alternative and credible modes of discourse exist within our culture, each of which when infused with a given moral theory yield contradictory moral conclusions.

I will use utilitarian and Kantian moral theory to illustrate my thesis. I suggest that my thesis extends to pluralistic or mixed deontological theories such as just war theory. Little imagination is needed to see how similar arguments extend to other paradigmatic moral theories or to other complex social issues. Finally, I propose a perspective outside of philosophical moral theory from which intelligent discussion of deterrence can occur.

I

The utilitarian argument to defend deterrence is long-standing. Although Gregory Kavka gives it its most recent and, perhaps, most persuasive formulation, one can find the germ of the argument among the earliest attempts to defend deterrence strategy from the moral point of view.[2]

The argument goes as follows. Deterrence is the best means to prevent the other side from either launching a nuclear war or of using nuclear blackmail as a means of dominating and controlling its adversary. When the other side is assured that the first will retaliate with a nuclear strike sufficient to cause unacceptable damage, one can rest assured that the other side would be irrational to launch a first-strike. Utility is maximized not only for one's citizenry but also for most of the rest of the world if nuclear war is avoided, since the economic and ecological effects of such a war are bound to be globally catastrophic. Hence, it seems to follow that deterrence strategy is optimific.

Although not as noticeable in the media, the utilitarian argument against deterrence is almost as old. While Douglas Lackey's arguments are among the most recent and persuasive in this tradition, they have their roots in the arguments of Bertrand Russell.[3]

Lackey argues that if one side unilaterally disarms, it is in the interests of the remaining nuclear power to use its nuclear weapons sparingly, if at all. There is little point in occupying an economically destroyed, highly irradiated nation covered with rotting corpses, and where diseased rodents and insects run wild.[4] The user of nuclear weapons is expected to suffer so severely from even a limited nuclear attack against another nation that it is reasonable to believe that the user's own attack would be deterred by the expected consequences of the action.

Nuclear blackmail, involving only a few surgical strikes, *may* be more likely should one side unilaterally disarm; but, again, it is irrational for the attacker to cause anything approaching the destruction of even a limited war. Moreover, the attacker must still consider the possible effects of a world combined against it both militarily and economically, which could provide a credible deterrent unto itself. Hence, it is reasonable to believe that the negative effects of nuclear blackmail would be far lower than those of not disarming, more than off-setting any increased probability. So it seems to follow that unilateral nuclear disarmament and not deterrence strategy is optimific.[5]

Kavka counters that unilateral disarmament risks not only lesser Soviet nuclear strikes but also worldwide domination by the Soviets. In combination, so the argument goes, the two smaller threats times their higher probability of occurrence is not orders of magnitude different from the greater threat of total nuclear war times the much lower probability of occurrence should we maintain present deterrence policy. Hence, if we choose the alternative that minimizes the probability of disaster occurrence, we should choose deterrence, since the probability of war under it is less than the probability of war and domination under unilateral disarmament.

Lackey counters that under unilateral disarmament one could expect that 20 million Americans would die in a one-sided strike, while under deterrence one could expect 120 million combined Soviet and American deaths in a two-sided war. Lackey concludes that, "100,000,000 (more) dead. . .is a matter of very great magnitude," and not as marginal as Kavka seems to conclude.[6] Hence, we have greater reason to avoid the potential invoked by deterrence strategy. Further, Lackey argues that it is not obvious that the likelihood of war under unilateral disarmament is greater than the likelihood of war under deterrence.

The debate between the conservative followers of Kavka and the liberal followers of Lackey continues. Each presents its own interpretation of the history of US/USSR relations to defend its claims about present Soviet intentions regarding such issues as global conquest, communist domination, and willingness to engage in nuclear conflict. For instance, the conservatives see the Soviet occupation and domination of Eastern Europe and, more recently, Afghanistan as examples of the Soviet drive for worldwide domination. Liberals see the same events as evidence of the Soviet fear of the West generated by our invasion of the USSR after the 1917 revolution, the Soviet loss of 25 million people during World War II, and provocative statements about invasion of the Soviet homeland made by the Allies since World War II. These events, the liberals argue, lead the Soviets to surround themselves with a buffer zone as a protection against potential invasion from its enemies.

Similarly, the conservatives see each new Soviet weapon system as an example of the Soviet effort to gain superiority in the arms race, and liberals see the same new weapon as a defensive Soviet reaction to a preceding nuclear buildup by the US. The conservative finds the Soviets guilty of an excessive will to power, while the liberal merely finds evidence of a fearful Soviet nation engaging in a catch-up game of self-defense.

Along with their interpretations of the history of Soviet intentions, the conservative and the liberal present their own theory of risk assessment to yield the desired conclusion on the arms race. The conservative usually encourages us to engage in worst-case reasoning to protect ourselves from the horrors of nuclear conquest and communist domination. The liberal usually appeals to such notions as the principle of charity and encourages us to place the most reasonable interpretation upon Soviet intentions, while reminding us that worst-case reasoning all too often yields the worst case as its self-fulfilling prophecy.[7]

Each side presents a consistent and seemingly persuasive interpretation of the history of Soviet intentions which supports its claims about present Soviet designs. Each side presents a plausible case for adopting its own particular theory of risk assessment, including theories of how to act in situations of uncertainty. How are we rationally to adjudicate these conflicting theories of Soviet intentions and risk assessment?

My point is a simple one. I do not think we have the means to adjudicate this dispute on solely rational grounds. The facts of the history of Soviet intentions *severely* underdetermine the choice of theory. One's prior ideological commitments tend to hold sway in terms of which side of the debate one finally embraces.[8] Theories of risk-assessment are a-dime-a-dozen, and the committed conservative or liberal can always find a suitable one. Whether it is more rational to engage in worst-case reasoning or adopt the principle of charity in interpretation of the behavior of others seems to be nonadjudicable for similar reasons and to depend in part on one's assessment of Soviet intentions. There simply is no one answer which either fact or reason provides concerning the arms race.

The utilitarian, like most of us, is bewitched by the view that we can empirically or rationally determine which is *the* true perspective about the history of US/USSR relations. According to him, if we merely allow ourselves to become objective, or perhaps if we look at the issue from an omniscient god's point of view, the facts will reveal themselves and we can determine the truth of the matter such that any rational inquirer would consent. Unfortunately, all too often the interpretation of the facts is invented along with the theory.

We are left with a variety of perspectives each of which, within its own framework of assumptions, seems to best describe the world. Unfortunately, none of these frameworks is value-neutral. No one views the issue *sub specie aeternitatis*. Nor does such a Archimedean ideological perspective seem plausible. By assuming the conservative perspective about US/USSR relations, the conservative begs the question against the liberal. By assuming the liberal perspective about

US/USSR relations, the liberal begs the question against the conservative. What lies behind the intractability of the debate between the conservative and the liberal is the mistaken and shared assumption that Archimedean epistemological points prevail, that there is *one* perspective which is assumptionless and demands the consent of all rational beings or, at least, is the best explanation.

II

Let us now turn our attention to Gerald Dworkin's Kantian approach to deterrence.[9] Dworkin argues that our intention to use nuclear weapons is wrong because one cannot justify to those affected by our actions what we are doing to them. One cannot justify to the innocent noncombatants of the Soviet Union "who neither use force against us nor aid those who use such force, and whose welfare we risk by our deterrence intentions, an argument to the effect that they (can expect) to gain (both prudently and morally) from our policy of deterrence."[10] Deterrence fails to respect the rational autonomy of innocent noncombatants. As such, deterrence involves treating the innocent noncombatants one targets as a mere means to one's political ends. Accordingly, deterrence violates the second formulation of Kant's categorical imperative.

But what can we make of the claim that we cannot justify to the noncombatants of the Soviet Union what we are doing to them? Does the point go through as easily as Dworkin assumes? I think not. It suffers the problems of the consequentialist debate between Lackey and Kavka. If one adopts the conservative ideological perspective envisioned during our discussion of utilitarianism, then one can plausibly argue that we could justify to the Soviet noncombatant our policy of deterrence. Just as Kavka argues that deterrence is justified because it avoids worldwide Soviet domination, one can argue that if Soviet citizens are stripped of false ideology and are free to choose their beliefs in a free market system, they too would consent to such an argument. Freed from totalitarian influences, the Soviet citizen would realize that the only hope of removing the bitter yoke of communism lies in preventing Soviet domination.

Moreover, the conservative can argue that the arms race helps to weaken communist control of its citizenry by diverting finances, resources, and attention away from totalitarian concerns and toward the technological race with the US. An explosive arms race will help bankrupt the Soviet economy and allow the Soviet people to overthrow the oppressive Soviet government, bringing an end not only to communist repression but also to the arms race.

Such arguments show that the Soviet citizen can expect to benefit from the American policy of deterrence on both prudential and moral grounds. Whether one finds such arguments plausible seems to rest on one's own prior ideological commitments. The liberal will take us in one direction, the conservative in the other. Each position seems internally consistent, self-contained, and capable of explaining the facts as it interprets them.

But there is another problem here. Must we convince the actual Soviet citizen, or some idealized Soviet citizen? If the former, the project seems hopeless. One can no more convince all Soviets that each benefits (or fails to benefit) from deterrence, than one can convince all Americans to wear seat belts. Consensus is difficult at a Quaker meeting, let alone within an ethically and culturally heterogeneous society of several hundred millions.

If our project is to convince some idealized Soviet citizen, which does seem to be Dworkin's intent, which one? An omniscient ideal observer who is impartial yet benevolent? Or one who is not benevolent? Or a group of rational contractors, prudently considering self-interest, and fully informed about their society and environment, but ignorant of their own individual personal characteristics, role in society, and conception of the good? Or simply someone who is willing to universalize moral prescriptions when performing the "role-reversal test?" Or any one of several other plausible alternatives?[11] There are no rational, a priori grounds for accepting one interpretation of Kantian ethics rather than another. Yet in terms of action, everything hinges on the choice. Kantian ethics is as useless in practice as utilitarianism.

What can we make of pluralistic or mixed deontological theories like Just War Theory? Traditionally, such theory has rested upon the criterion of proportionality—the level of force used must be proportional to the good it is intended to achieve—and the criterion of discrimination, i.e., intentional killing must respect the distinction between noninnocents and innocents, among others. While the criterion of proportionality leads us directly into the utilitarian disputes between Kavka and Lackey, the criterion of discrimination leads us to nasty and irreconcilable disputes about the nature of intention and the distinction between combatants and noncombatants. While such pluralistic approaches have the strength of combining both utilitarian and Kantian approaches, they also have all of their weaknesses plus all of the problems of providing an algorithm for melding the two into a moral judgment. These problems are, I believe, endemic to mixed deontological theories and render them useless in practice.

III

How then do we make ethical decisions? Reflection reveals to me that ethical judgments are made free from the concerns of moral philosophy. Sometimes I must do what I must, in Bernard Williams' sense of practical necessity. Other times the choice is more difficult and deliberation occurs. On such occasions, I find that I run through the various courses of action, considering each in turn. Finally, I reach a practical judgment that one course of action satisfies me as a person better than the other various available options. It simply has a better fit with my web of belief. While my choice reveals who I am, it also helps to make me into the person I would like to become. No theory is consulted. No algorithm is solved. Yet on other occasions I find that I cannot decide which course of action is most satisfactory, which is a better fit. Here I seek advice, or simply choose, or decide to wait. Over time, I find that some of my practical judgments lead me to regret my actions. My recognition of my failings in practical judgment serves to correct my future judgments.[12]

Ethical decision-making takes place at the level of perception and human practical judgment, not at the level of universal theory and moral algorithm.[13] It is a facet of the human condition that we lack certitude and a priori solutions to our practical problems. Experience teaches me that moral philosophy enters the game only as a means of rationalization after one has already decided what to do, or as a means of self-deception when one tries to bring imagined certitude to one's choice through a commitment to some supposed moral algorithm. Both are futile given that moral theory cannot provide the needed rational guide to action.

What does this have to do with the ethics of deterrence? A great deal, I believe. What I know best I cannot prove.[14] I know that there are physical objects. I know that the future will resemble the past. I know that other people are conscious. I also know that risking the deaths of hundreds of millions of innocent lives by intending their deaths daily is wrong.[15] Risking, intending, working toward such an ultimate catastrophe with all the means we can muster is, quite simply, unconscionable. Justifications based on communist domination, self-defense, prevention of conventional war, or the positive effects of the arms race on the economy, miss the point. These ends can be accomplished by other means, means that do not threaten ultimate catastrophe. I do not understand deterrence any more than I understand any preparation for mass, ritualized suicide. It is, to my mind, a moral surd.

I go to conferences. I read the journals. I see the detailed arguments to justify risking our civilization as well as millions of innocent lives across the globe in the name of peace, or justice, or utility, or democracy, or freedom, or whatever other abstract idea one can marshall. But by what right do we Americans threaten and plan daily for the destruction of a planet filled with people? To advance our ethnocentric notions of peace, or justice, or utility, or whatever? Or, more to the point, to advance our economic, neocolonial interests? That the Soviets do so? Such misdirected retributivism is not acceptable even from a five-year-old. The hundreds of millions of people whose lives we risk are not the ones who do the nasties. Many of those at risk are children. In fact, about 20 percent of the world's children quietly starve while we spend trillions preparing for instant civilizational death, and all in the name of peace and self-defense. This too is a moral surd.

There is the sickening feeling that there is too much *argument* on this issue, just as there is too much argument to prove that the physical world exists, or that the future will resemble the past, or that other people are conscious. There is the suspicion that the purpose of such argument is to change the nature of the truth, that we philosophers raise a dust and then complain that we cannot see. Such debates may reveal how clever we are, but they also reveal our lack of wisdom and understanding. One cannot prove the better known with the less well known.

The ethics of deterrence is, for me, simple. Deterrence strategy is just wrong. I acknowledge that those with different perspectives come to the opposite conclusion on this issue. But I find myself estranged from such perspectives. While I am willing to defend my observations,

I would only do so as part of a conversation in which the participants were open to a discussion free from some predesigned logical space of reasons, or mode of discourse, or rules for inquiry. Some of that may eventually be borrowed, but only as a conscious decision including a consideration of the presuppositions involved. I seek a decentralized, democratic conversation that returns power to people.

Finally, I remind you that I offer these observations not as sound, no-question-begging, philosophical arguments for the stand I take on nuclear deterrence. I offer them because practical, no-question-begging, sound philosophical arguments do not exist on the topic. I offer them because if we are to become effective in changing the world rather than merely interpreting it, we must become both practical and intelligent.

Hamilton College

Notes

[1] This is a shortened version of an article that originally appeared with the same title in *The Monist* 70 (1987) 357-76.

[2] Gregory Kavka, "Some Paradoxes of Deterrence" *Journal of Philosophy* 75 (1978) 285-302; "Doubts about Unilateral Disarmament" *Philosophy and Public Affairs* 12 (1983) 255-260; *Moral Paradoxes of Nuclear Deterrence* (Cambridge, 1987)

[3] D. Lackey, "Ethics and Nuclear Deterrence," *Moral Problems*, ed. James Rachels, (NY, 1979, 3rd ed.); "Missiles and Morals: A Utilitarian Look at Nuclear Deterrence" *Philosophy and Public Affairs* 11 (1982) 189-231; *Moral Principles and Nuclear Weapons* (Totowa, NJ, 1984).

[4] *The Effects of Nuclear War*, Office of Technology Assessment, US Congress, May 1979; "The Prompt and Delayed Effects of Nuclear War" *Scientific American* 241 (1979) 35-47.

[5] For criticisms of the claim that deterrence has worked to date, see Richard Wasserstrom, "War, Nuclear War, and Nuclear Deterrence," *Nuclear Deterrence,* ed. Russell Hardin et. al. (Chicago, 1985); Marc Catudal, *Nuclear Deterrence: Does it Deter?* (London, 1984).

[6] Lackey "Missiles and Morals" 204.

[7] See Jan Narveson, "Getting On the Road to Peace: A Modest Proposal," ed., Hardin, for a defense of the liberal position. Narveson's arguments fail for the reasons given in the following paragraphs.

[8] Kavka's and Lackey's ideological perspectives are a confirming instance for my claim. I can say the same for myself since I find Lackey's arguments more convincing and I am also inclined to accept the liberal account of US/USSR relations.

[9] I take Kantian morality to include *both* the first and second formulations of the categorical imperative. Hence it will not do to argue that deterrence can be justified on Kantian grounds as long as one is willing to universalize the practice of deterrence. One would also need to show that deterrence does not treat innocent noncombatants as mere means, in so far as it is they who are targeted, either directly or indirectly, by the practice of deterrence.

[10] Gerald Dworkin, "Nuclear Intentions," *Nuclear Deterrence,* ed. Hardin, (Chicago, 1985). My additions in brackets. I have used similar Kantian arguments in "The Immorality of Nuclear Deterrence," *Political Realism and International Morality,"* ed. Kenneth Kipnis and Diana T. Meyers (Boulder, CO, 1987).

[11] The first formulation yields an early Richard Brandt, the second Roderick Firth, the third John Rawls (or Bernard Gert), the fourth R. M. Hare. Bernard Williams' *Ethics and the Limits of Philosophy* (Cambridge, MA, 1985) explains why these theories are not extensionally equivalent and why they fail.

[12] For an account of ethical deliberation similar to the one I have sketched, see John Dewey, *Theory of the Moral Life,* (NY, 1980) especially 10-16 and 134-136.

[13] For further explanation of this claim see my "Ethical Realism," *Ethics* 93 (1983) 653-697, and "Ethical Realism Defended," *Ethics* 95 (1985) 292-296.

[14] I use the word "know" in John Dewey's sense of warranted assertability, not in G. E. Moore's sense of certainty or C. I. Lewis' sense of justified true belief.

[15] It is the risking of ultimate catastrophe which is most morally repugnant. Yet as Dworkin indicates, the intending is also morally wrong. This is so if for no other reason than that the intending makes the risking possible.

Robert Litke

I

We can distinguish between two types of change. In the first place, there is a change *within a framework*. We can think of this as change from state to state within a system which itself remains unchanged. An example would be the sequence of changes one goes through during a game of chess. In the second place, there is change *of the framework*. This can occur in a number of ways. The system itself can be changed; one can stop operating within the system; one can change from one system to another. For example, one could modify the rules of chess; one could stop playing chess; one could change to a game of checkers.

Watzlawick *et al* refer to these as first-order and second-order change:

> A person having a nightmare can do many things *in* his dream—run, hide, fight, scream, jump off a cliff, etc.—but no change from any one of these behaviors to another would ever terminate the nightmare. *We shall henceforth refer to this kind of change as first-order change.* The one way *out of* a dream involves a change from dreaming to waking. Waking, obviously, is no longer a part of the dream, but a change to an altogether different state. *This kind of change will from now on be referred to as second-order change.*[1]

These authors claim to find this distinction explicated by the Theory of Groups and the Theory of Logical Types.[2] For my purposes it is enough that this distinction is intuitively clear.

I find that moral theory is used to justify a call for both types of change in nuclear policy. I want to suggest that each use is legitimate and that there is no necessary tension between them. We can think of the one as a "conservative" use of morality and the other as a "radical" use. By conservative I mean a use which tends to preserve the established arrangements and which allows for gradual rather than abrupt change. A radical use is one which requires thorough and fundamental change.

II

Conservative discussions of the morality of nuclear war are conducted with a view to first-order change. War is taken as the given framework: it is assumed that some international problems will be settled by armed conflict (according to established practices and conventions of warfare) and that it is legitimate to do so (the right to self-defense). The problem is to determine in a precise way morally acceptable limits on the conduct of war and to work out the implications of these limits for nuclear policy.[3]

A paradigm example of this type of use of morality is the recent article by James Sterba, "Moral Approaches to Nuclear Strategy."[4] I consider the framework within which Sterba operates that of a morally constrained war system. Once he has this framework sufficiently explicated, Sterba works out the practical implications it has for nuclear policy. Here is his list of four morally legitimate uses of nuclear weapons:

(1) Under present conditions, it is morally justified to possess a survivable nuclear force in order to be able to quickly threaten or bluff nuclear retaliation should conditions change for the worse.

(2) If conditions do change for the worse, it would be morally justified at some point to threaten a form of limited nuclear retaliation.

(3) If conditions worsen further so that a massive nuclear first strike can only be deterred by the bluff or threat of a massive nuclear retaliation, it would be morally justified to bluff but not threaten massive nuclear retaliation.

(4) Under certain conceivable but unlikely conditions, a limited retaliatory use of nuclear weapons against tactical and strategic targets would be morally justified in order to restore deterrence.[5]

I think it is evident from this list and the details of his account that Sterba is calling for substantial changes in nuclear strategy and nuclear arsenals. It is to be noted, however, that these are first-order changes within a war system which is morally constrained.

In passing, Sterba mentions that establishing political, economic and cultural ties might eventually eliminate all morally legitimate uses of nuclear weapons. He does not suggest that such ties might eliminate all morally legitimate uses of *war itself*. Nor does he suggest that changes which would move us in precisely such a direction are morally required. To do so would be "radical." In this article Sterba is consistently conservative in his use of morality.

For a more general discussion of the same type one can read Wasserstrom, "Noncombatants, Indiscriminate Killing, and the Immorality of Nuclear War."[6] Again the framework of morally constrained warfare is taken as a given and the focus is on the implications of the framework for nuclear war. Since this framework requires that wholly innocent noncombatants should not be indiscriminately harmed, and because Wasserstrom believes that the weapons and strategies of nuclear war would lead to just such harm on a massive scale, he condemns nuclear war as "the morally worst and most despicable act conceivable."[7] He does not in this article raise moral questions about the legitimacy of the framework itself. In fact in the final paragraphs he concludes on a conservative note by saying that in bleak circumstances we may be required to harm people in unjust ways for the sake of self-defense. He ends where he began: entirely within the framework of a morally constrained war system.

III

· By way of contrast, radical discussions of the morality of nuclear war are conducted with a view to second-order change. In such cases the war system itself is criticized. There is a call to change the framework rather than to work out acceptable changes within it.

There is a considerable range of radical responses to nuclear war. I will mention a few. Some authors claim that nuclear weapons have so altered the war system that it must be abandoned as a framework for settling conflicts of national interest. The claim is that nuclear war makes war obsolete. For example, Einstein came to the view that we have only two options: we can prepare for war, which will mean universal destruction, or we can prepare for the abolition of war.[8] Another example: Somerville argues that nuclear war is not really war but omnicide.[9] What makes this reframing plausible is the assumption that even limited uses of nuclear weapons carry with them an unacceptably high risk of leading us into unlimited and omnicidal conflict. We need only add that conventional warfare with nuclear backup carries with it the same kind of morally unacceptable risk and brings the entire framework into question.

Further accounts can be given of how this alleged morally obsolete framework came into being. For example, in "Realism, Deterrence, and the Nuclear Arms Race," Brunk argues that the fundamental assumptions underlying the war system framework inevitably lead to arms racing which is now pushing "the whole world onto the increasingly precarious edge of the nuclear precipice."[10] In Brunk's view the solution to the problem of nuclear war will be found only in some other framework.

Beyond condemning the framework of the war system, radical thinkers sometimes consider alternatives. For example, civilian-based defense is being researched as an alternative to preparing for armed conflict.[11] Models of world federal government are also being explored. Beyond that, the possibility of a global peace system is being investigated. For example, Woodward suggests that it would require at least six interdependent elements: (a) universal and complete disarmament, (b) international institutions to settle disputes, (c) international unarmed peace-making forces and national forms of nonviolent self-defense, (d) massive peace educational efforts, (e) more effective institutions to protect basic political, social, and economic rights, and (f) the development of less resource-consumptive economies.[12] Evidently, this is a call for radical changes in a whole range of global frameworks, including the war system. This is second-order change at the maximum.

IV

Obviously, radical and conservative critiques of nuclear war are different from each other. Are they compatible? Their respective proponents believe they are not.

Consider the radical who is entirely certain that a nuclearized war system is itself immoral. From such a perspective the spectacle of a conservative who is (morally?) content to work within the immoral framework is at least disconcerting. Does the conservative mean to give tacit approval to the framework? Is it that he/she believes some plausible versions of nuclear warfare are not evil? In other words, if the conservative does not in the end arrive at a wholesale condemnation of nuclear war (which is tantamount to a second-order change), the radical suspects that the conservative is giving moral comfort to those who advocate nuclear warfare.

Consider now the conservative who has worked out precise

arguments demonstrating morally prescribed limits on the conduct of war. Such work requires a well-defined and stable framework. From such a perspective the spectacle of a radical attacking the framework itself is disconcerting. Does the radical intend to weaken the very basis for a strong and systematic critique of nuclear war? Does she/he have a plausible alternative framework which would support an equally sound critique? If not, radical discussions often appear to be intuitive, emotional, or inadequately conceived. In general, if a substantial replacement for the condemned framework is not offered, the conservative suspects that the radical is playing into the hands of those who favor less restricted kinds of nuclear warfare.

Thus each is tempted to regard the other's critique as countering the moral force of one's own. Despite such appearances I want to claim that conservative and radical critiques are not competitive but complementary to each other.

We may begin with Sterba's conservative use of the veil of ignorance principle: "Do those actions that persons behind an imaginary veil of ignorance would unanimously agree should be done."[13] He argues that the social contract approach which is specified by this principle "strongly endorses all the basic requirements of a traditional just war theory."[14] I do not wish to take issue with this claim. It seems to be correct. I do wish to insist, however, that it relies on the conservative assumption that one is confined to first-order choices, that is, one must choose among various kinds of war. Clearly if one were behind a veil of ignorance and one were asked to choose between a war system of any kind and a peace system of the kind, for example, envisioned by Woodward—a second-order choice—one would choose the peace system. We see then that conservative and radical uses of moral principles occur at different levels. That is why they do not compete with each other.

There is, however, a kind of nascent tension between conservative and radical approaches: each carries within it in embryonic form devastating critiques of the other. The radical is clear that *beyond a certain time* to go on discussing morally preferred choices within a substantially immoral framework is morally decadent. Similarly, the conservative is clear that after a *reasonable measure of time* to go on undermining a workable framework without offering a viable alternative is intellectually irresponsible. Precisely when such criticisms would be appropriate is a matter of judgement. At this time they seem premature. Each approach can respect the work of the other.

Nevertheless we can wonder whether one approach is more appropriate, more realistic, or superior to the other? The answer, I believe, depends on one's interests. In the first place we clearly have short-term interests of an urgent kind. For example, the arms race has become extraordinarily dangerous and expensive; it must be stopped. Since first-order changes are typically easier to comprehend and implement than second-order changes, conservative critiques may be the most useful in this regard. On the other hand, we also have long-term interests of an urgent kind. Since we cannot dismantle our ability to make and deploy nuclear weapons, our safety eventually requires that we render them obsolete by making the war system unnecessary. Radical critiques address this larger matter. Thus, rather than competing with each other, conservative and radical critiques are complementary.

Beyond that, there are relevant subjective differences in interest. Some thinkers have an intellectual preference for working within the constraints of a well-defined framework. There is a kind of satisfaction in that. Others prefer the excitement of challenging established ways of thinking and of working out untested possibilities. In general, we recognize each approach as a legitimate form of philosophical activity. In the case of our nuclear situation it is hard to imagine that we could not benefit from both types of orientation.

Wilfrid Laurier University

Notes

[1] P. Watzlawick, J. H. Weakland, R. Fisch, *Change* (New York: W. W. Norton & Co., 1974) 10-11.

[2] Watzlawick, chapter 1.

[3] In chapter thirteen of *The Leviathan,* Hobbes suggests that war is not only the act of fighting but also the known disposition to settle our conflicts in such a way. It is arguable, from such a perspective, that arms racing is warfare.

[4] J. Sterba, "Moral Approaches to Nuclear Strategy" *Canadian Journal of Philosophy* (Supplementary) 12 (1986) 75-109.

[5] Sterba 107.

[6] R. Wasserstrom, "Noncombatants, Indiscriminate Killing, and the Immorality of Nuclear War," *Nuclear War,* eds., M. Fox and L. Groarke (New York: Peter Lang, 1985) 39-55.

[7] Wasserstrom 45.

[8] A. Einstein, *Ideas and Opinions* (New York: Dell Publishing Co., 1973) 165-66.

[9] J. Somerville, "Nuclear 'War' is Omnicide," *Nuclear War* 3-9.

[10] C. Brunk, "Realism, Deterrence, and the Nuclear Arms Race," *Nuclear War* 224.

[11] Gene Sharp, *Making Europe Unconquerable: The Potential of Civilian-Based Deterrence and Defence* (New York: Taylor and Francis, 1984).

[12] B. Woodward, "The Abolition of War," *Nuclear War,* 245-56.

[13] Sterba, 80.

[14] Sterba, 91.

James Sterba

For many people a legitimate defense must meet the requirements
of just war theory.[1] This theory has a "just cause" component which
determines when it is right to go to war, and a "just means" component
which determines legitimate conduct in war. I have argued elsewhere
that, analogous to just war theory, there is a just threat theory whose
requirements must also be satisfied by a legitimate defense.

The *just cause* component of just threat theory can be put as follows:

There must be a substantial threat or the likelihood of such a threat,
and non-threatening correctives must be hopeless or too costly.

The *just means* component contains the following requirements:

1) The risk of harm resulting from the use of threats (or bluffs) should
not be disproportionate to the military objective to be attained.

2) Actions that are prohibited by just war theory cannot be threatened
as an end or a means.

3) The risk of harm to innocents from the use of threats (bluffs)
should be minimized by accepting risks (costs) to oneself that would
not render it impossible to attain the military objective.

In this essay I want to determine what constraints just war theory and
just threat theory taken together impose on a policy of Strategic
Defense.

Unfortunately, Strategic Defense is anything but a clear idea.
Following President Reagan's first use of the notion in his address to
the nation on March 23, 1983, the most frequently heard question in
the halls of the Pentagon was "What is strategic defense?" The source
of the lack of clarity is that the term does not refer to just one thing.
Strategic Defense is used to refer both to a research program and to the
deployment that could result from that program. Moreover, when the
term is used to refer to a possible deployment, it sometimes refers to
an umbrella defense of both military and civilian targets and sometimes

refers to a limited or point defense of missile silos and command centers alone.

These different referents must be kept in mind when assessing the following justifications that have been offered for Strategic Defense.

1. Strategic Defense is a means of promoting U.S. security that does not depend upon the (increased) good will of the Soviet Union for its effectiveness. (Here Strategic Defense is understood as a possible deployment. In addition, the justification is directed at those who tend to favor technological solutions to political problems.)

2. Strategic Defense is a morally preferable means of promoting U.S. security. (Here again Strategic Defense is understood to be a possible deployment, and the justification is clearly directed at those who find current nuclear strategy morally objectionable.)

3. Strategic Defense is a stimulus to arms control. (To serve this end, Strategic Defense is usually understood to be a research program whose deployment will eventually be bargained away. This is how Strategic Defense has tended to be interpreted by leaders of our European allies such as Prime Minister Thatcher and Chancellor Kohl.)

4. Strategic Defense enables us to keep up with the Russians and to keep them from breaking out with a deployment of their own. (This justification only seems to make sense if Strategic Defense is confined to a research program, assuming that the Russians do likewise.)

5. Strategic Defense enables us to save lives in the event of a nuclear attack. (Here Strategic Defense is understood to be a possible deployment, most likely an umbrella defense of both military and civilian targets.)

6. Strategic Defense serves the economic interests of the military industrial complex. (This justification might appear to apply equally to Strategic Defense as a research program or as a possible deployment, but as any defense contractor will tell you, deployment is much more profitable than research.)

Keeping these different referents in mind, let us critically examine each of the proposed justifications in turn.

The first justification, as we noted, takes Strategic Defense to be a possible deployment, either as an umbrella defense or as a point defense. Viewed as an umbrella defense, Strategic Defense was proclaimed by President Reagan as making nuclear weapons "impotent and obsolete." The appeal of this form of Strategic Defense was captured by a television commercial which aired in the fall of 1985. Quoting from the description in the *New York Times*:

> The 30-second commercial [produced by the Coalition for Strategic Defense Initiative] opens with a child's crayon drawing of a family of stick people outside their house, with a large sun in the background. A little girl is heard wondering what "Star Wars" is all about. She then says her father told her that "right now, we can't protect ourselves from nuclear weapons and that's why the President wants to build a Peace Shield." While she is speaking, a dome is drawn over the house and family. Missiles come crashing into the dome and are destroyed. When the attack is over, the Peace Shield becomes a rainbow, and the sun can be seen smiling in the background. The scene dissolves into a rainbow with "Support the Peace Shield" underneath, along with a phone number and address of the coalition.[4]

However, most proposed umbrella defenses do not claim to be able to achieve anything as complete as this commercial suggests. For example, in Daniel Graham's original High Frontier study, three layers of defense against ballistic missiles alone were envisioned:

> The first layer would consist of 432 orbiting battle stations, each armed with 40-50 non-nuclear kill devices. These weapons would radically reduce the effectiveness of Soviet missile attack in the early stages of flight.
>
> The second layer would involve battle stations using advanced beam weaponry to further reduce the effectiveness of a missile attack.
>
> The third layer—a ground-based system—would consist of weapons surrounding U.S. missile silos, for example, swarms of projectiles or rocket-powered interceptors that would be launched to destroy the surviving incoming ICBMs.[5]

Other proposed umbrella defenses differ in various respects, but they all incorporate Graham's layered approach and they all share the following problems.

The first problem with Strategic Defense viewed as an umbrella defense is that it defends only against long range ballistic missile attack. As Richard DeLauer, then Under Secretary of Defense for Research and Engineering, told the Senate Armed Services Committee: "The Strategic Defensive Initiative is a technological program against ballistic missiles, not against the air-breathing threat."[6] So conceived, Strategic Defense provides no defense against strategic bombers and cruise missiles which could deliver thousands of highly accurate nuclear weapons by going under any Peace Shield that was constructed. Moreover, since most Strategic Defense systems could not be ready for deployment until after the year 2000, the Soviets would also have over 10 years to develop still other forms of air-breathing delivery systems and low trajectory missiles to attack the U.S. without encountering the proposed defense.[7]

The second problem with Strategic Defense viewed as an umbrella defense is that it faces numerous technical difficulties. In order for space-based weapons to be effective against ICBMs, they would require targeting capabilities far beyond anything ever accomplished to date. The weapons would have to maintain near-perfect accuracy long enough to inflict damage upon targets traveling at more than 10,000 miles per hour, up to 3,500 miles away. This targeting challenge has been compared to that of "being on top of the Washington Monument, shooting a rifle, and hitting a baseball on top of the Empire State Building."[8]

An even more serious technical difficulty to be overcome in order for Strategic Defense to be a viable weapons system is computer software. According to David L. Parnas who resigned from the Strategic Defense Initiative Organization, discussion of Strategic Defense often ignores computers, focusing instead on new developments in sensors and weapons.[9] Yet since all software is to some extent unreliable, bugs have to be routinely worked out during use. In fact, programmers spend at least as much time testing and correcting errors as they spend writing initial programs. Big producers have separate groups of testers to do quality assurance. This is because programmers cannot be trusted to test their own programs adequately. Moreover, software is released for use not when it is known to be correct, but when the rate of discovering new errors slows down to one that management considers acceptable. Obviously, then, any large-scale software system requires extensive testing under realistic conditions. For example, to make even minor modifications in operational software for military aircraft requires extensive ground testing, followed by flight testing that closely approximates battle conditions. And despite these tests, bugs can and do show up in battle conditions.[10] Thus, Parnas contends that the inability to test a strategic defense system under field conditions before we actually need it, will mean that no knowledgeable person could ever put much trust in the system.

Yet Strategic Defense cannot be tested under realistic conditions and must perform with near perfection in an actual attack. The size of the program that is needed, which is estimated to be between 10 and 100 million lines of code, also gives rise to special problems.[11] Despite attempts to develop new programming techniques more appropriate for mammoth projects, Parnas reports that working programmers still use the conventional "think-like-a-computer" approach, which is unreliable for large, complicated programs. Finally, Parnas contends that the new technologies sometimes offered as remedies for these software ills—such as artificial intelligence, automatic programming (the use of computers to program other computers), and program verification (the use of mathematical proofs to establish that the program will work) —are not capable of providing reliable software for a system as large as that required for Strategic Defense.[12]

In contrast, Solomon Buchsbaum, executive vice president of A.T.& T.'s Bell Laboratories, maintains that the necessary computer network is available because an equally complex system exists in the U.S. Public Telecommunication Network.[13] But Karl Dahlke, who is engaged to design and maintain the same A.T. & T. system, disagrees with Buchsbaum. He writes:

> . . .despite our best efforts, the software that controls the telephone network has approximately one error for every thousand lines of code when it is initially incorporated into the phone system. Extensive testing and simulation cannot discover these errors. If SDI contains ten million lines of software (a credible estimate), and its quality is comparable to the telephone network, we can expect ten thousand errors embedded in this software when the Soviets attack.[14]

So it would seem that any software system that was adequate for Strategic Defense would have to be radically different from the systems we currently have.

As further evidence of the technical difficulties surrounding Strategic Defense, in a recent survey the membership of the American Physical Society, the nation's leading organization of professionally trained physicists, considered Strategic Defense as a step in the wrong direction by a margin of nearly 2:1 (54% to 29%).[15] In fact, those who knew the most about Strategic Defense tended to be the most skeptical about the program. Of those who responded, 61% said they knew a great deal or quite a bit about Strategic Defense; and of these, 63% describe the program as a step in the wrong direction for U.S. national security. Only 25% view it as a step in the right direction.

More recently, a panel of experts drawn from the same professional society reported that so many breakthroughs are required to develop the laser and particle beam weapons proposed for Strategic Defense that it will take a decade or more of intensive research just to determine whether the job can be done.[16] The co-chairs of this 15 member study group were Nicholas Bloembergen, a Harvard University physicist who won a Nobel Prize for work on lasers, and C.K.N. Patel, who is an executive director in research at A.T. & T. Bell Laboratories and a laser inventor. The group also included top scientists from the Government's own weapons laboratories. Their report was then reviewed by a six-member committee that included two other scientists who won Nobel Prizes for their laser work and two scientists who held top positions in military research. In addition, a majority of the members of the National Academy of Sciences believe that Strategic Defense is unwise, and 57 Nobel Laureates from this group, more than half of the living American recipients of this prize in the sciences, have endorsed the Union of Concerned Scientists' "Appeal to Ban Space Weapons." And more than half of the professors at the top twenty U.S. physics departments have gone so far as to sign a pledge not to accept funding for Strategic Defense research. Even a Strategic Defense that relies upon rockets rather than upon lasers would probably suffer "catastrophic failure" at the moment when it was needed, according to a recent study by the U.S. Government's own Office of Technology Assessment.[17]

A third difficulty with Strategic Defense is that whatever military advantage it might otherwise produce, that advantage could be overcome by a variety of countermeasures the Russians might take, countermeasures which are often cheaper than the proposed defenses themselves. The simplest Soviet countermeasure would be a massive buildup of offensive nuclear weapons in an attempt to overload the defense system. Other possible countermeasures are: 1) warheads that fly erratically toward their targets; 2) warheads that confuse radar tracking abilities by releasing clouds of metal from their tips; 3) decoys that behave like warheads and thus work to saturate the defense; (According to MIT's Henry Kendall, "They could give each decoy the ability to maneuver and emit spurious radar signals. You'd have a million objects maneuvering, sizzling and sparkling. All they need is wristwatch electronics to run all this. You'd have to shoot at everything."); 4) hardened and reflective materials that would blunt the effect of lasers; 5) rotating missiles that would disperse laser beam energy; 6) warheads that emit smoke screens as a shield against lasers; and 7) missiles with a shortened booster phase so as to make them less a target for lasers. With respect to this last countermeasure, even General Abrahamson, the manager of the Strategic Defense Initiative Organization, has been quoted in the *Washington Post* as saying, "You probably could not handle the fast-burn booster."[19] In addition, most of the countermeasures that have been mentioned would also exploit existing technology in contrast to the unproven technology on which Strategic Defense would rely.[20]

In sum, when viewed as an umbrella defense, there are three basic problems with Strategic Defense: it defends only against long-range ballistic missiles, it is subject to numerous technical difficulties, and its effectiveness can be reduced, if not cancelled out, by a variety of countermeasures that the Russians might take. Clearly, then, when viewed as an umbrella defense Strategic Defense is not a means of increasing U.S. security independent of the (increased) good will of the Soviet Union.

When Strategic Defense is viewed as a limited or point defense, it suffers from the very same problems that undermine Strategic Defense as an umbrella defense: it defends only against long-range ballistic missiles, it is subject to numerous technical difficulties, and its effectiveness can be reduced, if not cancelled out, by a variety of countermeasures that the Russians might take. Granted, the technical difficulties facing a point defense are not as severe as those facing an umbrella defense. Nevertheless, the decreased effectiveness of a point defense against a nuclear attack makes it easier for the Russians to cancel out any advantage such a defense might otherwise provide by simply increasing their own offensive nuclear forces. The only way to prevent this from occurring, assuming the Russians are not going to show increased good will in the face of our military build-up, is if the development and deployment of such a defense were linked with a significant cut-back in the development and deployment of offensive nuclear weapons, such as MX missiles, B-1 bombers, Trident submarines and cruise missiles. Without such a cut-back, it would not be possible to deploy a Strategic Defense that promotes U.S. security without relying upon the (increased) good will of the Soviet Union for its effectiveness.

Now the second justification for Strategic Defense is closely tied to the first. Whether Strategic Defense is a morally preferable means of promoting U.S. security depends upon its effectiveness, and that, as we have seen, depends upon both overcoming the relevant technical difficulties and combining development and deployment with a significant cut-back in the development and deployment of offensive nuclear weapons. Moreover, without a cut-back in the development and deployment of offensive nuclear forces, Strategic Defense will appear to be part of a first-strike force. This is because supporters of Strategic Defense contend that such a system should be built even if it is only 30% effective against a nuclear attack.[21] But what defensive purpose could be served by a Peace Shield that lets in 70% of what the Russians could throw at us? Even if Strategic Defense were 90% effective against a Soviet nuclear attack, 10% of the Soviet nuclear force would suffice to utterly destroy the U.S. Accordingly, the only strategic use for such a porous shield would seem to be to defend against a second strike by Soviet nuclear forces following a first strike by our own nuclear forces. It is not surprising, therefore, that the Soviets view Strategic Defense in conjunction with the combined deployment of MX missiles, B-1 bombers, Trident submarines and cruise missiles to be a part of a first strike force in the making. Yet, according to the just means component of just threat theory, no nation should have to endure the threat of a first strike from another nation when that threat is not necessary for maintaining the other nation's national security. Consequently, if Strategic Defense as a limited point defense is to be morally justified, it would have to be combined with cutbacks in the development and deployment of offensive nuclear weapons systems in ways that were not envisioned by the Reagan administration.

As we noted, the third justification tends to view Strategic Defense as a research program to be bargained away to achieve arms control. But this need not be the case. If Strategic Defense were combined with a deep cut in the development and deployment of offensive nuclear weapons as required by just threat theory, then it could serve as a stimulus to arms control even when viewed as a possible deployment. But if Strategic Defense is not combined with a deep cut in the development and deployment of offensive nuclear weapons, then it would most likely serve as a stimulus not to arms control but to an arms race possibly on a scale previously unknown.

Similarly, although the fourth justification would seem to require that Strategic Defense remain a research program, a deployment that was linked with a deep cut in the development and deployment of offensive nuclear weapons may still achieve the goals of this justification in a manner that accords with just threat theory.

With respect to the fifth justification, it is relevant to ask how many lives would be saved by the proposed deployment. If the number is small relative to those that are lost, then just war theory would require that some more productive approach to saving lives be tried. In addition, even if Strategic Defense is capable of saving a goodly number of lives from a nuclear attack, we need to know whether such a defense would not make a nuclear attack more likely in the first place. If it did, Strategic Defense would not be justified, since it would clearly violate the just means component of just threat theory.

From a moral point of view, the sixth and final justification for Strategic Defense is clearly only appropriate after a strong case has been made for Strategic Defense in terms of one or more of the other justifications and, thus, ultimately in terms of just war theory and just threat theory. But in the real world, this justification seems to be determining events, at least determining the relevant defense appropriations. Thus, we find defense contractors influencing the decisions to buy weapons by a variety of means, such as advertising, hiring former Department of Defense employees, making political contributions and maintaining expensive lobbying efforts in Washington D.C.[22] For example, four contractors alone spent a total of $31 million on advertising in 1985. During a ten year period (1976-85) TRW, a major military contractor, spent at least $100 million on advertising, while McDonnell Douglas spent $50 million. In addition, the hiring by contractors of former military officials increased nearly 500% between 1975 and 1985, and the twenty top defense contractors poured $3.6 million into congressional and presidential campaigns in 1984, double their 1980 level.[23]

Is it any surprise, therefore, that military work is more than twice as profitable as commercial work, that over the last thirty years only five military programs valued over $1 billion were terminated, that 45% of space-weapons prime contracts went to President Reagan's home state of California, and that 77% of the prime contracts went to states or districts represented by Congress persons or Senators who sit on the armed services committees and the defense appropriations subcommittees?[24] Accordingly, the need for the recent FBI investigations of the relationship between Pentagon officials, military contractors and our elected representatives comes as no surprise at all.

In sum, I have evaluated each of the six proposed justifications for Strategic Defense and argued that from the perspective of just war theory and just threat theory none of these justifications supports Strategic Defense unless the program is combined with a radical cut-back in the development and deployment of offensive nuclear weapons. For only when combined with a radical cut-back in the development and deployment of offensive nuclear weapons can Strategic Defense succeed in providing a morally preferable means of promoting U.S. security that does not depend upon the (increased) good will of the Soviet Union for its effectiveness.

The University of Notre Dame

Notes

[1] An earlier version of this paper appeared in *Public Affairs Quarterly*, 2.4 (1988).

[2] The requirements of just war theory can be stated as follows. *Just Cause:* There must be substantial aggression and nonbelligerent correctives must be hopeless or too costly. *Just Means:* (1) The harm resulting from the belligerent means employed should not be disproportionate to the military objective to be attained. (2) The harm to innocents should not be directly intended as an end or as a means.

(3) Harm to innocents must be minimized by accepting risks (costs) to oneself that would not render it impossible to attain the military objective.

[3] James P. Sterba, "Moral Approaches to Nuclear Strategies: A Critical Evaluation *Canadian Journal of Philosophy* 12 (1987) 75-109. See also "Just War Theory and Nuclear Strategy" *Analyse & Kritik* (1987) 155-174.

[4] *New York Times,* October 12, 1985.

[5] Daniel O. Graham, "Defense and Development on the High Frontier" *Imprimis* 11.6 (1982); Union of Concerned Scientists, *Briefing Paper* 5 (October, 1983).

[6] Center for Defense Information, *The Defense Monitor,* XV.2 (1986) 2.

[7] Center for Defense Information, 2

[8] Union of Concerned Scientists.

[9] David Parnas, "Why I Quit Star Wars" *Common Cause Magazine* (May/June, 1986) 32-35; "Software Aspects of Strategic Defense Systems" *American Scientist* 13 (1985) 432-440.

[10] Parnas, "Software Aspects" 434.

[11] Union of Concerned Scientists, *Nucleus* 7.3, (1985) 2.

[12] Parnas, "Software Aspects" 437-39.

[13] See Lord Zuckerman, "Reagan's Highest Folly" *New York Review of Books* (April 9, 1987) 39.

[14] Zuckerman 39.

[15] Union of Concerned Scientists, *Nucleus* 8.2 (1986) 1, 4.

[16] *New York Times,* April 23, 1987.

[17] *New York Times,* April 25, 1988.

[18] Union of Concerned Scientists, *Briefing Paper;* Jerry Hartz, "Star Wars: Panacea or Poison?" *Sane World* 24.4 (1985) 1-2.

[19] *Washington Post,* January 18, 1987.

[20] Hartz 1. In fact, these are the countermeasures the U.S. is currently developing! See Union of Concerned Scientists, *Briefing Paper.*

[21] See Colen Campbell, "At Columbia, 3 Days of Arms Talks," *New York Times,* February 11, 1985, and "Star Wars Chief Takes Aim at Critics," *Science,* (August 10, 1984).

[22] Center for Defense Information, *The Defense Monitor* 16.3, 1-8.

[23] Center for Defense Information, 16.3 1-8.

[24] Center for Defense Information, 16.3 1-8, and E. P. Thompson, "Folly's Comet," *Star Wars,* ed. E. P. Thompson (New York: Pantheon 1985) 133.

The Man in the Teflon Suit:
A Flaw in the Argument for Strategic Defense

David Hoekema

The heated public debate over the scientific and political merits and shortcomings of the system of defense against strategic nuclear weapons proposed by President Reagan in 1983 has been largely dominated by discussion of the technical feasibility of such a system. The fundamental morality of strategic defense is more often assumed than explicitly defended. If philosophers have a contribution to make to this important discussion, it lies above all in critically assessing the ethical underpinnings of a policy of defending against nuclear attack, and it is to that task that the present paper is devoted.[1]

The central argument for the desirability of strategic defence —the argument commonly advanced by proponents and challenged in various ways by critics—can be reconstructed and summarized as follows:

(1) *Each nation has both a right and a duty to protect its people and territory against military attack, subject to reasonable constraints of cost, absence of corollary harm to the innocent, and fulfillment of other duties.*

(2) *The threat of nuclear retaliation, although it may be an effective deterrent to attack, is both potentially unstable and morally disquieting as a permanent basis for national security.*

(3) *Defense is morally preferable to offense; i.e., to defend against attack by means which neutralize or deflect aggressive acts is better from a moral standpoint than to retaliate against an attacker.*

Since our concern is not with the actual use but with the intention to use defensive or offensive measures, we need a narrower premise than (3):

(4) *Having the intention and the capacity to defend against attack is morally preferable to having the intention and the capacity to retaliate against an attacker.*

At this point an empirical claim must be made:

(5) *An effective and reliable system of defense against strategic nuclear attack, a system that has no offensive capability, can be constructed at reasonable cost using technology that is now, or soon will be, available.*

Around this assertion, needless to say, endless controversy swirls; we will return to the point below. But we can infer from (2) and (4):

(6) *Strategic nuclear defense is morally preferable to the threat of nuclear retaliation as a basis for national defense.*

All that prevents us from drawing the desired conclusion is an additional empirical premise, which might be stated thus:

(7) *The nature and source of the threat of military attack against the United States morally justifies the counterthreat of nuclear retaliation as a means of preventing any such attack.*

Needless to say, the same claim might be made for any number of other nations generating precisely parallel arguments. At this point, from (1), (6), and (7), we can infer the desired conclusion:

(8) *The United States is morally justified in seeking to construct a. system of strategic nuclear defense.*

This is not the only possible argument that could be advanced for building a strategic defense system. It might be argued that nuclear deterrence is categorically immoral, for example, but that strategic defense escapes its weaknesses. The argument reconstructed here, however, reproduces in outline the moral case that is put forward by many adherents of strategic defense and is frequently accepted even by critics.

Let us consider each step of the argument in turn. The first premise is a straightforward application of a widely shared moral consensus regarding the moral standing of nations. As a statement of principle it could be granted by pacifists as well as militarists, however great their differences over how to apply the constraints of cost and of avoiding harm to others. The third constraint, concerning the fulfillment of other duties, serves to deny to a thoroughly unjust and oppressive political order the right to self-preservation.

Only a few years ago premise (2) was vehemently rejected by most conservatives; but no more. One of the remarkable results of the unexpected shift in defense policy in 1983 has been a broad consensus in both liberal and conservative camps regarding the fundamental immorality of nuclear deterrence.

In 1983 the U.S. Conference of Catholic Bishops issued its long-anticipated pastoral letter, "The Challenge of Peace," and its key conclusion that nuclear deterrence could be only temporarily and provisionally tolerated as a means to disarmament was roundly attacked by the Reagan administration.[2] But during the same spring President Reagan reported to the nation that he had "become more and more deeply convinced that the human spirit must be capable of rising above dealing with other nations and human beings by threatening their existence," and he called on the scientific community to "give us the means of rendering these nuclear weapons impotent and obsolete."[3] At a major conference of evangelical Christians concerned with peace issues held during the same period, few of the pacifist theologians among invited speakers condemned nuclear deterrence as vehemently or as categorically as did conservative Senator William Armstrong, who described nuclear deterrence as "impractical and unrealistic," a policy that is "intellectually and morally bankrupt."[4]

There is, then, widespread acknowledgement of the moral as well as practical imperfections of nuclear deterrence. No doubt those who have long condemned nuclear deterrence on moral grounds have motivations quite different from others lately come to the cause whose misgivings have surfaced only in the debate over strategic defense. But ours is not to scoff at moral progress, whatever its motives.

Premise (5) is the focus of the public controversy over strategic defense. Proponents of strategic defense support it by pointing to the rapid progress of the past decade in microprocessor and sensor technologies. In an age when yesterday's $3 million mainframe computer is outpaced by today's $3000 desktop machine, when cruise missiles use detailed electronic maps to skim along treetops for thousands of miles, is it not churlish even to raise questions about the technical feasibility of a task such as strategic defense, given a few more years and an appropriate research budget? Critics counter that the complexity of the imagined strategic defense system and the need for flawless coordination and extremely high reliability relegate it to the realm of scientific fantasy. A study commissioned by three Senators in 1986, they observe, found scientists at the major strategic defense weapons laboratories skeptical of their prospects for success because of "intractable problems" both of constructing a defensive system and of shielding the system itself from attack. Scientists at one laboratory agreed that "space-based, boost-phase defense can never be made survivable, except by treaty."[5]

In the debate over technical feasibility, philosophers' voices ought to be heard, not only as concerned citizens but also as careful observers of both the genuine achievements and of the overblown claims of science in our day. But I propose for the moment to set this issue entirely aside in order to turn instead to basic issues of morality. Let us assume, therefore, for purposes of this discussion, that premise (5) above is sound. Let us suppose that a highly reliable "missile shield" can be built within the next decade, promising to destroy or harmlessly deflect every strategic nuclear weapon that might be launched against our nation or its allies.[6] Let us suppose further that the cost of the system will be modest—some small fraction, let us say, of present defense spending—and its failure rate negligible, so that if a thousand missiles were launched against us it would be highly unlikely that even one would penetrate our defenses. These assumptions are far more optimistic than even the most enthusiastic supporters of strategic defense would be willing to defend. But for purposes of argument we grant them.

I propose similarly to grant premise (7) rather than attempt to assess its soundness. No reasonable person would deny that the Unites States, like the other nations of the world, faces serious threats of many kinds to its territorial integrity and national security. But the appropriateness and effectiveness of nuclear deterrence in meeting such threats is disputed by many reasonable persons, and I have argued elsewhere that there are both practically and morally better alternatives.[7] For our present purposes, however, let us simply stipulate that the world is a nasty enough place and that even the extreme threat of nuclear attack can be morally condoned. Granting this premise provisionally grounds the case for building a system of defense to replace the threat of retaliation.

It would be permissible, if not a positive duty, to build such a system if the argument sketched above is sound, and its conclusion does follow plausibly from its premises. But we have not yet considered the soundness of premise (3) or its corollary (4). It has seemed obvious to most of the disputants in the debate that defense, if it is possible, is morally superior to offense. But what seems obvious is not infrequently wrong. And if as philosophers we have learned anything from the tangled issues surrounding nuclear deterrence, we have learned that our moral inclinations may fail to guide us, or even lead us seriously astray, when they are applied to matters of life and death on a global scale.

In the remainder of this discussion I will argue that premise (3) is not, after all, a sound premise, and that (4) is similarly flawed. Both premises can be amended in ways that enhance their appeal, but the results then fail to support the conclusion of the argument above. As a result, the argument fails to provide clear moral support for strategic nuclear defense.

At the end of Book I of the *Republic*, Plato suggests that the quest for justice can more fruitfully be pursued if the object of inquiry is enlarged from the individual to the state. In the present case, we can see the flaws of premise (3) more clearly if we shift our attention from issues of global life and death to more mundane circumstances of individual action. Let us turn for the moment from strategic nuclear weapons and the potential death of billions to consider a more homely example of defending oneself against attack.

The ring of Gyges, Plato reminds us, in conferring invisibility would exempt its wearer both from aggression and from moral accountability. It would be, in a sense, the perfect means of personal defense, and at the same time a license to unbridled immorality. The same ambiguity attends less perfect and more realistic means of personal defense.

A flak jacket, as all cultured persons have learned from television cop shows, is a vest heavily reinforced with synthetic fibers capable of absorbing and diffusing the impact of a bullet fired at the wearer. Such a jacket offers partial but imperfect protection. Suppose we have invented a head-to-toe Teflon suit that reliably deflects all bullets and bazooka rounds. The suit is a potent means of personal defense, yet it cannot harm anyone. Can there be any moral objection to such a defensive device? Should we make it available to anyone who requests it?

Imagine first that a police captain asks for Teflon suits to outfit a team preparing to negotiate with a deranged man holding a family hostage in their apartment. Surely no one would refuse such a request on ethical grounds. The wearers of our suits will be taking a considerable personal risk in order to attempt to rescue several innocent people from death or injury, and the suits will protect them in doing so.

The next request, let us imagine, comes from Jesse James, and his gang is known to be plotting a daring series of bank raids. If we have any moral scruples at all we will refuse his request, since outfitting bank robbers with protective suits will only embolden them and increase the risk of harm to others. None of the reasons why police officers should have such jackets apply to Jesse James, who deserves no protection in carrying out his planned crimes.

These contrasting cases make it evident that defense is not always morally permissible. Whether defensive measures are morally permissible, it is clear, depends on the context. For the police in the situation I have described, the Teflon suits diminish the harm that can be caused by a deranged man. A strong case might be made for requiring the police officers to turn in their service revolvers when signing out their suits. To carry a deadly weapon while effectively immune from attack is an invitation to use excessive violence, and in any case a team of trained policemen able to walk up to the hostage-taker without fearing for their own safety can subdue him by nonlethal means. For the police officers, our Teflon suits make both practical and moral sense, for they broaden their range of choices and protect their lives.

But the James gang with Teflon suits is in no way morally preferable to the James gang in standard-issue denims. At their next bank job, Teflon suits will only increase their willingness to take risks in wrongdoing, since they need not fear being killed if their gunfire is returned. Their nefarious activities deserve no protection, certainly not the protection of our suits. More than that, the Teflon suits provide a means of defense which multiplies both the likelihood and the potential harm of their aggressive violence. Here the addition of defensive to offensive capacities would make a bad situation much worse.

Premises (3) and (4) above imply that there could be no moral objection to my selling Teflon suits to whomever I wish. But this is a confusion. To provide means of defense may facilitate wrongdoing. To give Jesse James a Teflon suit and a pistol is worse than to give him only a pistol.

Furthermore, the moral dubiousness of defense is not limited to felons and criminal gangs. Indeed, the considerations that would lead us to deny Jesse James a Teflon suit would apply to ordinary law-abiding citizens as well. If ordinary citizens are entitled to purchase firearms for sporting use, to permit them to have Teflon suits as well would serve no significant purpose, and it would increase the danger to others when their weapons are turned to harmful purposes.

An armed man who can laugh off bullets is an extremely dangerous man. The danger of such an outcome is so great that seemingly harmless defensive devices may properly be denied to anyone except police officers. Even for the police, only an emergency such as the situation I have described would warrant the use of such suits, and temporarily giving up deadly weapons should be a condition of their use. Even for the police, to wear them routinely, or to wear them while carrying a sidearm, might make trigger fingers too quick.

Returning to the argument sketched at the outset, we must amend premise (3) by inserting an appropriate proviso:

(3') *Defense is morally preferable to offense, provided it does not protect offensive capacity.*

And we could similarly revise (4):

(4') *Having the intention and the capacity to defend oneself against attack is morally preferable to having the intention and the capacity to retaliate against an attacker, provided that defensive capacities do not themselves augment offensive capacities.*

But this shift in a key premise throws into question the entire argument in support of strategic defense. If strategic defense is to *replace* deterrent threats as the foundation of natural security, then the misgivings voiced in the preceding section do not apply. President Reagan spoke in the speech quoted earlier of "eliminating the threat posed by strategic nuclear missiles." Moreover, at the Reykjavik summit in October 1986 the leaders of the two nuclear superpowers evidently devoted serious discussion to a rapidly negotiated elimination of all strategic nuclear weapons. But their talk issued in no serious negotiations.

It is evident from the statements of many other military and political leaders that strategic defense is envisioned as a *supplement to*, and not a substitute for, the destructive capacity that our nation already possesses. Defense Secretary Caspar Weinberger, for example, called in January 1987 for early deployment of a partial defensive system, and his annual reports to Congress made it clear that even the full system of strategic defense would supplement rather than replace nuclear deterrent forces.[9] A strategy analyst writing in a philosophy journal in defense of strategic defense has described it as a means of "strengthening deterrence" that might lead in three or four decades after its deployment to substantial steps toward nuclear disarmament.[10]

With the revised premises (3) and (4) in mind, the conclusion (8) conflates two distinctly different possibilities. We can distinguish them—the two alternative conclusions to our argument—as follows:

(9) *The United States is morally justified in seeking to construct a system of strategic defense after destroying all of its nuclear weapons.*

Presumably such destruction would occur at an advanced stage in a coordinated program of global disarmament—total and unilateral disarmament is scarcely within the realm of political possibility. But from the moral standpoint, the essential point is that defense should replace deterrence. This is one possible conclusion of the argument. The other is the following:

(10) *The United States is morally justified in seeking to construct a system of strategic defense while retaining its nuclear weapons.*

Of these alternative conclusions, only (9) can be reasonably inferred from the revised argument. Even this may be too sweeping a conclusion, for there may be other means of serving the ends cited in premise (1) which involve less cost or less risk of harm. Nevertheless, we can legitimately draw a measure of support, if not conclusive support, from the premises identified for the first of our two conclusions.

But (9) clearly does not support active efforts to create a system of strategic defense at present. If we are convinced of the truth of (9), our first step toward implementing it would be to redouble efforts to remove nuclear weapons from the arsenal of the world's weapons.

Having done so we would then assess whether strategic defense would remain a prudent hedge against future violations of disarmament pacts, or whether the process of achieving disarmament had created other means of security which make strategic defenses unnecessary.

(10), unlike (9), would support strategic defense efforts in the near term, while our deterrent force remains in place. But (10) quite clearly does not follow from the preceding argument when we substitute (4') for (4).

Hence the argument I have sketched, one commonly invoked by defenders of strategic defense in support of their position and equally commonly attacked by critics, fails to provide support for any deployment of measures of strategic defense unless they are preceded by effective nuclear disarmament. The argument fails not because of any presumption that the purposes for which the deterrent is held are immoral purposes. Indeed, we have explicitly specified that the alternative measures we are considering rest on the legitimate need for protection against attack. Yet even legitimate purposes do not justify extremely dangerous means. Strategic defense, even if it were harmless in isolation, becomes both dangerous and threatening to others when conjoined with offensive capacity.

It should be added that the argument of the present paper does not bear directly on the question of whether a limited program of research on the feasibility of strategic defense might nevertheless be justified, even while deterrence stands. Such a program would be intended to determine the truth of premise (5)—that a strategic defense system can be built at reasonable cost and without offensive capability—on which the present argument rests. If a research program offers clear evidence for the truth of this premise, its results would have at least some potential relevance to future policy choices. If, on the other hand, the preliminary results of research contradict (5), we would have strong grounds for discontinuing the research program itself.

In *Leviathan* Thomas Hobbes observed that human society needs civil government because of the approximate equality of man with man, giving even the weakest the power, through stealth or conspiracy, to kill the strongest. Had the Creator endowed us like the insects with rigid exoskeletons, Hobbes implies, we would need no government but would live lives of complete freedom. But the Creator has left us soft and vulnerable, and for security we must turn to the commonwealth.

Nuclear weapons are the great equalizers of international affairs, affording even the smallest nation the capacity to destroy the largest. In an era of conventional warfare, the strongest army offered the greatest immunity to attack, but in the nuclear age we all stand exposed.

The vision of strategic defense is a dream of a national exoskeleton. But just as a man in a shell would be a danger to his neighbors, so would a nation in a strategic shell, at least if, in each case, defensive measures supplemented offense.

If there is an escape for nations from the solitary, brutish, and potentially short life that the security of nuclear deterrence affords, it is not to escape vulnerability but, in Hobbes's terms, to establish covenants. The moral superiority of a perfect defense, in a world of offensive threats, is illusory.[11]

The University of Delaware

Notes

[1] Readers may note an absence of acronyms and of derogatory terms derived from science fiction films. Whatever the merits and originality of the present paper by other standards, the author aspires to write the first piece of English prose about strategic nuclear defense which employs neither device.

[2] The U. S. Conference of Catholic Bishops, *The Challenge of Peace:. God's Promise and Our Response, Origins,* 13.1 (May 19, 1983).

[3] Ronald Reagan, speech on defense spending and defensive technology, March 23, 1983, *The Star Wars Controversy: An. International Security Reader,* eds., Steven E. Miller and Stephen Van Evera (Princeton, NJ: Princeton University Press, 1986) 257-258.

[4] William Armstrong, "The Challenge of Nehemiah," *Perspectives on Peacemaking: Biblical Options in the Nuclear Age,* ed., John A. Birnbaum, (Ventura, CA: Regal Books, 1984) 210. The conference at which the papers in this volume were presented was held at Fuller Theological Seminary in May, 1983.

[5] The report to Senators William Proxmire, Lawton Chiles and Bennet Johnston was released in a declassified version in March, 1986.

[6] I incorporate both the motivational and the physical criteria for "pure

defense" identified by Gregory Kavka in his "Critique of Pure Defense" *Journal of Philosophy* 83.11 (1986) 625-633. Kavka's discussion, which came to my attention during the writing of the present essay, is a helpful outline of the moral issues surrounding nuclear defense in a realistic context, and my discussion is largely an elaboration of the third of the "four ways" he identifies in which pure defense may be morally questionable, namely, by making an aggression safer.

[7] See Hoekema, "The Moral Status of Nuclear Deterrent Threats," *Social Philosophy and Policy,* 3.1 (1985) 93-117.

[8] The appropriate material is actually not Teflon but Kevlar, a synthetic substance whose extremely strong but pliable fibers lend themselves to use in garments. I mention this fact only in a footnote for security reasons, since terrorists and agents of foreign powers generally do not read footnotes. Should they be inspired by the example in the text to outfit themselves in Teflon suits, they will be well protected against stubborn food stains but not against police bullets.

[9] "Weinberger Gives Strategy Outline on Missile Shield," *New York Times,* Jan. 13, 1987; Caspar Weinberger, *Annual Report to Congress, Fiscal Year 1984* (Washington, D.C.: Government Printing Office, 1984) 30.

[10] Colin Gray, "Strategic Defense and Peace," *Ethics* 95.3 (1985) 671.

[11] I wish to acknowledge helpful comments and criticisms of an earlier version of this paper provided by Ronald Santoni, Charles Beitz, and Kenneth Kemp, and by members of the audience at Calvin College and at the first national conference of Concerned Philosophers for Peace.

Section III

Criticizing Modern War and Promoting Peace

One of the functions of philosophy is clarification and criticism. Use of these tools could be observed in the previous sections, but with a focus on the ideological—those issues that set the people of the United States and the Soviet Union in opposition—and on the moral—evaluating the justification of various ethical methodologies for nuclear war and deterrence. In this section other issues are raised that also need to be taken into account when modern warfare is examined. These issues go beyond superpower ideologies and established ethical methodologies. They probe nontraditional concerns that challenge orthodox orientations. As such, they critique the entire modern war apparatus, and thus can be placed under the umbrella of peacemaking. Issues include the environment, sexism, warism, and democratic control of foreign affairs. The essays that follow treat these broader concerns.

In "Experiencing the Death of Humanity," Robert Ginsberg suggests that one thing is indispensable for understanding war and peace in the nuclear age: grasping the enormity of the threat posed for humanity by the very existence of the nuclear arsenals. Intellectual grasp of the threat of human extinction is one thing; experiential or existential grasp is another. Ginsberg tries to enter into this existential grasp by first centering on one's own death and then expanding to the death of humanity. Ginsberg views nuclear war as "omnicide" or "anthropocide," which means the killing of all or all humans. He wonders whether we will face nuclear death squarely or continue the process of psychological denial. Will we begin the process of stepping back from the nuclear horror, or will we numbly make excuses for our actions in the manner of human addicts?

In "From Nuclear Winter to Hiroshima," William Gay, too, is concerned about educating the public. Gay's orientation is environmental philosophy. He disagrees, however, with those like Ginsberg who argue that nuclear war is immoral on account of its potential for killing all humanity. The enormity of the potential horror is not what propels humans to act; change at the political level is not affected by such scares. Instead, Gay suggests that we come to grips with evil on a smaller scale. Hiroshima was wrong, he says, even though it did not reach the level of nuclear winter. Chernobyl was a

173

disaster of lesser magnitude that did great damage to the environment. We do not have to project nuclear war as killing all human life in order to acknowledge it as wrong. A more balanced view of what is morally unacceptable damage to the environment is thus given by the environmentalists. Moreover, environmentalism entails globalism, while nuclear armamentation is a product of nationalism. Globalism, in turn, embodies opposition to war, racism, sexism, autocracy, and violence, issues that are taken up in the remaining essays.

"Warism" is Duane Cady's name for the widespread presumption that war is both morally justifiable in principle and often morally justified in fact. Cady's essay, "Exposing Warism," is a call for our reexamination of that presumption. Cady suggests that so many people have accepted the "truth" of warism that they do not question whether warism might be false. Warism has become embedded in our culture, romanticized in our media and games, and accepted by our academic scholars. But what if warism is like racism and sexism? What if war, like slavery, were to be abolished? Why, asks Cady, is peacemaking not considered normal human activity, and war not required to be justified? By "justifying war" Cady does not mean a particular war or battle, but the institution of war. Peace activism comes in many forms and degrees, and need not be dismissed as an extreme. In the process of coming to understand peace we also need to appreciate healthy change in the status quo.

John Howie, too, in "Our War Problem and the Peacemaker Attitude," supports nonviolence and peacemaking as the optimal ethical option. He begins by reflecting back upon the history of philosophical commentary on war and shows the disagreement that has arisen, not surprisingly, among philosophers themselves on the question of whether war is justifiable. Aristotle, Augustine, and Thomas Aquinas are remembered for having mounted "just war" arguments which are still widely advocated. Over the centuries, philosophers have joined their voices to both sides: Rousseau, Fichte, Mill, Hegel, and others have advocated the conditional justifiability of warfare, while Kant, Emerson, and Thoreau have opposed it. Howie then details four aspects of our war problem, and concludes by sketching the rudiments of a serious peacemaker approach. His approach includes commitment proportionate to the immensity and complexity of the problem, an employment of nonviolent means for mitigating injustice and resolving conflict, a growing sensitivity to injustice within our own society and in international relations, and a massive redirecting of energies to the global problems of humankind.

Paula Smithka's article, "Nuclearism and Sexism: Overcoming Their Shared Metaphysical Basis" approaches issues of war and peace from the feminist perspective. Smithka links nuclearism with classism and sexism; all three, she claims, are symptoms of a deeper metaphysical crisis: the quest for radical autonomy which regards persons and nations as objects to be manipulated and controlled. The arms race, classism, racism, and sexism, she says, are severe forms of oppression which arise when human beings adopt an attitude of psychological *disassociation* from one another and from nature generally. This deep disassociation splits mind from body, humans from nature, males from females, autonomy from caring. In this regard, nature, body, and women have been oppressed, repressed, and exploited throughout history by masculine patriarchy. Patriarchy tends to be egoistic and atomistic, and feminism, interrelationist. Overcoming disassociation requires a fresh sense of integration, connectedness, rootedness in others and in nature. While some feminists call for a swing of the cultural pendulum toward interrelationism, Smithka believes such a move would only continue the alienation from the opposite pole. Instead, Smithka calls for an interconnectedness—what she calls "the autochthonic attitude"—wherein the differentiated masculine/feminine traits complement one another. To pursue a global society and to overcome the oppression manifest in sexism, classism, racism, and nuclearism, requires nothing less than an alternative metaphysics, global autochthony.

In a democratic country, who should decide nuclear weapons policy? Paul Churchill opens up some dimensions of this delicate and difficult question in his essay, "Democracy and the Threat of Nuclear Weapons." At present, the American decision to launch or not to launch nuclear missiles lies solely with the President. But this is not all. The entire strategy of nuclear deterrence has been devised and implemented over the years by a changing, but relatively small group consisting of the President, some members of the cabinet, and a few top national security advisors. Churchill calls this inner decision-making group a "nuclear autocracy," and asks whether this is the proper decision-making apparatus in a democracy for matters of such global importance. Is secretive and autocratic decision-making really necessary for national security? Churchill examines several arguments offered in support of our current policy, such as the argument from tacit consent and the argument for guardianship. He finds these arguments unconvincing. He concedes that the problem is delicate: there are very real dangers connected with nuclear-weapons policies that are likely to emerge from more democratized policy-making processes. Yet, in the end, Churchill stands by his judgment that nuclear weapons policies are made in a manner inconsistent with fundamental principles of democratic and constitutional government, and that some of the most basic policies—those which involve principles rather than procedures—should be made in a more fully democratic manner. Certain kinds of information and principles might well require secrecy, but other kinds of information and policy-principles should be subjected to open and public debate on a scale not even dimly approached by current policy-making practices. Throughout this essay Churchill does not presume that nuclear policies would change if they were made in a more democratic manner; rather, the author is concerned about the plight of democracy should more and more major decisions be made autocratically. A more democratically based decision would only change nuclear policies to the degree that men and women take seriously the new peacemaking perspectives offered in this section.

Smithka's search for a metaphysics of personal rootedness and Cady's effort at making nonviolence more culturally acceptable are echoed in the thesis of the last piece in this collection. In "On Stories, Peacemaking, and Philosophical Method" Lawrence Bove emphasizes the role of tradition, narration, and personal stories in ethical decision making. Bove draws upon the work of Stanley Hauerwas, Barbara Deming, and Bernard Lonergan in going beyond the traditional perspectives of utilitarianism and deontology. Science and absolutes form only a part of human history. Bove recommends instead a method for enlarging our sense of human interrelatedness: emphasis upon *stories* and *interpretive communities* as a foundation for ethical choices. Bove remembers Deming explaining her personal history of nonviolent resistance to war, racism, and sexism, and Lonergan developing a generalized method for the natural and human sciences. Bove shows how these approaches offer promising new modes of discourse for the study of nonviolence.

Robert Ginsberg

Verily, verily, I say unto you, Except a corn of wheat fall into the ground and die, it abideth alone: but if it die, it bringeth forth much fruit.

The text for today's sermon is from the Gospel according to St. John, 12:24. Jesus is calling for the abandonment of one's old form of life and a rebirth in Him. Though we lose that old life, the reward is life eternal (John, 12:25). But let us turn from this Christian notion of a dying that is linked to immortality to Dostoyevsky's *Brothers Karamazov,* for the biblical verse is the novel's epigraph as well as cited within it (Pt. II, Bk. 6, Ch. 2). Something deep in one's being must die out if a profoundly new life is to flourish. The saga of the three Karamazovs, which Dostoyevsky did not finish due to his death, was to be a dying and rebirth for each. Love—universalized fraternal love—would be their salvation, overcoming their excesses: heedless sensuality, detached intellectualism, and unworldly spirituality.

The psychological reality of loss and redemption is attested to by the world's religions. By a sudden stroke, as if of lightning, the old self falls away, dies out, and the new you is reborn. Perhaps the powerful Hindu doctrine of reincarnation owes its psychological strength to the experience in life of this kind of rebirth. The quantum leap to the new life brings with it a magnified sense of vitality, a maximization of meaning, and the heightened presence of reality, so that the experience is easily outfitted in religious terms. This kind of breakthrough may take the form of an epiphany or conversion. Accompanying the sudden life change is a vibrant joy, a dynamic peacefulness. One is ready to face life actively but with an abiding contentment.

Existential death and rebirth need not be experienced in religious categories or analyzed in those terms. People claim to go through life crises in which they are totally at a loss only to suddenly emerge as new persons with a fresh grip on life. Such crises often occur at stages of life: emergence from adolescence, marriage, childbearing, the celebrated middle-age crisis, and old age. Events in life can trigger the trauma of rebirth: a death in the family, going off to war, being violated, losing one's career, moving to another culture. A person may live four or five lives within the span of one eventful life. A human being always has the possibility, even on the deathbed or mounting the gallows, to undergo a sudden radical transformation. Zen may strike anyone at any moment.

Let us concentrate on the secular experience especially as it centers around the recognition of one's death, for this may be the most important crisis one faces in life. We may be intellectually aware that we are mortal without knowing this existentially. Is it an accident that the Scholastics used as sample premise to illustrate syllogistic form, "All men are mortal"? Yet the sample for the minor premise was that "Socrates is mortal," rather than that you, or I, are mortal. Death thereby is logically deflected from us. Freud argued that the primitive *It* which is ourselves cannot countenance its negation. So what the I knows about its death is subject to veto by a more powerful force of personality within. Unamuno analyzed the human being as a creature with an insatiable longing for immortality and a critical intellect aware of mortality. For Unamuno we are a sick animal, a living, and dying, contradiction, at best a tragic awareness. For Freud we are an animal in conflict, whose best bet is to bring peaceful balance between the competing internal powers. Yet for both thinkers, crucial to the dignity of individuals is that we face our death. Philosophical reflection has an eminent tradition of concentrating upon one's death as a point of departure for one's life. Philosophers are at home in death, though we intellectualize about it more than confront it existentially.[1]

To grasp one's own death may be the moment of opening a new lease on life. Terror and negation may give way to joy and affirmation. One's life may be redeemed as one "dies" when the rebirth experience occurs. Literary examples are Tolstoy's *Ivan Ilyich* and Camus' *The Stranger.* One may experience one's death early in life by experiencing the death of someone close, by absorbing the power of imaginative works, or by narrowly escaping death. Some people are reported to have died briefly and then been revived to relate after-death experience. A case can be made for the value of experiencing one's death while alive, for this may be the key to awareness of the value of one's life. You have not really lived if you have not experienced your

180

death. Instead of leaving morbid and depressing after-effects, such an experience may be the spirited rebirth that carries one forward in life with renewed energy.

The death at stake is the real death: the extinction of the individual. One ceases to be, forever. Death is not death if there is resurrection, reincarnation, eternal life, or entering the divine presence. Death in its finality, life in our finitude, is experienceable without any escape hatches. But if those forms of salvation are embedded in the experience, then the rebirth experienced is deflected from this life to some other mode of existence. We circumvent our death in this brilliant displacement of vital energy, though some of that energy renews one's engagement in life. Life can become fuller because of a discovered confidence in something much better to come. Thus, those who experience the escape hatch from the finality of death may appear similar to those who are reborn to value the fragility of the life that remains upon recognizing no escape from death. But in the long run, when the chips are down, one reborn to otherworldliness will give up sooner on the world, for that individual's fundamental insight is that life is never really lost or else it is not worth what we are to gain. This divergence of commitment in the crises of life and death is crucial. Those who experience the finality of death are tempted to save themselves by the displacement of otherworldliness. And those who experience otherworldliness may suddenly face the real death of the individual, and thus may experience rebirth in this world. The two movements are in struggle within each individual's breast. One is experienced in the face of the other, for one can only be the heroic denial of the other.

A special case of experiencing one's death must be mentioned before we turn to experiencing the death of humanity. We may be engaged in activities that unknowingly are contributing to our death. Smoking, alcohol addiction, and drug abuse are popular examples. These habits may be enjoyed as sociable, stimulating, or relaxing, with no intention of self-destruction. But one day we may discover that, in effect, we are killing ourselves. That discovery may be so moving as to give us the strength to break the habit. Three discoveries are tied up in the event: (1) we are heading for death, (2) we are the cause of our dying, (3) we can prevent our death by this cause by turning over a new leaf. By taking action corrective of ourselves we do not win immortality.

Instead, in the face of the finality of death, we save ourselves from a premature and inadvertent death. Moreover, we save ourselves from victimization by our own inappropriate actions. Our dignity triumphs over our folly. We are reborn with heightened self-respect and a deeper value for life.

Now let us apply this analysis of the rebirth of the individual faced with death to the problem of facing the death of humanity, anthropocide. At once a difference strikes the intellect, for whereas individual human beings are perforce mortal, the human species is not necessarily destined for extinction. While a comet may collide with the earth, a virus may overcome our species, or we may destroy ourselves, there is no necessity that we be eliminated. We know that the sun will eventually burn out, but that event is sufficiently far off to give us the opportunity to either provide another energy source or another home for the human species. That the species can continue the human adventure indefinitely is a consolation to the individual who must shuffle off this mortal coil.

Humanity need not die: a crucial insight when coupled with the recognition that humanity is engaged in those activities whose likely outcome will shortly be the extinction of the human race. The species while intending to deter nuclear war is moving ever closer to inflicting nuclear war on itself. Intellectually, we should be able to recognize this. Soon, 100,000 nuclear weapons, each 100 times as destructive as the atomic bomb dropped over forty years ago on Hiroshima, may be ready for release on a moment's notice. Within an hour 10,000,000 times the destructivity experienced by Hiroshima may be experienced worldwide. The firestorm, the radiation, the tidal wave, the black rain, and the nuclear winter will wipe out those unlucky enough to have survived the first hours. We can recognize this can happen, this is about to happen, and this need not happen. It can be prevented, although I do not as yet know how, but if it is not prevented it will happen.

Intellectually, this likelihood of the death of humanity is denied in several ways: (1) No nuclear power has an interest in starting a nuclear war which would lead to its own destruction. (2) Nuclear powers have a tacit understanding to refrain from escalating conflict to the point where nuclear weapons are used. (3) Nuclear weapons have not been used since the Second World War, demonstrating that their very existence does not lead to use. (4) Indeed, nuclear weapons by their very existence and deployment for use deter their use by opponents. (5) A nuclear war, once started, could be stopped and won with survivors, although hundreds of millions of lives may be lost. (6) Defenses may be constructed to protect part of humanity from the nuclear weapons of another part. (7) Nuclear-free zones are designated where non-combatant peoples will survive. (8) Finally, even at its worst, all-out nuclear war is sure to leave survivors of the human species in remote lands, in caves, in special buildings, or in submarines. If nuclear war were ninety-nine percent effective, fifty million human beings would remain alive to reclaim the earth and continue the adventure of the species.

These arguments must be taken seriously and answered calmly with evidence and reason. Each argument has its weakness. None is worth pinning our hopes upon. Though some may have strong probabilities in their favor, the margin of failure, though small, is too dangerous to tolerate. If all the arguments that total nuclear destruction will not occur were ninety-nine percent accurate, the world will be blown up in the next century.

While the logic of each argument is to be assessed, something familiar is suggested by the psychology these arguments appeal to. People engaged in self-destructive activities, such as alcoholism, are wont to dismiss the threat to their life by rationalizations. The threat cannot be taken seriously because one cannot yet confront one's mortality. One's own death in such a case remains an abstraction. It is intellectually held at a distance from one's existence. Hence, one becomes overconfident that one's activities, justified on this or that ground, will not lead to one's death. The energy that goes into the self-destructive activity also spills over into the cover-up of the threat and the protection of the activity which is addictive. So the several accounts of how we may continue to safely live with nuclear weapons seem to be intellectually distant from what is really at stake: the death of humanity. Moreover, the confident attachment to some logical position may evade psychological recognition of the impending death of the species. If the alcoholic refuses to take responsibility for addictive behavior because the death of that individual is not really, existentially, experienced, then we may be collectively refusing to take responsibility for our addictive behavior in preparing for nuclear war because as individuals we have not really faced the threat of human extinction.

One can, one must, experience existentially the impending death of humanity. It is a mind-boggling experience. It is an ultimate experience, a grasp of absolute finality. One's heart is grasped by the end of things—their termination, not fulfillment—since all access to things concludes for humanity with its eradication. Anthropocide, which each of us can experience before the event, is the end of all of us. It is the destruction not only of all presently alive but also of the future. This act which we have been preparing during forty years is the end of the human adventure. Thus, it also destroys the earlier chapters. Anthropocide kills the past along with us, for no one will be left to cherish it.

Anthropocide, caused by humanity, is total evil, since it irreversibly destroys everything of human value and every living human being. This experience is like a revelation of hell. No other experience, except that of one's own death and that of genocide, can be brought close to this existential crisis.

The shock of one's own death, which is absolute, may be so faced that a rebirth occurs and one goes on living with renewed intensity. But then the shock of anthropocide seems to veto that individual experience. Anthropocide removes the consolation of a continuing humanity that may have softened the former. By anthropocide, which is likely to occur in our lifetime, one loses one's own life again. Having been reborn to value life more than ever, we are staggered by the threat to all life, including our own, that would wipe away all values. What good is it to continue living in such a world racing toward its self-destruction? The individual who has squarely faced private mortality may have worked out an attitude or project for living one's precious few years. But can we plan our lives to make the most of them in face of this universal disaster? To live joyfully in the world cognizant of our own individual death is one thing, while to live joyfully in the world cognizant of its death is quite another. The value of our individual lives seems diminished by the threat to the continuity of humanity. Thus, recognition of the species problem may well interfere with the successful rebirth of the individual who has faced private mortality.

The experience of humanity's death fills the individual with terror and despair. The individual is terrorized by such absolute evil. Nothing worse is conceivable. The experience is a plunge into the terrible abyss of helpless, hopeless solitude. All the previous generations of humanity had to face as individuals only the death of the individual. The five billion human beings now living have this additional, unprecedented terror to face. While the experience is of all of us dying, we remain isolated in the experience. "How can I save humanity?" is the overwhelming question that mocks the poor individual.

All humanity is about to die because of activities we are engaged in, presumably for our benefit. You and I are guilty of taking a hand in the suicide of our species. That is a strong accusation which many will reject with careful reasoning. The acts of humanity, their logic will run, cannot be ascribed to individuals. Moreover, humanity as a whole is not engaging in self-destruction. At most, certain large nations are the responsible parties, and then merely their governments rather than the people are responsible. The acts are defensive in intention; no one is really aiming at world destruction. Therefore, if the world is destroyed it will be by inadvertence. No one will be guilty then. Finally, argues the individual, I have denounced nuclear weapons, marched in peace demonstrations, contributed to the anti-war movement, and voted for peace candidates.

All these exculpatory accounts are plausible and may be intellectually justified. But they may not be true to the ultimate experience. Psychologically, we recognize that if we continue to live in the world in the usual way, then we share in the responsibility for its death. We are profiting, while we live, from the world about to die. To protest against evil in the usual ways is not sufficient when facing ultimate evil. Indeed, the usual gestures on behalf of peace ease the conscience while allowing the systemic evil to continue its fatal advance. The members of an alcoholic's family, though not technically guilty in that person's unwitting self-destruction, may feel they have a responsibility for assisting that person to change. But the disease has an in-built mechanism which fuels itself upon the usual efforts of relatives to interrupt what the alcoholic takes to be self-directed choices. Only by radical intervention, producing the shock of a dying, can such family members really help. As members of the human family our usual efforts for peace are also absorbed by the disease of addiction to weapons of mass destruction. Our arguments and pleas seem to make no dent. The world is either deaf to our warnings or takes them to heart only to be displaced by habitual activity. The peace movement functions within a world system geared for self-destruction.

Often those who have had the ultimate experience and speak out against destruction only convince others who have had the same experience. We preach our sermons to the converted. I have been deeply moved by many conferences on peace, and by many demonstrations for peace, but I have come home from them wondering if they have been of any good other than to the dignity of the goodwilled participants.

Extraordinary measures are called for to face ultimate evil. The disaster for the species is total; therefore, the effort of prevention must be exceptional. Psychologically, I discover both my responsibility for stopping the ultimate death and my puniness as mere individual. I cannot escape the terror by proclaiming it is not my fault. For if I have not done all I can to avert a disaster involving myself, then I am responsible for the fatal omission. Nor can I get myself off the hook by saying, "I can't do anything about it," though I do experience the despair of not being able to do enough for saving humanity. Hence, something in me dies in this experience.

But the lesson of our text is that from such a dying within may arise a new springing forth into life. As illustrated in the Romance languages, such as French, the smashing of despair (*désespoir*) produces hope (*espoir*). I may spring forward to face the threatened world with newfound power. At one moment the ultimate experience overwhelms us as victims, but in the next moment we respond heroically. How curious and wonderful a thing is the human being. Crush it, and it refuses to remain crushed. Let it overwhelm itself and it renews itself. This is what fascinated Dostoyevsky as well as St. John. There is no estimating the power of human beings to arise to unprecedented heights of insight and ability when faced with unfathomable depths of terror and destruction.

If such a rebirth experience occurs in the individual facing his own inadvertent death, then it may also occur when we individuals face the approaching death of humanity. While the death of all might seem infinitely greater than the death of one, yet that extinction of humanity is not necessary. I am mortal, but we may live on. What exactly do we need to do in order to save humanity?

From initial despair that nothing will work comes invigorated recognition that a thousand plausible things may be tried. I will not go into them here, as many of my fellow writers as well as you, my readers, may be ably pursuing them. Instead of arguing for a solution, I have been probing the existential grounding for any solution. Just as a prerequisite to leading a fully responsible life may be the experience of one's death, so if humanity is to save itself it may very well have to share the ultimate experience. Many people try to escape that experience by displacement to an eternal, guaranteed realm. Many people are so busy with their lives that they do not allow themselves access to experiencing the likely loss of all human life. Some people live in conditions so remote from mass destruction that their spirit cannot turn toward this despair. In many villages of the world, in the countryside, even on the back streets of great cities, I have met ordinary people who had no intellectual inkling of the threat to the world, much less an existential feel for it. The greater part of humanity, I fear, is ignorant of its danger and of its choice. Hence, humanity is largely out of touch with its true humanity.

Whatever solutions you work out and argue for, please make the first step, the growth of worldwide recognition in everyone's heart of hearts of who we are as a species at risk in the universe. Without the experience of our death, we may not find the strength to survive.

The Pennsylvania State University
Delaware County Campus

Notes

[1] At this point in my reflections I was unaccountably struck by a persistent fever which kept me suspended between life and death for a few weeks so that I could not deliver this paper scheduled for a philosophical conference. My intellect could not function to complete the argument in the typewriter as I was buffeted on the ocean of experience.

William Gay

I. Introduction: A Puff of Smoke

And since a dead man has no substance unless one has actually seen
him dead, a hundred million corpses broadcast through history are no
more than a puff of smoke in the imagination.

—Camus, *The Plague*.

What is the meaning of recent discussions about nuclear winter? Is
it that several hundred million of us are doomed even in a low-level
nuclear war? This meaning is frequently stressed in discussions about
nuclear winter, but does this prospect make us act in decisively
different ways? So far, the prospect for nuclear winter has been little
more than a puff of smoke in the imagination of the public. Nuclear
winter sounds scary and deplorable, but we manage those terrible
images without altering our politics.

My concern is with altering politics, and I want to see how
philosophical reflection on nuclear winter might shed light on the real
obstacles to such change. In applied philosophy nuclear weapons and
the environment are each receiving growing attention.[1] While I will
argue for a larger role for environmental philosophy in the assessment
of nuclear weapons, I also will present philosophical reflection on
nuclear weapons and the environment as parts of a larger struggle.

II. Nuclear Winter and Hiroshima: More Than a Little Smoke

A. Nuclear Winter: Imagining the Worst

Of all the potential catastrophic consequences of nuclear war,
nuclear winter most strongly points toward the prospect for biocide.
Our knowledge of nuclear winter is, of course, indirect.[2] Because the
research is based largely on computer simulations, some refer to it as
the 'theory' of nuclear winter. Nevertheless, although the research is
partly theoretical and speculative, it is also partly empirical and relies
on well-warranted analogies. Despite the political motivations of some
of the researchers, the scientific work is serious. The projections should

be taken neither as mere propaganda for the antinuclear movement nor as gospel.

What is nuclear winter? Physically, nuclear winter is not a function of radiation, EMP, ozone depletion, or medical crises; those are other potentially catastrophic consequences of nuclear war. Rather, nuclear winter is related to the blast and heat of nuclear detonations. Following nuclear detonations on or near the earth's surface, massive fires are likely. Forests and cities with their numerous combustible fuels will burn and produce enormous amounts of smoke, soot, dust, and other particles. As this material is taken up into the atmosphere, it will form massive dark clouds that eventually will blanket much, if not all, the earth's atmosphere.

For a couple of weeks perhaps only a few percent of the average amount of sunlight will reach earth and temperatures may drop to between -15 and -25 degrees centigrade. Sub-freezing temperatures could last for months, wiping out many crops and livestock. Ecosystems would suffer major disruptions for at least a year, and numerous species would become extinct. Particularly in the Northern Hemisphere, survival would be precarious.

This image of nuclear war has emerged only during the 1980s. Perhaps the first major study relevant to nuclear winter is the June 1982 issue of *Ambio*.[3] The article by Paul Crutzen and John Birks, "The Atmosphere After a Nuclear War: Twilight at Noon," has received the most attention. Three months later Birks testified before Congress.[4] Nevertheless, two other research groups got the initial media attention. The findings of these separate research teams, which were associated with Mark Harwell and Carl Sagan, were initially published in the December 23, 1983 issue of *Science*.[5] Sagan then drew policy implications in his frequently cited article in *Foreign Affairs*.[6] The following year Harwell published *Nuclear Winter*, the first full-length book on the topic.[7]

The list of scholarly texts on nuclear winter continues to grow.[8] Though some experiments are being conducted to test the theory and despite some dissent, the scientific literature conveys a strong consensus that the environmental effects of nuclear war would be very severe. Nevertheless, these researchers, as opposed to some of the popularizers, are rather cautious about drawing apocalyptic conclusions. None of the major writers say that human extinction is probable, though each stresses that it is possible. Basically, these writers, more than others, factor in environmental consequences. Many earlier studies focused much more on the direct and immediate effects.[9] So what does research on nuclear winter add to our knowledge? A careful reading of the scientific literature suggests that when environmental effects are included, one needs, at the least, to double the estimates of casualties that are obtained from calculating only the immediate physical effects.[10] While the suggestion that we need to increase our estimates of the lethality of any nuclear war by at least a factor of two may not sound particularly apocalyptic, it brings out the importance of the effect of nuclear detonations on the environment and the resulting hardships that follow even long after the smoke clears. As Harwell notes, "Human recovery could not proceed more rapidly than the recovery of natural systems."[11] Clearly, this fact shows the relevance of environmental philosophy to the nuclear debate.

Some writers, however, draw much more sweeping conclusions about nuclear winter. Regarding nuclear winter, Robert Lifton notes that "In making concrete the idea of the nuclear end, it clarifies our existential situation and helps us liberate ourselves from illusion."[12] I am all for eliminating nuclear illusion.[13] However, politically speaking, I hold no special hope that by itself reflection on nuclear winter will be more than a puff of smoke in the imagination. Lifton and others, on the contrary, stress the need for such an apocalyptic vision.[14] I suspect such imagining is neither necessary nor sufficient for continuing the life of the species.

Actually, it does not take much imagination or reflection to reach the conclusion that nuclear winter needs to be prevented. I find it odd that some paint nuclear winter in even more harsh terms, as if such added horror will propel us to act. Sagan warns that nuclear winter might even follow a nuclear war in which only 500 to 2000 strategic nuclear weapons are detonated.[15] He calculates that as a result, as many as 500 trillion people might "not live," that is, never be born. How does he reach the conclusion? After all, the current global population is about 5 billion. Assuming that biocide will occur, he calculates how many people would have lived if our population rate remained constant, our lifespan averaged 100 years, and our species were to have lasted the 10 million years typical of successful species.

Of course to deny life to billions and billions of people, let alone trillions, is wrong. But must it be possible for nuclear war to deny life to billions before it is clearly wrong?

I have argued elsewhere that rational and moral objections can be raised against much less severe nuclear wars.[16] You do not have to kill everyone before it is wrong. Michael Walzer is of course correct in his assessment of General Okamura's order during World War II to "Kill all! Burn all! Destroy all!" Walzer notes:

> Any war that requires the methods of General Okamura, or anything approaching them, is itself immoral, however exalted the purposes in the name of which it is being fought.[17]

Even if nuclear winter follows, a major nuclear exchange may not kill all and burn all, but it will at least approach it sufficiently in the targeted areas to require moral condemnation.

B. Hiroshima: The Destruction of a 'World'

For the same reason that nuclear winter would be wrong, Hiroshima was wrong. "Little Boy," the 12.5 kt uranium bomb dropped on Hiroshima on August 6, 1945, carried out rather efficiently the order to "Kill all! Burn all! Destroy all!" The order was issued by U.S. President Harry S. Truman. This blast pretty much leveled a square mile, and the resulting fires consumed an area four times larger. While the U.S. government estimates 78,000 people died, the city of Hiroshima says that by November 1945 some 130,000, or 37% of those present, had died.[18] Whatever the number, it is still rising. Even though over forty years have passed, the body count must continue, particularly because of the deaths from cancers developed as a result of radiation exposure. As far as I am concerned that bomb was enough to "Kill all! Burn all! Destroy all!" It destroyed a world, the one known to thousands as Hiroshima. But for Truman, once was not enough, and the order was issued again. "Fat Man," a 22 kt plutonium bomb, was dropped on Nagasaki on August 9th.

In assessing Truman's order, Douglas Lackey states:

> To begin to take the moral measure of what happened at Hiroshima, we must ask what moral estimate we would make of a person who fired a flame thrower into the faces of 40,000 children, one by one. . . . If the person with the flame thrower were put on trial, we would demand

an *extraordinarily* powerful excuse indeed before letting him or her escape. What was Truman's excuse?[19]

Lackey finds it unlikely that Truman or anyone else who gives a similar or even more extensive order can provide a morally acceptable excuse. And Lackey was restricting himself to the *killing* of the innocent.

I have been arguing that nuclear winter and Hiroshima are wrong and for the same reason. Nevertheless, there are some differences, and I want to stress some of these differences. Whereas reference to "nuclear winter" signifies a *possibility* that *might* follow multiple nuclear detonations, reference to "Hiroshima" signifies an *actuality* that *did* follow a single nuclear detonation. I concur with the popularizers of the *theory* of "nuclear winter" that the consequences of multiple nuclear detonations *would* be *catastrophic*, and I agree with the popularizers of the strategic bombardment of Hiroshima that the consequences of that atomic blast *were catastrophic*. I describe as "catastrophic" both the projected consequences of nuclear winter and the actual consequences of Hiroshima. My question is this: Does nuclear winter represent a difference in degree or in kind? Unless the most apocalyptic visions of nuclear winter are correct, the distinction is probably one of degree. Regardless, I want to stress that nuclear winter would be a catastrophe and Hiroshima was a catastrophe.

I am aware that some catastrophes are worse than others. Nevertheless, I still deem it important to designate as "catastrophes" the "lesser" cases. Moreover, in the cases of those catastrophes, whether great or small, that are the result of questionable human decisions, rather than uncontrollable natural forces, I add my moral condemnation. So, nuclear winter and Hiroshima, since both are catastrophes and results of questionable decisions, are subject to moral condemnation. What kind of moral assessment is in order? I agree with Duane Cady when he states, "Even if all war is morally wrong, still some wars might be more wrong than others."[20] So, while Walzer gives me a criterion for saying both nuclear winter and Hiroshima are immoral, Cady allows me to concede that nuclear winter would be more wrong than Hiroshima. However, I want to push my argument further. In terms of nuclear weapons, moral condemnation is in order even at levels much lower than Hiroshima.

III. Environmental Philosophy: The Need for a Nuclear Smoke Alarm

Whereas I take it for granted that nuclear winter would be unacceptable in any viable approach to environmental philosophy, I am prepared to argue that any use of environmental philosophy to assess nuclear weapons which cannot also show the unacceptability of the environmental consequences in Hiroshima is inadequate. Environmental philosophy does not lose its relevance once one moves beneath the threshold of nuclear winter: it can serve as a "nuclear smoke alarm" and alert us to dangers well below and before the detonation of nuclear weapons.

A. Less Than Nuclear Winter

Environmental philosophy does give the necessary condition for assessing the effect of human action on the environment. As Colwell notes, "a natural community. . . cannot fail to achieve balance in the pattern of energy utilization. This is the first law of the morality of Nature."[21] However, if environmental philosophy *only* gives necessary conditions, then some nuclear wars would be exempt from violating its criteria. Some writers on nuclear winter seem to hold up primarily this necessary condition, and the result, I wish to argue, is environmentally and ethically problematic.

In his critical assessment of nuclear policy, Carl Sagan uses the prospect for nuclear winter as his normative criterion. With a sigh of environmental relief, he mentions "subthreshold" nuclear arsenals.[22] He conceives of a new system of several thousand very low yield, high accuracy, earth-burrowing warheads. While such a system may be technically feasible and may not violate the necessary condition of environmental philosophy, it still leaves as strategically viable and perhaps morally justifiable nuclear wars of very great destruction. Even with current arsenals, Sagan views as "below the threshold for severe climatic consequences" such options as "the destruction of 10 or 20 cities, or 100 silos of a particularly destabilizing missile system."[23]

While it is not necessary to turn to environmental philosophy to argue that such destruction is morally unacceptable, can environmental philosophy provide sufficient grounds for such condemnation? In terms of traditional ethics, John Ford argued in 1944 that saturation bombing was morally unjustified.[24] And the bombing of Europe to which he referred was nonnuclear and was less destructive than what Sagan describes. If environmental philosophy cannot match Ford's criteria, then it will be inadequate.

Fortunately, there are several environmental perspectives which show "subthreshold" nuclear war to be environmentally unacceptable. For example, the Fox and Groarke anthology *Nuclear War: Philosophical Perspectives* includes an entire section on the environment. Kristin Shrader-Frechette's essay "Nuclear Arms and Nuclear Power" is particularly useful for making the environmental argument that is lacking in Sagan.[25] In the same volume Michael Fox explicitly addresses the *environmental* unacceptability of nuclear war even down to the level of the explosion of a 1 Mt warhead over a major city.[26] So, from an environmental point of view, while it is necessary to avoid threshold nuclear war, even subthreshold nuclear wars are sufficient for warranting condemnation.

B. Chernobyl and Challenger

If some subthreshold nuclear wars are wrong, are all subthreshold nuclear wars wrong? I want to address very briefly what a low-level nuclear war might entail and reflect on the environmental implications. In so doing, I will note the relevance of Chernobyl and Challenger to the environmental assessment of nuclear weapons.

Whereas current global stockpiles of nuclear weapons have reached 16,000 Mt, World War II only involved about 6 Mt, and virtually any plausible scenario for strategic nuclear war would exceed this level.[27] Even the use of a dozen average strategic weapons would exceed 6 Mt, and such limited use, as governmental officials have conceded, makes little, if any, military sense.[28]

But let us consider such restricted use. The difference between the 6 Mt of World War II and the 6 Mt of a limited strategic exchange is that, with the exception of the 34 kt involved in the bombing of Hiroshima and Nagasaki, the 6 Mt of World War II did not produce radiation. Of course, that 34 kt presented a radiation problem that is still killing people today. Try to imagine what *just* 6 Mt of nuclear detonations would do, not the 100 Mt or so "needed" for nuclear winter.

For comparison, consider the Chernobyl explosion. The medical and environmental consequences of the Chernobyl accident have caused considerable alarm, and that explosion was only .1 kt.[29] Chernobyl killed and is still killing, though not at the level of Hiroshima and Nagasaki. The difference between Chernobyl and Hiroshima, however, is one of degree *and* kind. Whereas Hiroshima involved 140 times more explosive force than Chernobyl, it was, unlike Chernobyl, *not an accident.*

Even limited tactical nuclear war would be worse than Chernobyl.[30] Short-range to medium-range nuclear weapons are from 1 to 1000 kt, or each about 10 to 10,000 times more forceful than the Chernobyl blast. Even battlefield nuclear weapons are rather potent. They range from .1 kt to 100 kt, the power of the Chernobyl blast to 1000 times the Chernobyl blast. And when would it make military sense to use only a few battlefield weapons?

While the military value of very limited strategic or tactical nuclear wars is questionable, the environmental effects are considerable. In addressing the effects of low level ionizing radiation, Jim Garrison notes the parallel between the accident at Three Mile Island, which was much less severe than Chernobyl, and the nonaccident at Hiroshima: both produced 'invisible contamination' that caused and will cause cancer, leukemia, and genetic defects.[31] The immorality of this kind of effect was put in more concrete terms by Albert Schweitzer back in 1958 when, along with Linus Pauling and many other scientists, he opposed above-ground nuclear testing. In his little book *Peace or Atomic War?* Schweitzer writes:

> We must not be responsible for the future birth of thousands of children with the most serious mental and physical defects simply because we did not pay enough attention to that danger. Only those who have never been present at the birth of a deformed baby, never witnessed the despair of its mother, dare to maintain that the risk in going on with nuclear tests is one which must be taken under existing circumstances.[32]

In the late 1950s and 1960s, these effects were not a mere puff of smoke in the imagination. They were sufficiently real to enough parents for the political movement for a Partial Test Ban Treaty to succeed. I worry that it is not the level, but the location, of effects that seems to make the difference. Hiroshima and Nagasaki, like the prospect for nuclear winter, can remain puffs of smoke in the imagination. Unless and until we have the corpses before us, action is too easily postponed.

Our luck may run out. We have gone over forty years since Hiroshima and Nagasaki, and, so far, we have had no more nuclear wars. But can we take the risk? The accident at Chernobyl happened. And consider the Challenger explosion. That too was an accident. Our technology fails us. The cost that time was seven lives. Yet the next launch was to carry 46.7 pounds of plutonium for a reactor to power a Jupiter space probe.[33] Far more than seven might have died had it been that launch of the Challenger that exploded. One ounce of plutonium can cause a million cases of lung cancer. Of course, the plutonium might not have been released, and even if it were, much might not have returned to earth, the distribution would not have been even, etc. But these mitigating factors show that were such a disaster to occur, it might be a lesser rather than a greater catastrophe. Such factors should not obscure the point that accidents happen. The Challenger explosion happened. The Chernobyl explosion happened. Accidental nuclear war might happen as well.[34]

Perhaps environmental philosophy can alert us to the more subtle signs of the damage we are doing and may do to ourselves with nuclear weapons. Environmental philosophy could serve as a "nuclear smoke alarm," providing an early warning of the dangers we face. In *Deep Ecology*, Bill Devall and George Sessions devote an entire chapter to "Why Wilderness in the Nuclear Age?" They, and other radical environmentalists, surely will sound the alarm. In fact, they state, "No testing of nuclear weapons or disposal of nuclear wastes should be permitted in wilderness areas, on land or water."[35] This maxim can be followed only if the production of nuclear weapons ceases. So, how can such a significant political change be achieved?

IV. Conclusion: From Environmentalism to Pacifism

Unhappily, the mere threat of death is too abstract in itself; the only time it will be real enough is when it is too late to do more than kiss goodbye . . . .Antinuclear politics must do more than scare people. It must offer an affirmative vision as well.

—Joel Kovel, *Against the State of Nuclear Terror*

197

What will be the political effect of knowledge of nuclear weapons, including the prospect for nuclear winter? Political systems can give way to evidence about the catastrophic environmental consequences of nuclear weapons but in a manner which will "assimilate ecological necessities as technical constraints, and adapt the conditions of exploitation to them."[36] For this reason, Andre Gorz argues that *"the. ecological movement is not an end in itself, but a stage in the larger struggle."*[37] From a proper ecological perspective, the issue is not so much the form of socio-political organization, be it capitalist or socialist, as their import for the future of the species on this planet and the ecosystems that sustain them: there is an ecological critique of capitalism and socialism.

As is often noted, the environmental and antinuclear movements point to new ways of thinking and acting, yet their message often falls on deaf ears. Military decision making, like decision making in international politics, is "prejudicially anthropocentric,"[38] because each is tied to a *particular* group of the *human* community. We are in a situation in which leaders put national interest before human interest, and yet even stress upon human interest still does not go beyond anthropocentrism. Thus, while environmental philosophy may give us criteria for criticizing nuclear winter, Hiroshima, the testing and even the production of nuclear weapons, it may well remain as irrelevant to the transformation of politico-military thinking as traditional ethics with its concern for the protection of the noncombatant. We need to find ways to make globalism relevant to the prejudicial anthropocentrism of nationalism. The issue is not the fine nuances among geocentrism, biocentrism and nonanthropocentrism.[39] Rather the issue is how to alter nuclear states.

Joel Kovel has noted the role that the nuclear threat can play in delegitimating politics as currently practiced. He states:

> By pushing society to the edge of doom, the nuclear state bursts asunder the seams of rationalization within which the West's domination of nature and other people has been contained.[40]

The issue concerns how to turn the nuclear threat into an "unmanageable steering problem" for the state.[41] In employing Habermas's term, I am suggesting not that nuclear weapons get out of control but that populations get out of control, out of the control of their nuclear states.

As much as anyone, Gene Sharp has shown the myth of distinguishing the people and the state. The people are the loci of power. Sharp's nonviolent methods for social change are:

> Based on the theory that rulers are dependent on those they rule, and that persistent withholding of the necessary cooperation, obedience, and submission means an inevitable weakening and possible collapse of the regime. . . .[42]

But, as Kovel makes clear, before the nuclear state *apparatus* can be defeated, the nuclear state *of being* must be defeated.[43]

The nuclear state of being is the postwar equivalent of what in *Being and Time* Heidegger termed average everydayness–the They-Self. Our everyday way of being, our state of being, is the nuclear state. And it is inauthentic. Nuclear discourse is just one example. Such discourse is "idle talk"[44] and a form of linguistic alienation.[45] So long as we remain in the nuclear state, we are alienated and voiceless.

Keeping ourselves out of the nuclear state of being requires protracted effort or else we slip back into the postwar everydayness of nuclearism. However, as Kant noted, the unlikelihood of genuine peace is not the issue. He stresses the importance of possibility; otherwise, if we knew we absolutely could not achieve it, any "duty" to try to advance genuine peace would be eliminated.[46] To live authentically is not easy. Unless we are vigilant, we fall back into the nuclear state of being. We need to be on guard. In this regard, Heidegger provides the image of the House-Friend: "The House-Friend is a friend to the house which the world is."[47] The House-Friend watches for threats to our planet, and takes action.[48] We need to be the careful shepherd of all beings, not the prisoners of the nuclear state of being.

Insofar as we rise above the nuclear state of being we can take on the nuclear state apparatus which our quiet obedience otherwise legitimates and sustains. But effective delegitimation, effective refusal, is not an isolated act. It requires solidarity. Our goal should be to integrate antinuclearism and environmentalism, along with antiracism and feminism, into the general struggle for pacifism. Kovel gives us the vision. It is of:

> A social transformation—non-nonviolent, anti-militaristic, anti-imperial, anti-technocratic, libertarian, feminist, non-racist,

decentralized, ecological, emerging from a new mode of production and a new mode of relationship to humans and nature. . . .[49]

We start from where we are. We join together. We are part of a larger struggle, one in which, together, we just might ensure that the prospect for nuclear winter and the memory of Hiroshima are not a mere puff of smoke in the imagination.

University of North Carolina at Charlotte

Notes

[1] To learn about the most recent work, *Concerned Philosophers for. Peace Newsletter* and *Environmental Ethics* are especially relevant.

[2] William Gay and Michael Pearson, *The Nuclear Arms Race* (Chicago: American Library Association, 1987) 86. For nuclear winter, see 102-104.

[3] Jeannie Peterson, ed., *The Aftermath: The Human and Ecological Consequences of Nuclear War* (New York: Pantheon Books, 1983).

[4] U.S. Congress, House, Committee on Science and Technology, subcommittee on Investigations and Oversight, *The Consequences of Nuclear War on the Global Environment* (Washington, D. C.: Government Printing Office, l983).

[5] R. P. Turco et al., "Nuclear Winter: Global Consequences of Multiple Nuclear Explosions" *Science* 222 (December 23, 1983) 1289-1292; Paul R. Ehrlich et al., "Long-term Biological Consequences of Nuclear War," *Science* 222 (December 23, 1983) 1293-1300.

[6] Carl Sagan, "Nuclear War and Climatic Catastrophe," *Foreign Affairs* (Winter 1983/84) 257-292.

[7] Mark A. Harwell, *Nuclear Winter: The Human and Environmental Consequences of Nuclear War* (New York: Springer-Verlag, l984).

[8] See, for example, Curt Convey, Stephen Schneider and Starley Thompson, "Global Atmospheric Effects of Massive Smoke and Dust Injections From a Nuclear War" *Nature* (March 1, 1984) 21-25; Paul R. Ehrlich, Carl Sagan, Donald Kennedy, and Walter Orr Roberts, *The Cold and the Dark* (New York: W. W. Norton, 1984); Owen Greene, Ian Percival, and Irene Ridge, *Nuclear Winter: The Evidence and the*

Risks (Cambridge, UK: Polity Press, 1985); Lester Grinspoon, ed., *The Long Darkness: Psychological and Moral Perspectives on Nuclear Winter* (New Haven: Yale University Press, 1986); Mark A. Harwell and T. C. Hutchinson, *The Environmental Consequences of Nuclear War: Volume II Ecological and Agricultural Effects* (New York: John Wiley, 1986); Julius London and Gilbert F. White, eds., *The Environmental Effects of Nuclear War* (Boulder, CO: Westview Press, 1984); National Research Council, *The Effects on the Atmosphere of a Major Nuclear Exchange* (Washington, D.C.: National Academy Press, 1985); J. Peterson, "Scientific Studies of the Unthinkable–The Physical and Biological Effects of Nuclear War," *Ambio* 15.2 (1986) 60-69; A. Pittock, T. Ackerman, P. Crutzen, M. MacCracken, C. Shapiro, and R. Turco, *The Environmental Consequences of Nuclear War: Volume I Physical and Atmospheric Effects* (New York: John Wiley, 1985); Starley L. Thompson and Stephen H. Schneider, "Nuclear War Reappraised" *Foreign Affairs* (Summer 1986) 981-1005; and Nicholas Wade, *A World Beyond Healing: The Prologue and Aftermath of Nuclear War* (New York: W. W. Norton & Co., 1987).

[9] See esp. Samuel Glasstone and Philip J. Dolan, eds. *The Effects of Nuclear Weapons,* (Washington, D.C.: The Government Printing Office, 1977, third edition); U.S. Congress, Office of Technology Assessment, *The Effects of Nuclear War* (Washington, D.C.: Government Printing Office, 1979); and U.S., Congress, Senate, Committee on Banking, Housing and Urban Affairs, *Economic and Social Consequences of Nuclear Attacks on the United States* (Washington, D.C.: Government Printing Office, 1979).

[10] Of course, the need to calculate long-range effects is not new. See esp. K. Lewis. "The Prompt and Delayed Effects of Nuclear War" *Scientific American* 241 (1979) 35-47, and Committee to Study the Long-Term Worldwide Effects of Multiple Nuclear-Weapons Detonations, Assembly of Mathematical and Physical Sciences, National Research Council, *Long-Term Worldwide Effects of Multiple Nuclear-Weapons Detonations* (Washington. D.C.: National Academy of Sciences, 1975).

[11] Harwell, xvii.

[12] Robert J. Lifton, "Imagining the Real: Beyond the Nuclear 'End'," *The Long Darkness*, ed., Grinspoon 93.

[13] See Gay essay, "Myths About Nuclear War: Misconceptions in Public Beliefs and Governmental Plan" *Philosophy and Social Criticism* 9 (1982), 115-44, reprinted in revised form as "Nuclear War: Public and Governmental Misconceptions" *Nuclear War*, eds., Fox and Groarke 11-25. See, too, Trudy Govier, "Nuclear Illusion and

Individual Obligations" *Canadian Journal of Philosophy* 13 (1983) 471-492.

[14] Lifton 98.

[15] Sagan 259f.

[16] Gay, "Myths" 127, and *Nuclear War* 16-17.

[17] Michael Walzer, "Moral Judgment in Time of War" *Philosophical Issues: A Contemporary Introduction*, eds. James Rachels and Frank A. Tillman (New York: Harper & Row, 1972), 280. This essay originally appeared in *Dissent* 14 (1967) 284-292.

[18] The Committee for the Compilation of Materials on Damage Caused by the Atomic Bombs in Hiroshima and Nagasaki, *Hiroshima and Nagasaki: The Physical, Medical, and Social Effects of the Atomic Bombings*, trans. Eisei Ishikawa and David L. Swain (New York: Basic Books, Inc., 1981) 32.

[19] Douglas P. Lackey, "The Moral Case for Unilateral Nuclear Disarmament" *Philosophy and Social Criticism* 10.3/4 (1984), 158-59.

[20] Duane L. Cady, "Backing Into Pacifism" *Philosophy and Social Criticism* 10.3/4 (1984) 177.

[21] Thomas B. Colwell, Jr., "Ecology and Philosophy," *Philosophical Issues*, eds., Rachels and Tillman 360. Originally published as "Some Implications of the Ecological Revolution for the Construction of Value," *Human Values and Natural Sciences*, eds., Ervin Laszlo and James B. Wilbur (Goredon and Beach, 1970) 245-58.

[22] Sagan 279-80.

[23] Sagan 277

[24] John C. Ford, "The Morality of Obliteration Bombing," *War and Morality*, ed., Richard A. Wasserstrom (Belmont, CA: Wadsworth, 1970) 15-41. Originally published in *Theological Studies* 5 (1944) 261-309.

[25] Kristin Shrader-Frechette, "Nuclear Arms and Nuclear Power:

Philosophical Connections," *Nuclear War,* eds., Fox and Groarke 85-100.

[26] Michael Fox, "Commentary: The Unacceptable Gamble," *Nuclear War,* eds., Fox and Groarke 109.

[27] Ruth Leger Sivard, *World Military and Social Expenditures 1986* (Washington, D.C.: World Priorities, 1986) 5.

[28] See, for example, U.S. Congress, Senate, Committee on Foreign Relations, Subcommittee on Arms Control, International Organizations, and Security Agreements, *Analyses of the Effects of Limited Nuclear War* (Washington, D.C.: Government Printing Office, 1975), esp. the study prepared by the Office of Technology Assessment's Ad Hoc Panel on Nuclear Effects and the Department of Defense's revised estimates (p. 45).

[29] Sivard 5.

[30] See William Arkin, Frank von Hippel, and Barbard G. Levi, "The Consequences of a 'Limited' Nuclear War in East and West Germany," *The Aftermath,* ed., Peterson 165-87. The figures in this paragraph are based on their data.

[31] Jim Garrison, *The Plutonium Culture: From Hiroshima to Harrisburg* (New York: Continuum, 1981) 167. See the extensive data on the results of above-ground nuclear testing in Harvey Wasserman and Norman Solomon with Robert Alvarez and Eleanor Walters, *Killing our Own: The Disaster of America's Experience With Atomic Radiation* (New York: Delacorte Press, 1982).

[32] Albert Schweitzer, *Peace or Atomic War?* (New York: Henry Holt and Co., 1958) 17.

[33] "The Lethal Shuttle," editorial in *The Nation* 242 (February 22, 1985) 193.

[34] *International Accidental Nuclear War Prevention Newsletter* (Santa Barbara, CA: Nuclear Age Peace Foundation).

[35] Bill Devall and George Sessions, *Deep Ecology: Living as if Nature Mattered* (Layton, Utah: Gibbs M. Smith, Inc., 1985) 129.

[36] Andre Gorz, *Ecology as Politics,* trans., Patsy Vigderman and

Jonathan Cloud (Boston, MA: South End Press, 1980) 3.

[37]Gorz, 3.

[38] The term "prejudicial anthropocentrism" is coined by Paula J. Smithka in her review of *Emancipation and Consciousness,* forthcoming in *Journal of Social Philosophy.* She argues that while an anthropocentric attitude places primary value on human interest, it also gets applied selectively and prejudicially and results in such chauvinisms as sexism, racism, and nationalism.

[39] I coin the expression "axiological geocentrism" in my essay "The Nuclear Debate and American Philosophers: 1945 to 1985," *Religion and Philosophy in the United States of America,* ed., Peter Freese (Essen, West Germany: Die Blaue Eule, 1987) 1, 315. One of the chief advocates of biocentrism is Paul W. Taylor. See his *Respect for Nature: A Theory of Environmental Ethics* (Princeton, NJ: Princeton University Press 1986). One of the leading advocates of nonanthropocentrism is Michael E. Zimmerman. For a connection with nuclear weapons, see his "Anthropocentric Humanism and the Arms Race," *Nuclear War,* eds., Fox and Groarke 135-49.

[40] Joel Kovel, *Against the State of Nuclear Terror* (Boston, MA: South End Press, 1983) xii.

[41] I am appropriating the terminology of Jurgen Habermas. Cf. his *Legitimate Crisis,* trans., Thomas McCarthy (Boston, MA: Beacon Press, 1975). See my article "Justification of Legal Authority: Phenomenology vs Critical Theory" *Journal of Social Philosophy* 11.2 (1980) 1-10.

[42] Gene Sharp, *Social Power and Political Freedom* (Boston, MA: Porter Sargent Publishers, 1980) 218.

[43] Kovel, xi.

[44] Martin Heidegger, *Being and Time,* trans., John Macquarrie and Edward Robinson (New York: Harper & Row, 1962) 210-212.

[45] See my article, "Nuclear Discourse and Linguistic Alienation," *Journal of Social Philosophy* 18. 2 (1987) 42-49.

[46] Immanuel Kant, *Perpetual Peace,* trans., Campbell Smith (London: George Allen & Unwin, Ltd., 1903) 136 & 161.

[47] Martin Heidegger, "Hebel–Friend of the House," trans., Bruce V. Foltz and Michael Heim, in *Contemporary German Philosophy* ed. Darrell E. Christenson et al., vol. 3 (University Park, PA: The Pennsylvania State University Press, 1983) 93.

[48] Heidegger, "Hebel" 94.

[49] Kovel, 224.

Duane Cady

> When you are criticizing the philosophy of an epoch, do not chiefly
> direct your attention to those intellectual positions which its exponents
> feel it necessary explicitly to defend. There will be some fundamental
> assumptions which adherents of all the variant systems within the
> epoch unconsciously presuppose. Such assumptions appear so
> obvious that people do not know what they are assuming because no
> other way of putting things has ever occurred to them.
>
> —Alfred North Whitehead, *Science and the Modern World*

Warism is the view that war is both morally justifiable in principle
and often morally justified in fact. While this general view can be
expressed in a variety of forms, the basic notion is that war can be moral
and thus that alternatives to war must be entertained only insofar as
they promise distinct advantage to a war option. In what follows I will
defend the claim that warism is just the sort of fundamental but
unconscious assumption to which Whitehead refers above. One task
of philosophers is to expose, examine and scrutinize such
presuppositions so that those holding them do so knowingly.[1]

In every culture there are fundamental concepts, assumptions, ideas
and values which together form a frame of reference, a conceptual
outlook, a world view or perspective through which members of the
culture experience the world. These fundamentals seem so obvious
from within that it rarely occurs to members of a given culture that
many of the most important ideas of their society are based on
foundations which are taken for granted. One example in the Western
tradition is the shift in perspective now called the Copernican
Revolution. While the way the solar system works did not change, the
perception of the workings of the solar system did change as we moved
from an earth-centered model of the relationship between sun and
planets to a sun-centered model. This change in basic outlook shook
dominant institutions to their foundations. Since we now take the
Copernican model for granted, it is hard for us to imagine the basic

conceptual shift involved.

An example of a fundamental shift in perspective closer to our own experience can be seen in the ongoing reactions to the theory of evolution. People touched by Western science struggle to imagine the human species as emergent from less complex life forms. They do so within the context of traditional views of a divine creation of the human species. Some see the two models as compatible but many see diametric opposition. Where the models are understood each to exclude the other, fundamental differences in perspective are at stake; one's entire orientation to reality, even to the meaning of life, may hinge on the difference between a divine source and a natural biological source of the human species. Questioning someone's perspective on such an issue can be threatening, not only because of the importance of the viewpoint but also because it may be a "given" to that individual.

Further examples of dominant societal conceptions can be seen in the significance of gender and race in determining economic, social and educational opportunities in traditional Western culture. Without malicious intent people have taken for granted that women interested in medicine become nurses while men with those interests become doctors; women become secretaries, men become lawyers, and so on. Minority races have been presumed fit only for unskilled labor while whites (white males) aspire to the professions. Here it should be obvious that the unconscious presuppositions about reality can have profound implications for values as well as beliefs. The cultural givens can be like normative lenses through which "reality" is conceived. Only after they are acknowledged and examined can resulting prejudices be exposed. Making explicit the fundamental concepts, the normative lenses, which form the basic perspectives of a culture is doing philosophy. So is questioning these fundamentals and imagining alternatives. The more basic the hidden concepts, the more difficult it is to examine them.

In contemporary Western culture, warism is a dominant outlook. There is no special justification burden which must be born by the warist; in fact, the greater burden of justification rests with anti-warists. There are a few people who consider themselves pacifists—those who oppose war in principle—but they are a small minority of citizens in modern nations. The overwhelming majority attitude in Western culture has been to regard pacifism as well-meaning but naive and misguided; warism, on the other hand, is almost universally accepted.

The Western inclination to take warism for granted is so pervasive as to form an unexpressed attitude which is manifest in virtually all aspects of the culture from the obvious cases of politics and the popular media to business, education and even religion.[2] There is no conspiracy required here; advertising, television, public and parochial school curricula all tend to reflect the dominant outlook, the fundamental attitudes of the culture. The traditional importance of autonomy of the individual, of personal integrity, of rights to privacy and property, of freedom from governmental interference in the lives of individuals, of fighting for what one believes in against all odds, all are examples of fundamental Western values which are for the most part uncritically adopted. In history and government classes students learn about our republic: born in revolution, expanded through numerous battles with native American Indians, solidified in civil war, internationally preeminent after two world wars, a super-power strong in defense of freedom. School curricula offer many opportunities to discuss battles, heroes, tactics and military leadership; one must dig to find mention of advocates of nonviolence, pacifists, models of cooperative rather than domineering domestic and foreign policy. The emphasis should be expected, given the fundamental perspectives taken for granted.

To complicate matters further, Western culture has a tradition of attempting "value-free" education, placing little emphasis on ethical or political questioning of current or past social policy. Increased awareness that all teaching is laden with hidden values has tended to make parents and school boards more inclined to restrict materials which are at all controversial, thus avoiding the introduction of values which might be at odds with those traditionally dominant. This tends to reinforce the momentum toward uniformity and underscore status quo values. Entrenched in tradition and forming the fundamental perspective by which all judgments are made, the basic conceptions and values of a culture are rarely made explicit, and even more rarely questioned from within the culture. When questions are raised, they tend to be met with defensive reactions, thus further underscoring the status quo values.

As a dominant attitude, warism is not limited to views reflected in popular culture and documented by mass opinion polls. Warren Steinkraus observes that "the great bulk of philosophers who have spoken on the question of war have supported and defended it as an instrument of social change."[3] Most often war is defended not for itself but justified as a means to important ends sought and achieved, such as peace or self-defense. Steinkraus goes on to describe professional philosophers' reactions to war, saying "studied aloofness which invariably means tacit acceptance" is the most common attitude followed by "overt defense of a particular national policy." The next most common attitude is "reluctant and even hesitant justification" and the least common is "direct criticism with or without consideration of alternatives."[4] This sequence could be extrapolated to describe academics in general, not just philosophers. John Dewey makes the point most clearly: "War is as much a social pattern as is the domestic slavery which the ancients thought to be immutable fact."[5]

Further indication that our common cultural disposition is to consider war as morally justifiable, even morally required, is the fact that anti-warists are much more frequently called upon to justify their views than are those who defend war as a legitimate activity of nations. It is presumed that the burden of proof rests on those individuals morally opposed to war and committed to alternative means of resolving conflict. This is because warism is a cultural given, almost a national presupposition in the modern West. This is not to say that Western nations are necessarily belligerent; rather, it is to say that the war system, the standard operating procedure of sovereign states constantly preparing for, threatening and employing military force in domestic and international affairs, goes almost wholly unquestioned. Given this context, criticism of the war system is typically met with hostility. Political candidates, understanding the dominant attitudes, need to present themselves as "tougher" than the other candidates, need to be wary of being characterized as "soft on the enemy," "weak on defense," "indecisive" with adversaries or reluctant to "stand firm." All this contributes to encouraging the dominant attitude and belittling its opposition. The result is that peace advocates are not seriously considered because "everybody knows" how patently implausible, politically naive and romantically idealistic peace theorists and activists must be; this conventional wisdom is confirmed through its own media and institutions.

Included in the cultural predisposition to warism is the widespread inclination to regard anyone sympathetic to peaceful alternatives to war to be pacifists of the most extreme sort. Characterizing, or better, caricaturing, all anti-warists in this way polarizes discussion, creates confusion and provokes defensive reactions. While absolute pacifism is one form of anti-warism, it is not the only one, and it certainly is not the most commonly held position. Not even all pacifists want to be called upon to defend absolute pacifism since their own commitment may be to pacifism of another sort.[6]

The widespread, unquestioning acceptance of warism and the corresponding reluctance to consider peace-ism as a legitimate option demonstrate the difficulty of proposing a genuine consideration of peace alternatives. Typically, either it does not occur to the warist to challenge the view that war is morally justified or the warist openly accepts warism. In either case, the conceptual framework of the culture, which takes warism for granted, goes unquestioned. If we assume, without realizing it, that war itself is morally justifiable, our moral considerations of war will be focused on whether a particular war is justified or whether particular acts within a given war are morally acceptable. These are important concerns, but addressing them does not get at the fundamental issue raised by many anti-warists: the morality of war as such. In *Just and Unjust Wars* Michael Walzer explains that "war is always judged twice, first with reference to the reasons states have for fighting, secondly with reference to the means they adopt."[7] The pacifist suggestion that there is a third judgment of war—namely, "might war, by its very nature, be unjust?" is considered only as an afterthought in an appendix where it is tossed off as naive. Perhaps Walzer should not be faulted for this since he defines his task as describing the conventional morality of war; the conventional morality does take warism for granted. To this extent Walzer is correct. And this is just the point: our warist conceptual framework, our warist normative lenses blind us to the root problems. The concern of those aware of the hidden warist bias is not merely to describe cultural values but to examine them and suggest what they ought to be.

The slow but persistent rise in awareness of racial, ethnic and gender oppression and the beginning efforts of liberation from within the oppressed groups offer hope that even the most deeply held and least explicitly challenged predispositions of culture might be examined. Such examinations can lead to changes in the lives of the oppressed. Perhaps even those oppressed by warism will free themselves from accepting war as an inevitable condition of nature. Just as the civil rights movement has helped us see that human worth is not determined by a racial hierarchy, feminism has helped us realize that dominant attitudes may well be values we choose rather than innate and determined features of human nature. By questioning the traditional role models of men and women, all of us are more free to choose the selves we are to be; we need not be defined by hidden presumptions of gender roles. Parallel to racial and gender liberation movements, the peace movement questions taking warism for granted. Various anti-warists seek an examination of our unquestioned assumption of warism in order to expose it as racism and sexism have been examined and exposed. Just as opponents of racism and sexism consider the oppression of people of color and women, respectively, to be wrong and thus to require fundamental changes in society, so opponents of warism—including pacifists of various sorts—consider taking war morally for granted to be wrong. Thus they too require fundamental changes in society.

When the dominant attitudes of a culture are predisposed toward some ideas and against others, defending those widely embraced and rejecting those widely discounted is great sport. Dewey opens *Human. Nature and Conduct* by drawing the reader's attention to just this point when he writes, "Give a dog a bad name and hang him."[8] That is to say, people and ideas can be dismissed readily when they do not have to be taken seriously because they are widely regarded as deserving dismissal. If the reputation is bad enough, the hanging is easy. If the reputation is a function of a caricature and an unfriendly climate, it is too easy.

These cultural obstacles—the predisposition to warism, the popular caricature of peace advocates as mystical moral fanatics, and the summary dismissal of alternatives to war as unrealistic and naive—all contribute to and help create the hostile context in which peace issues are discussed. They come together in a dominant attitude: a good many people take "keeping the peace" to mean preserving the status quo. Those holding this concept of peace often enjoy an advantageous *relative* position within the status quo, that is, they see themselves as well off in comparison with the social, economic, political, educational, environmental, and physical health of their peers, friends and neighbors, near and distant fellow humans. Any threat to the status quo, to the relative advantage, is often seen to require "defense against aggression," often without considering the possibility that the favored status itself may have oppressive implications for others. The pervasive view that keeping peace is preserving current conditions, the notion that any threat to the way things are, any change, might "justify" the use of violence, is rooted in deeply entrenched assumptions about peace, war and the status quo. It is not surprising that those who regard peace to be the preservation of the status quo are inclined to regard the peace movement with suspicion. Anti-warists threaten the status quo, especially the pervasive presumption of warism with its implications for the political and economic activities of a society.

No doubt there are many conditions which hinder the serious consideration of legitimate alternatives to warism, conditions beyond the cultural presumption to warism, the inclination to dismiss peace theorists and activists as moral extremists, the disposition to regard alternatives to war as naive and unrealistic and the notion that peace is the preservation of the status quo. It is not just popular opinion which embodies these preconceptions; academics making the effort to address these issues often reflect the same negative dispositions, though they do so subtly and articulately.[9]

None of us can set aside all our preconceptions at will. But calling the possibility of their being prejudicial to our attention can make us wary and can help us to open our minds, to suspend disbelief, to listen and try to fathom how anyone could take peace seriously. It is not easy to make the effort to understand something which is at once respected for its moral strength and at the same time disregarded as utopian fantasy. Honesty and fairness demand a suspension of disbelief while recognizing the difficulty of the demand. As Karl Popper says, theoretical progress is made by a sympathetic grasp of the theory in question followed by the rigorous attempt to refute it. "There is no point in discussing or criticizing a theory unless we try all the time to put it in its strongest form, and to argue against it only in that form."[10] There will be no progress at taking peace seriously until the prevailing cultural dispositions to warism, academic as well as popular, are examined and exposed. Academics in general and philosophers in particular are especially well suited to this task. But they must be prepared to be treated like those returning to the cave in Plato's *Republic*.[11] This is always so for those probing the fundamental questions of philosophy.

Hamline University

Notes

[1] I am grateful to Nancy Holland and Karen Warren for helpful comments on an earlier draft of this essay. A more thorough development of this issue may be found in the opening chapter of my book, *From Warism to Pacifism: A Moral Continuum* (Philadelphia: Temple University Press, 1989).

[2] Concerning our cultural understanding of war, Iredell Jenkins observes, "We appear to act on the assumption that wars are ultimate and ineradicable features of reality, so there are only two things we can do about them: delay their occurrence and make sure we win them when they occur." In fact we take war to be such an essential feature of the nature of things that it seems natural to try to prevent war by threatening it. Iredell Jenkins, "The Conditions of Peace," *The Monist* 57.4 (1973) 508.

[3] Steinkraus, Warren E., "War and the Philosopher's Duty," *The Critique of War,* ed., Robert Ginsberg (Chicago: Henry Regnery Co., 1969) 3.

[4] Steinkraus 6.

[5] John Dewey, *Problems of Men* (New York: Philosophical Library, 1946) 186.

[6] For an overview description of varieties of pacifism, see Duane Cady, "Backing into Pacifism" *Philosophy and Social Criticism* 10.3/4 (1984) 173-180, or see Cady, *From Warism to Pacifism: A Moral Continuum* 57-75.

[7] Michael Walzer, *Just and Unjust Wars* (Basic Books, 1977) 21.

[8] John Dewey, *Human Nature and Conduct* (Henry Holt, 1922).

[9] For a useful discussion of how warist-biased language bars open dialogue on peace issues, see Thomas Merton, "War and the Crisis of Language," *Critique of War* 100-117. For a survey of academics' views on pacifism, see George W. Hartmann, "The Strength and

Weakness of the Pacifist Position as Seen by American Philosophers"
The Philosophical Review 53 (1944) 125-44.

[10] Popper, Karl, *Objective Knowledge* (Oxford, 1972) 266.

[11] Plato, *Republic*, 514a-517b.

John Howie

Philosophers are by no means agreed on the meaning and matter of war. Even a random sampling of their views uncovers a wide-ranging diversity.[1]

Aristotle observed that "the art of war is a natural art of acquisition, for the art of acquisition includes hunting, an art which we ought to practice against wild beasts, and, against men who though intended by nature to be governed, will not submit; for war of such a kind is naturally just."[2] Any war against barbarians was thereby a just war. (Of course, the assumption that such government established through conquest would automatically provide the needed framework for virtuous living is false). Although offering an implicit notion of a just war, Aristotle (in agreement with Plato) recognized the importance of economic rivalry as a prominent factor in bringing about war. He remarked, "poverty is the parent of revolution and crime."[3] If economic inequality is the cause of revolution within countries, then it is the same inequality among countries that contributes to international wars. But Aristotle shrewdly insisted that it is the gap between those who have wealth and property and those who do not have it that provokes revolution and that wealth itself feeds its own greed—an exaggerated preoccupation with money and material goods. People with luxuries want more luxuries just as people in desperate want desire the necessities. Such an appetite may be satisfied by war in a number of ways, especially through victors acquiring "spoils."

Centuries later "just war" receives some support from Augustine of Hippo[4] and detailed development from Thomas Aquinas. Holding that war and Christianity were not antagonistic, Thomas insisted that three conditions be met: (1) an authoritative sovereign must declare that the war is a "just" one, (2) a just war requires a "just" cause (at least one that is clear enough that the monarch can specify it), and (3) the belligerents must have rightful intentions so that good will be promoted and evil will be avoided. For Thomas this meant that the "guilt" of the enemy justified killing them.[5] For us these remarks may seem uncommonly vague or even ridiculous. The notion that the *guilt* of the enemy justifies killing them seems preposterous for modern warfare. Total destruction and saturation-bombing tactics make it absurd to claim *citizen* guilt or even *national* guilt covers the havoc wrought. At what cost in innocent lives are the allegedly guilty persons killed? Modern military technology makes it very difficult to limit the damage one inflicts to enemy soldiers alone or even to military installations. Civilians are often hurt or killed by the necessary efforts to prevent the production and transportation of military supplies.

To take the issue a step further, *whose guilt* serves as a warrant for the full-scale campaign of terror often waged against civilian populations? In the case of guerrilla warfare, the guerrillas themselves abolish the conventional distinction between soldier and civilian. They do so by attaining widespread support from the local population. It must at least be admitted that guerrilla warfare greatly complicates, if it does not make impossible, any argument for a "just" war. Richard Wasserstrom argues that it is difficult to imagine a set of circumstances that would *justify* war since innocent persons would intentionally be killed by modern warfare. Wasserstrom writes:

> The intentional, or at least knowing, killing of the innocent on a large scale became a practically necessary feature of war with the advent of air warfare. And the genuinely indiscriminate killing of very great numbers of innocent persons is the dominant legacy of the birth of thermonuclear weapons. At this stage the argument from the death of the innocent moves appreciably closer to becoming a decisive objection to war.[6]

In practice during the Middle Ages, the citizen, in the absence of overwhelming evidence wars were unjust, would ordinarily assume that wars were just. It is worth noting that no official Roman Catholic leader has ever declared that a war of his *own* nation was unjust.

Rousseau asserts that war is a relation between states rather than persons.

> War, then, is a relation, not between man and man, but between state and state, and individuals are enemies only accidentally, not as men, nor even as citizens, but as soldiers; not as members of their country, but as its defenders.[7]

We may think of war abstractly as a conflict between state and state, not one between individuals, and we do justify war most frequently on the ground of defense. But, to think of it in that way tends to blur the stark horror of it—its pain, suffering, death, and destruction.

J. G. Fichte believes that any violation of a treaty and any refusal to recognize a state are proper grounds upon which to wage war.[8] On Fichte's view, war is justified by what may be called *backward-looking. criteria.* What has already happened is, on this view, relevant to the justice or rightness of the war that is subsequently waged. Both of the grounds for waging war seem to overlook the countless *other* ways of gaining recognition as a nation and securing compliance to a treaty.

John Stuart Mill believes that to go to war for an idea, *if the war is. aggressive,* is as immoral as to do so for territory or for revenue. We are as unjustified in forcing our ideas on others as we are in compelling them to economic obedience. There are, however, some instances where intervention in the affairs of another nation might be justified. These circumstances may be present when the intervention by an advanced nation in the internal affairs of an undeveloped nation takes place, since presumably the undeveloped nation is likely to benefit from such intervention. It is no surprise that Mill's view is in step with the usual rationale for British empire-building.[9]

Hegel argues that war is inescapable, and insists upon its usefulness in the development of nations. For Hegel the state is the most significant organization to which persons may belong. The state bestows upon each individual person authentic meaning, and sacrifice for the state is the universal duty of all its citizens. He thinks of war as a way of settling international disputes and of "saving" nations. Lacking the vision of any international organization, he thinks of nationalism as at once the epitomy and limit of human loyalty.[10]

Kant, to his lasting credit, takes a different view. In *Perpetual Peace*, he urges a "league of nations" and a reassessment of the whole war issue in the context of some moral principles. He recommends the abolition of standing armies, and rejection of secrecy as a governmental strategy. By recommending an openness of action between nations he is attempting to get nations to discuss rationally their differences and to create a hospitable attitude among nations.

Turning to a couple of American philosophers, consider the views of Thoreau and Emerson. Henry David Thoreau reflects on the moral callousness of war and the peculiar inversion of values that it produces. War, after all, destroys the very things from which living gains its meaning.[11]

Ralph Waldo Emerson insists that war will one day pass away as a sign that man has finally become mature. At the higher stage of development, which will denote his maturity, man will "turn the other cheek."[12]

R. G. Collingwood seems to have taken an ambiguous view of war. On the one hand, he argues that war and peace are not contradictories. This means (as he views matters) that there is no impossibility of war serving the cause of peace and of being justified when there is no other way to curb belligerent tyranny. Collingwood also admits, however, that war is a sign of diplomatic indecision and political weakness.[13]

In a fascinating book called *The War Myth*, Donald Wells, a recent contemporary writer, declares,

> The definition of war, therefore, is conditioned by the wish to appear on the right side of the war, and thus, the general subject of the just war is handled with casuistry, sophistry, and self-deception. It is not that justice or injustice cannot be distinguished in a war, but rather that the nations involved are not in the proper position to make this distinction.[14]

His arguments leave us with a troublesome question: Is all talk of a just war merely a rationalization? Is our claim that there can be such a thing as a "just war" simply an exercise in self-deception?

L. T. Hobhouse, in *Social Development*, remarks that it should not take an advanced intelligence to see that pestilence, famine, and organized slaughter are not conditions for the advancement of culture.[15] Wars result in the loss of personal liberties in precisely those areas where the creative side of persons is most fruitful. Either a nation decides to work for those institutions that make peace possible, or it wages war with enthusiasm, and, as Nietzsche observed, pays the price by becoming insensitive, stupid, barbaric, and vengeful.[16] While the army will always get along without culture, no so-called civilized nation can. Herbert Spencer and William Graham Sumner both stress the fact that, while armed might may have served a progressive end in the childhood of the race, we have long since reached the stage where war no longer promotes civilization. (We may wish to add that this stage was reached long before the development of the atomic and hydrogen bombs!)

Norman Thomas entitles one of his books *War: No Glory, No Profit, No Need* to indicate the total pragmatic failure of war to fulfill any ends for which it was supposedly fought. War is supposed to promote patriotism, but the nationalism that results is better unlearned because it blocks hopes for world order and feeds the fires of new aggressiveness. War is claimed to bring about the redress of grievances, but in the end, we must all come to the conference table, and it is there that constructive decisions are made. Even the claim of war enthusiasts that it awakens the virtues of courage and self-sacrifice ignores the fact that such attributes are virtues only when they are directed toward worthy ends and when they utilize worthy means. When the ends and means are both foul, no virtue is present.

Let me share with you some insights from a recent book by a colleague of mine, Ronald Glossop, entitled *Confronting War* (1983). Glossop defines war as "violent conflict between organized groups that are or that aim to establish governments."[17] He then indicates that the "war problem"—"humanity's most pressing problem"—has four aspects, and any comprehensive solution must somehow deal with each of these facets of the problem.

These four aspects of the problem are the following: First, there are *preparations for war.* Huge expenditures of public funds are involved and vast amounts of human time, talent, and effort are expended on war projects, armaments, and military training of recruits. Even if an actual war never comes, this expenditure may be a great obstacle to our survival. Such expenditure is troublesome and detrimental to human progress for two obvious reasons: (1) use of resources, money, and human talent for war projects and the development of new weaponry diverts these instruments of power from being used creatively to solve pervasive human problems, and (2) once these preparatory steps have been taken and new weapons created, there is a stubborn inertia, whether economic or social, that impedes transforming these "swords" of destruction into "plowshares." Let me illustrate the second point first. There is now a nuclear stockpile of weapons sufficiently powerful to kill 58 billion people, or to kill every living person 12 times![18] Now, assume that all the nations of the world were to come to the conference table and decide to abandon nuclear weapons. What would these peaceful nations do with this enormous capacity for death and destruction? How could they transform these weapons of annihilation and use them to solve creatively the troublesome human problems?

Think with me about the first point: How could this money, human talent and resources be better employed? To answer this question you are invited to think about these mind-boggling contrasts in priorities: "In a world spending $800 billion a year for military programs, one adult in three cannot read and write, one person in four is hungry."[19] "The developed countries on average spend 5.4 percent of their Gross National Product (total earnings) for military purposes, .3 percent for development assistance to poorer countries."[20] "There is one soldier per 43 people in the world, one physician per 1030 people."[21] Are not our real human problems those of education, hunger and health?

The second part of our war problem is the *danger of a nuclear holocaust,* whether by accident or intent. The superpowers, the Soviet Union and United States, may unleash thousands of nuclear warheads that they have ready for launch. The warheads are ready; all it takes is a command and the turn of a couple of keys. And, these warheads are fast—30 minutes from launch to target (sometimes less). Some of the nuclear warheads on these missiles are 1500 times more powerful than the bombs dropped on Hiroshima and Nagasaki. It should come as no surprise that the radioactivity from an all-out nuclear exchange would eliminate or cripple in a hideous way higher life on this planet. "Nuclear winter" (our experts tell us) would likely involve a futile struggle (by those so unfortunate as to survive) for bare existence, while undergoing excruciating suffering and pain. Donald Wells remarks:

> Our ability to destroy has so far outstripped our ability to imagine the results that we have become uniquely insensitive and heartless. . . . In a potential war where the first strike could well be the last strike, leaders *still worry about* the damage they might be able to inflict in a robot-directed second strike.[22]

The third aspect of the war problem is the *occurrence of conventional wars.* These wars are very destructive and they seem to be on the increase in recent years. Since the end of World War II these conventional wars have generally been fought on the soil of the poorer countries. The number of maimings and deaths resulting from these wars is very great indeed. "Four times as many war deaths have occurred in the forty years since World War II as in the forty years preceding it."[23] Wars in these developing, or Third World, countries are especially crippling and sometimes damage or atrophy the development of the country for decades. In general, for these countries it has meant a five-fold increase in military spending since 1960.[24] This has diverted an enormous amount of resources from meeting the pervasive human problems—hunger, health, housing, and education—and has produced accompanying pain, suffering, and death.

The fourth aspect of the war problem is *intranational or civil wars*. Merely to give examples accentuates the way in which these wars "spill over" into international conflicts. One thinks of the Vietnamese War, the Cuban revolution, the Biafran separatist movement in Nigeria, the on-going battle between the Greeks and Turks on Cyprus, the struggle in Northern Ireland, the overthrow of the Shah in Iran, the revolution in Nicaragua, and the struggle for control in El Salvador. In all these, whether directly or indirectly, whether overtly or covertly, the United States and the Soviet Union have intervened decisively to influence the outcome. These wars may have been initially and essentially intranational or civil wars, but they did not stay that way for long.

Any lasting solution to our war problem would need to deal with these four aspects of the situation. Reduction in conventional arms and nuclear arsenals seems imperative. Challenging the massive military expenditures should be a primary concern. Redirecting funds to meet human needs wherever those needs are discovered could be an immediate goal. Since war is a complex problem, one should not expect a single, simple solution for it. Many proposals for trying to solve the problem need to be examined, and it seems plausible that some combination of them will be required to rid the world of war. To be rid of war or to have a warless world is perhaps a goal that is accepted by most rational humans. The effect of warlessness upon the human spirit is perchance not quite so apparent. One of my teachers, William Ernest Hocking, who, at one time approved of war, later (after the development of the nuclear bomb) rejected it entirely. Why? In part because of the inherent contradiction in war-making which treats human beings as things and yet presupposes that they will continue as persons, in part because warlessness will lift the cloud of nuclear war that hangs over life's total meaning and dispel the horror, degradation and shame of war, but, most importantly, because a warless world will free the spirit of man to work in cooperation for lasting peace.[25]

Leaving aside many matters that are essential to solving the war problem, focus with me on some changes in attitude that may provide a beginning (but only a beginning) in our approach to the complex war problem. The preamble of the constitution of the United Nations' Educational, Scientific, and Cultural Organization says: "Since wars begin in the minds of men, it is in the minds of men that the defenses of peace must be constructed." We can begin by reshaping ourselves, by changing our attitudes, if we are committed to a world in which peace and justice are to abide.

What sorts of changes in attitude would promote peace and cooperative effort? Let me mention four aspects of the peacemaker attitude. First, we need an *attitude of commitment that is proportionate to the problem.* War, as we have insisted, is a complex problem; it is also a long-standing problem; it has been with us for thousands of years. We need a *whole-hearted commitment* to the abolition of war. In the United States, for example, much ado has been made recently of the legislation signed October 1984, establishing a United States Institute of Peace. The Institute is to be an independent, nonprofit institution that will accomplish three goals: (1) promote research of the conditions that make peace possible, (2) train persons to bring about conflict-resolution (specialists at resolving conflicts), and (3) serve as a resource center for information on peace studies. Now, these are *noble goals,* and it is the hope of peace-loving peoples that the Institute will achieve them. The refusal to allow either political party (the Democratic or the Republican) to dominate the Institute through its 15 member board offers a ray of hope. However, the fact that the Secretaries of State and Defense of the U.S. government will be members of the board and that only $4 million was initially appropriated surely raises some doubts *about its independence* of governmental control and the *strength* of Congressional commitment to its objectives. Four million dollars is very little money in comparison to the 1985 defense budget of $274.4 billion! Our commitment needs to be proportionate to the difficulty of the task we confront.

Second, we need to concentrate on *nonviolent means* both for removing injustice and for obtaining justice. Peace is certainly something other than the mere absence of war, but there can be no peace when war is present. The organized violence and killing that are involved in war perpetrate additional injustices. The attitude of the peacemaker is that which employs nonviolent means for removing injustice and obtaining justice. If humankind is to achieve the maturity for which Emerson hoped, violence must be renounced.

Why? Using violence in situations of disagreement and conflict between nations is a radical error for many reasons. Here are a few. The use of violence is based upon a false assumption. Employing violence assumes erroneously that the stronger is "right." The person forcing or coercing the others is assumed to have the "correct" ideas. This assumption is so obviously gratuitous or false it is difficult to imagine why violence is viewed as a solution to anything! Again, if violence is employed, resentment is aroused among those who are coerced into acting against their wills. Rather than resolving the disagreements, violence fosters new and deeper conflicts and disagreements. Certainly the violence of war brings about injuries, pain, death, destruction, loss and sadness.

Third, as individuals we need to be especially *sensitive to injustice* within our own society and in the relations of one nation to another. The argument that is sometimes offered for waging "a just war" is that the armed conflict and killing will alone rectify the horrible injustices that are present. There are difficulties with this argument. An obvious defect is that those who are injured and killed in war are quite often not the individuals or groups inflicting the injustices within the society. Often it is the innocent who are injured or killed, while those within the society who brought about the injustice go untouched. But, the attitude that promotes peace is the *sensitivity to injustice* and the willingness to remedy the situation before it becomes severe or extensive. This sensitivity to injustice keeps people from turning to war by removing the underlying basis for resort to violence and killing. In brief, as an appropriate epigram states: "If you desire peace, work for justice!"

A fourth aspect of this attitude is the *redirecting of energies to the global problems of humankind.* The peacemaker must be acquainted with human problems regardless of the geographical boundaries in which they are found. This attitude would give highest priority to meeting urgent needs of human beings wherever they may be located. The problems of population explosion, world hunger, disease, health of peoples, unsanitary conditions, and enormous use of nonrenewable resources require our full effort and commitment.

In a word, the attitude and commitment of the peacemaker can be characterized by the word: *humatriotism*.[26] (It rhymes with patriotism but it differs radically from it.) It includes acquiring knowledge concerning other societies and, indeed, awareness of the global community and its problems. It must be a loyalty that is developed in young people and nurtured in older people. It is a loyalty to the whole human race. It requires continual renewal and recognition (in word and deed) that war, huge military expenditures, waste of resources, pollution, diseases, and natural disasters are "the enemy" against which rational human beings need to direct their united and unrelenting efforts.

Humatriotism would surely mean changes in our nationalism. It would require that loyalty to one's country be radically dissociated from the military. It would require that the interests of the nation not be promoted in ways detrimental to the larger world community.

Our war problem will not easily be solved. Let us make a beginning by adopting the attitude of peacemaker.

Southern Illinois University at Carbondale

Notes

[1] This paper is slightly revised from an article that originally appeared under the same title in *Dialectics and Humanism* 13.4 (1986), 69-77.

[2] Aristotle, *Politics,* Bk. I, Ch. viii, #1256, in Richard McKeon, *The Basic Works of Aristotle* (New York: Random House, 1941) 1137.

[3] Aristotle, Bk. III, Ch. vii, #1265.

[4] Augustine, *The City of God,* Bk. III, Section #4; See also Bk. III, Section #30, 86, 106. Random House Edition, 1950.

[5] Thomas Aquinas, *Summa Theologica,* Part II, Second Part, Question #41, Art. 1, Vol, IX, (London: Burns, Oates, and Washburne, 1916).

[6] Wasserstrom, "On the Morality of War: A Preliminary Inquiry," *War and Morality,* ed., Wasserstrom (Belmont, CA: Wadsworth Publishing Co., 1970) 100-101.

[7] Rousseau, *The Social Contract,* Bk. I, Ch. 4, p. 11. (New York: Hafer, 1957).

[8] Fichte, *The Science of Rights* (Philadelphia: J. B. Lippincott Co., 1969) 482.

[9] J. S. Mill, "A Few Words on Non-Intervention," *Dissertations and Discussions,* (London: John Parker, 1859-1875) 166-167.

[10] Hegel, *Philosophy of Right,* (Oxford: Clarendon Press, 1942), 333-334.

[11] *Thoreau's Writings* (Vol VII), in *The Journal,* Vol, I. (Boston: Houghton Mifflin Co., 1870), 101, 335, 246.

[12] *Essays,* "War" (Boston: Houghton-Mifflin Co., 1903-1911), 166-175.

[13] *The New Leviathan* (Oxford: Clarendon Press, 1942), 244.

[14] Wells, *The War Myth* (New York: Western Publishing Co., 1967), 23. It has sometimes been claimed that "the principle of double effect" can be used to *justify* wartime obliteration bombing in which civilians are killed and their homes and property destroyed. This "principle" may be stated in this way: an individual or group is not morally accountable for the foreseen evil effects of his (or the group's) action, provided that (1) the action in itself is directed immediately to some other result, (2) the evil effects are *not* willed either in themselves or as a means to the other result, and (3) the permitting of the evil effect is justified by reasons of proportionate weight. It should be underscored that this principle does not allow the use of evil effects *even* as means to the "good" result. This means (in my opinion) that the principle is wholly incapable of justifying wars in which civilians are wantonly maimed and killed. For an interesting discussion, see John C. Ford, "The Morality of Obliteration Bombing," in *War and Morality,* edited by R. Wasserstrom (Belmont, CA: Wadsworth Inc., 1970), 15-41

[15] Hobhouse, *Social Development* (New York: Henry Holt, 1924), 110.

[16] Nietzsche, *Human, All-Too-Human* (London: George Allen & Unwin, 1910-1930), Part I, Par. #444.

[17] R. Glossop, *Confronting War* (Jefferson, NC: McFarland & Co., Inc. 1983), 7.

[18] Ruth Leger Sivard, *World Military and Social Expenditures 1985* (Washington, D. C.: World Priorities, 1985), 5.

[19] Sivard, 5.

[20] Sivard, 5.

[21] Sivard, 5.

[22] Wells, 93-94.

[23] Sivard, 5.

[24] Sivard, 5.

[25] See Hocking, "The Spiritual Effect or Warlessness," *A Warless World* ed., Arthur Larson. (New York: McGraw-Hill Book Co., 1963) 169-172.

[26] As Glossop indicates, the term "humatriotism" was apparently first used by Theodore F. Lentz in his book, *Humatriotism* (St. Louis: The Futures Press, l976) 28. Many of the same ideas had found expression in Lentz's earlier book, *Towards a Science of Peace* (New York: Bookmans, 1961). Interestingly, one of the practical suggestions he makes is to establish a "peace center," which would house a library and provide meeting rooms for peace action groups. Lentz, 178-179.

Paula J. Smithka

Introduction: The Crisis Of Nuclearism

> What are the roots that clutch, what branches grow
> Out of this stormy rubbish? Son of man,
> You cannot say, or guess, for you know only
> A heap of broken images, where the sun beats,
> And the dead tree gives no shelter, the cricket no
> relief,
> And the dry stone no sound of water.

> —T.S. Eliot, "The Wasteland"

Currently, the world's two superpowers have stockpiled over 48,000 nuclear weapons. The U.S. has about 27,000 nuclear weapons: 12,000 strategic weapons and 15,000 tactical weapons. The U.S.S.R. has about 21,000 nuclear weapons: 9,000 strategic and 12,000 tactical.[1] An additional 1,390 nuclear weapons are in the collective arsenals of France, the U.K., and China.[2] What these figures show is that the planet and all its life forms are at the mercy of—that is to say, the slaves of—50,00 nuclear weapons. According to Ruth Leger Sivard (1985):

> The megatonnage in the world's stockpile of nuclear weapons is enough to kill every person now living 12 times.[3]

What greater form of oppression than this can exist? Of course, even in modern times persons have systematically oppressed/exploited other humans, as was exhibited in the enslavement of Black Americans and the death camps for Jews under the Nazi regime. But now, the fate of the entire planet, the possibility of the annihilation of this eco-system as a whole, is in our hands. Humanity can now control not only its own destiny, but that of the entire planet as well. This control lies in the ability to press a few fateful buttons. Herein we have outgrown ourselves; we have created a technology which extends beyond our human control should it be activated.

Consider even the "weakest" leg of the triad: bombers. Each bomber can deliver 8,000,000 tons of TNT equivalent explosive, compared to the Hiroshima bomber which delivered 15,000 tons of TNT equivalent explosive.[4] If activated, their fury, like that of a tremendous hurricane, could not be effectively stopped or controlled, but only awaited, anticipated, assuming one even got a few minutes warning. The difference between a hurricane and a nuclear attack is both one of kind and degree. On the one hand, while a hurricane is a blind force, in that its "attack" is random, a nuclear attack would be a conscious and planned decision. On the other hand, while the former does not threaten globally, but locally, the latter threatens each existing form of matter, both organic and inorganic, on a global scale. Since we may well be unable to exert control once a nuclear exchange has begun, have we not, in effect, signed and sealed our own and the planet's death certificates? Have we not, with such exploitive technology, placed upon ourselves and on the planet, constraints such that no form of matter is free from the possibility of annihilation? What greater form of oppression than this can exist? Indeed, the *Angst* of extinction has peaked with nuclear terror. Not only are we aware of our own personal mortality, but we recognize the possibility of the extinction of our species (global genocide), and of all living things (omnicide), indeed the possibility of planetary annihilation (ecocide).

Although these prospects are depressing, they should be known by all. However, we cannot allow ourselves to wallow in our despair. Despair is stagnating, and, for that reason, we need to look beyond our despair; we must retain or attain hope. We must have, and work toward, a future vision, a vision which seeks to reduce the oppression of persons and Nature and one which seeks to conserve and preserve the planetary ecosystem. In order to articulate what such a future vision might be, it is important to investigate the origins, or sources, from which the oppression manifested in the nuclear arms race stems. This oppression, this *Angst* manifested with the escalation of the nuclear predicament, has as its source an even deeper metaphysical problem, the problem of dissociation. Humans tend to perceive themselves, that is, they are socially and culturally taught to be, radically autonomous creatures. In the quest for radical autonomy the individual attempts to sever his/her relationship with others and with Nature; this severance, or attempt to completely sever these relationships, is dissociation.

Historically, the oppressions/exploitations that get manifested, such as classism, racism, sexism, and more recently, nuclearism can be seen to emanate from a single locus; that locus, or epicenter, is dissociation.[5] Though such "-isms" exploit and oppress persons, they may also exploit the natural environment, which is termed "naturism."[6] Each of these "-isms" is a symptom of the disease called dissociation. Similarly, though nuclear weapons are oppressive and exploitive of both persons and Nature to a degree that "nuclearism" may perhaps be the most severe form of oppression, the arms race itself, I contend, needs to be viewed as a symptom of the disease, rather than the disease itself. While I am presenting the arms race as "only" a symptom of the disease called dissociation, I recognize it to be the most acute symptom, one which demands immediate attention and effective alleviation. Nevertheless, I wish to stress that even if this acute symptom called the arms race is arrested, and even eventually alleviated, the disease remains. While the symptoms require treatment, they will not be effectively eliminated until the disease itself is remedied, that is, until the reinforcement and facilitation of the attitude of dissociation, from others and Nature, is overcome. The purpose of this essay is to introduce the concept of dissociation to philosophers concerned about the threat posed by nuclear weapons and to suggest an alternative attitude. This alternative attitude is one which facilitates and reinforces integratedness or connectedness, a rootedness in others and Nature. This alternative is the "autochthonic" attitude. In so doing, I will be showing how both the problem with and solution for nuclearism are inseparable from the struggle against classism, racism, and sexism.

I. Consequences Of Alienated Dissociation

What is this disease that I have called dissociation, and how was it contracted? While the historical origins of dissociation are complex, I will simply note here the connection between alienated dissociation and what Ken Wilber describes as the successful emergence of ego-consciousness, what Wilber calls the solar ego.[7]

This dawning of self-consciousness in the evolution of mind serves as the hallmark for the emerging dualism. In this evolutionary process, the dualism between body and environment first emerged. Here, the body is regarded as something independent, that is, separate from its environment. Later, the emergence of the ego marks the dualism between mind and body. Such dualistic tendencies facilitate recognition of the other, whether it be Nature or persons, as wholly distinct from self. It also facilitates the treating of these others as objects, objects to be manipulated, controlled, repressed, oppressed. Thus, the ego, in its dualism from Nature and other persons, not only accomplishes *differentiation* between ego and Nature and ego and others (negation of their immediate unity), but *dissociation* as well. Wilber states:

> The ego rose up arrogant and aggressive and. . .began to sever its own roots in a fantasy attempt to prove its absolute independence.[8]

Thus, the Western ego, in its quest for independence or for radical autonomy, in its blind arrogance actually severed its own roots—its rootedness in Nature and in others. Wilber argues:

> . . .once the ego was cut loose from seasonal nature and from the body, it had no *felt* roots in which to *ground* its otherwise higher order awareness. It then seemed perfectly acceptable to the ego to begin a premeditated assault upon nature, regardless of the *historical* consequences of such activity, because history and nature were no longer integrated in a mutually dependent fashion.[9]

In an analogous manner, an assault was made upon the body by the ego. Because a dualism was created between mind and body, the body, as well as the bodies of others, began to be perceived as objects to be controlled and/or exploited. Just as there was "No longer harmony with the Heavens, but a 'conquering of space'; no longer respect for nature, but a technological assault on Nature,"[10] there was no longer harmony with the body; rather there was a coercive assault on the body. How have such coercive assaults manifested themselves in Western societies? They are depicted in our obsession with sex and violence. Each of these aspects is frequently viewed with an attitude of control and dominance. Two outgrowths from this attitude of control and dominance have been patriarchy and the advent of the machine, which I will connect with sexism and nuclearism.

A. The Rise of Patriarchy
Wilber suggests that patriarchy emerged as a product of a "mixture

of natural tendencies and unnatural inclinations."[11] He thus distinguishes between "natural patriarchy" and "unnatural patriarchy." Natural patriarchy reflects those "natural tendencies" which may have initially disposed the heroic mentality to be masculine.[12] Under this category, Wilber presents the traditional sex role stereotypes based on body differences. He notes that the more the human mind evolves, the less sexual stereotypical attitudes and behaviors are displayed. This tendency moves toward a more balanced identity between males and females and higher mental androgyny forms. Such mental androgyny is the transcendence (*Aufhebung*) of the male/female body differences. The movement toward such mental androgyny, I argue, will be an important step in the reduction (perhaps eventually *Aufhebung*) of the oppression of both persons and Nature. Moreover, given the relation between language and consciousness, I will argue that such a change goes hand in hand with the reduction (and eventually *Aufhebung*) of alienating discourse. However, the appreciation of these arguments requires a full explication of Wilber's "natural patriarchy."

Since the woman-female-mother image had been traditionally so embedded in the "birth-body-earth realm," that is, associated with Earth, and since Earth/Nature was being transcended in the evolution of ego-consciousness, the development of mental culture "naturally" fell into the realm of the fathers-males.[13] The mind, associated with the masculine, reinforced the dualism developing between mind/ego and body. This emergence of patriarchy did not fulfill the *Aufhebung* of the lower levels of evolutionary consciousness; rather, it reinforced repression, not only of mind over body, but the masculine (heaven-male) over feminine (earth-female). Since this new acquisition of masculine status was accomplished through oppression and exploitation, Wilber terms it "unnatural patriarchy." He argues:

> . . .because historically the body was equated with femininity and the mind with masculinity, then the inward and psychological dissociation of the body from the mind meant an outward and sociological oppression of the feminine by the masculine. . . .[14]

Thus, the oppression, repression, and exploitation of Nature, body, and woman were viewed as one entity, according to Wilber. This "trinity" was to be suppressed if the masculine principle (heaven-male) was to remain the preferential status over the feminine (earth-female).

Despite his elaborate historical and interpretative account of the rise of the masculine as dominant in the human ego, Wilber does not consider fully the possible psychological roots of this dissociation which manifests itself as outward and sociological oppression of the feminine. In this regard, Elizabeth Dodson Gray presents an interesting account in her book *Green Paradise Lost*. She argues that the male's need to prove himself is rooted in his envy of the female's intrinsic worth, a worth which needs no proving and is based on a woman's capability to bear children. Using excerpts from the works of Bruno Bettelheim, David Riesman, and Karen Horney, she establishes the existence of "uterus-envy." While Freud made a big issue of a woman's envy, "penis-envy," he seems not to have recognized the possibility of a man's envy.

Bettelheim argues that there is much evidence that substantiates the existence of "uterus-envy." Such envy apparently emerges as a result of the male's awe and admiration of a woman's capability to produce, that is, to create, life. While men realized their role in procreation, they themselves could not *bring forth life* and were frustrated, or never fully satisfied in their producing. Charles Ferguson captures this frustration when he observes:

> For all his growing sense of strength and his power to destroy by means of a gun, the male could not get any real satisfaction from producing. A god could, but he couldn't. And a woman could. She could bring forth life, produce it, hand it to him. Of course the male could procreate. He had an essential part in the life process. He could start it, but it was the woman who finished. By the time of the birth act, his role seemed remote and obscure, far away and all but forgot . . . .[15]

The woman, like the earth, could bring forth new life, whereas the male could not. This awe and admiration that males had for this process eventually became resentment and led to the "dread of women." Males then sought immense achievements in other ways. Karen Horney notes:

> It was this life-creating power of woman, an elemental force, that filled man with admiration. And this is exactly the point where problems arise. For it is contrary to human nature to sustain appreciation without resentment toward capabilities that one does not possess. Thus a man's minute share in creating new life became, for him, an immense

incitement to create something new on his part. He has created values
of which he might well be proud. State, religion, art, and science are
essentially his creations, and our entire culture bears the masculine
imprint.[16]

In the male's resentment toward the female, we again see the role of
repression by the ego in dissociation. There is the reinforcement of the
repression of the body by the ego that becomes manifest in the
oppression of women and Nature in patriarchal society. Riesman
comments:

> On the whole, men, by virtue of the very patriarchal dominance which
> puts them on top, must repress the extent of their longings for the
> simplicities and indisputable potentialities of being a woman, whereas
> women are much freer to express their envy of the male's equipment
> and roles.[17]

Riesman's latter point expressed in Freudian terminology is the
familiar diagnosis of "penis-envy."

B. The Advent of the Machine

In a patriarchal society where men perceive the need to repress those
"natural/feminine" feelings, thus exemplifying the attitude of control
over a "docile body" as brought out in the philosophy of Foucault, they
turn their attentions toward male achievement.[18] This immense
incitement for achievement has manifested itself in perhaps one of the
greatest, yet potentially most detrimental or oppressive, forms of
advancement: the machine. Machines were man's creation. These
machines opened up the possibility for man to produce, literally, to
create and, sadly, to destroy. The vision involved recognized the
potential for man's becoming nearly as important as woman in the life
process. Ferguson states:

> The machine, if fully developed, offered Man the prospect that he
> might become as important as woman in the life process. . . .With the
> machine he could produce. Like an ancient deity, it would enable him
> to do what he could not do otherwise. More exciting, it would enable him
> to feel what he had not been able to feel before. . . .Except as menials, there
> would be no woman in the process of production. . .just as there was no
> man around in any significant way at the birth of a child.[19]

With the production of the machine, man has indeed achieved his goal, namely, "to become as important as the woman in the life process," for in this modern age of technology, not even the "life process" has remained untouched: *in vitro* fertilization and "freezing" embryos for future implantation are merely two examples of a vast array. Man has not only *created* independent of woman, but is now involved in "her" creation process in ways never before seen. Of course, some argue that this type of technology is positive since it allows for otherwise sterile couples to have a child with the genetic contributions of both parents. Yet, such technologies also entail a dark side which can reinforce dissociation. They frequently facilitate and legitimate the exploitation and oppression of persons in the forms of classism, sexism, and racism and Nature (naturism).[20]

The irony is that the masculine ego, while attempting to *create* and overcome death and mortality, has actually succeeded in securing the certainty of both with the "advancement" of technologies. Perhaps this masculine ego has most effectively secured death and mortality in the production and deployment of nuclear weapons. Nuclear weapons are potentially the most detrimental/oppressive of all the technologies, since within them lies the power to change the planet and all the life forms on it; indeed, they introduce the potential for ecocide, the annihilation of the planet's ecosystem as a whole.

The realization that there is a connection between machines and the desire to control, to atomism (that is, the attitude that persons are radically autonomous, or dissociated beings) and to destruction, occurred even before the advent of nuclear weapons. Lewis Mumford, writing in the 1930's, noted how machines facilitate power. He observed:

> . . .it was not until the machine culture became dominant that the doctrine of untrammeled power was, practically speaking, unchallenged.[21]

Thus, the advent of machines dramatically advanced patriarchy in its quest for control. Yet, while men in their desire for creation turned to machines for a surrogate, they got destruction as well. Mumford thematizes this negative side of machines and shows the close relation between the development of machines and war. Further, he characterizes the type of atomistic people that the military mind produces:

> The regimentation and mass production of soldiers, to the end of turning out a cheap, standardized, and replaceable product, was the great contribution of the military mind to the machine process.[22]

In order to achieve power, men used machines and people: they produced ever more destructive machines and continued to reduce people (soldiers) to the status of near machines, that is, unthinking, well-controlled 'atoms' whose output response is programmed by input commands. Mumford not only recognizes, but laments these destructive consequences:

> The alliance of mechanization and militarization was, in sum, an unfortunate one: for it tended to restrict the actions of social groups to a military pattern, and it encouraged the rough-and-ready tactics of the militarist in industry. It was unfortunate for society at large that a power organization like the army, rather than the more humane and cooperative craft guild, presided over the birth of the modern forms of the machine.[23]

Clearly, our present nuclear age is the product of this combination of machines, atomism, and destruction.

Thus, we have seen that the advent of the machine has furthered, that is, facilitated and legitimated, the dissociation evolved between ego-body, ego-others, and ego-Nature. It has done so by providing an "easy" means for implementing control, the production of the "docile body" and employing the earth as a "standing reserve." This dissociation is the metaphysical root which has allowed the West to retain atomism as the predominant model of relations toward others and Nature. In the next part, I characterize this model and the alternate "web" model proposed by feminist theories, as an alternative, and I will show some problems inherent in both models. On this basis I will proceed to sketch my own alternative model in the third part and conclude on a note of hope.

II. Patriarchal Atomism Vs. Feminist Interrelationalism

Recent psychological studies have demonstrated that there seem to be differences in the ways in which the sexes view and experience the world, that is, in the ways in which they relate to others and to their environment. Carol Gilligan's studies indicate that little boys identify themselves in terms of the "I," or the centered-separate self. On the other hand, little girls tend to identify themselves in relation to others. Girls do not see the self as the center and separate; rather, their orientation is decentered and interrelated. These contrasting themes reflect the attitudes entailed in the atomistic and "web" models, respectively. While these differences between males and females are perhaps reflected biologically, they are certainly reinforced culturally. Of course, such attitudes are not restricted to gender and these differences do not imply a need for dissociation. Gilligan states:

> The different voice I describe is characterized not by gender but theme. Its association with women is an empirical observation, and it is primarily through women's voices that I trace its development. But this association is not absolute, and the contrasts between male and female voices are presented here to highlight a distinction between two modes of thought and to focus a problem of interpretation rather than to represent a generalization about either sex.[24]

Indeed, one of the mistakes on both sides has been the exclusion, or alienation, of an Other on the basis of sex/gender. Both sexes contain within themselves aspects of the other. In other words, what is human nature is present in both sexes, but perhaps with a differing degree of emphasis.

This point is reflected in Arthur Deikman's presentation of the two modes of consciousness: the "object mode" and the "receptive mode." According to Deikman, "The 'object mode' is functional, adapted to the need to act on the environment."[25] Whereas the object mode is related to Wilber's dissociated ego-consciousness, the receptive mode has connections with Gilligan's "web" model. Deikman notes that in the receptive mode, "The separate self dissolves, permitting the experience of connection or merging into the environment."[26] Deikman emphasizes that both modes are necessary, as is illustrated in creative problem solving. The danger emerges when one mode is taken as dominant over the other. Generally, when one mode dominates, it is the object mode.[27]

Just as Deikman recognizes that both modes are necessary and calls for a balance between these modes, so also both relational models are necessary, but require a blending for balance. In such a blend there would remain differentiation, but not dissociation.[28] In other words, men and women would be cognizant of their differentiation—for example, perspectives and roles in procreation—but would not perceive a dissociation: each sex as a threat to the other. This blending of relational models will facilitate the reduction, perhaps eventually *Aufhebung*, of oppression/exploitation of both persons and Nature. However, in order to establish a foundation for such a blend, it is necessary to characterize the two "ingredient" models.

A. The Atomistic/Masculine Model: Patriarchy

As has been sketched throughout Part I, the main theme of the atomistic/masculine view has been dissociation. Boys and men tend to perceive themselves as isolated, separate, autonomous individuals. According to Nancy Chodorow,[29] this attitude of isolation begins very early in childhood. Little boys, like little girls, initially identify themselves with their mothers. But because mothers perceive their sons as "male opposite" and the son recognizes this sexual difference, he seeks to establish his own identity apart from his female-mother. Thus, boys tend to break this association much earlier than girls. Because girls recognize that they are "like their mothers," identity formation comes through this attachment rather than separation. Gilligan states:

> Consequently, relationships, and particularly issues of dependency, are experienced differently by women and men. For boys and men, separation and individuation are critically tied to gender identity since separation from the mother is essential for the development of masculinity. . . . Since masculinity is defined through separation while femininity is defined through attachment, male gender identity is threatened by intimacy while female gender identity is threatened by separation.[30]

Because the "male ego" is threatened by intimacy and relationship, in order to preserve his identity, he "tends to define himself in a negative way as *not female*."[31] He seeks control of all that is. Traditionally, what is considered feminine includes both women and Nature, as was alluded to in Part I; thus, the attitude of domination as well as domineering behavior, is manifested in his relationship with both women and Nature. According to Michael Zimmerman:

> From a masculine perspective, the self appears not to be constituted

239

by relationships with others, but instead is a self-contained entity which constitutes temporary external relationships with other self-contained entities.[32]

Because all relationships are perceived as external, it is easily seen how the other may be treated as object. When the other is perceived as object, the autonomous ego may exploit the other. An effective example of this treatment applied sexually is offered by Deikman:

> . . .if lovers treat each other as objects, attempting to control their partners and maintaining a clear and separate sense of self, they are likely to experience "screwing" rather than "making love."[33]

Hence, one may be "screwed" because of race or class, and Nature may likewise be "screwed" by such exploitive measures as the dumping of toxic waste and stripmining, to say nothing of the exploitation that would result from nuclear war.

Concerning the matter of how technological "advancements" have brought further oppression on Nature, Heidegger observes that Nature has become "a gigantic gasoline station, an energy source for modern technology and industry."[34] Such an attitude toward Nature reflects a radically autonomous model. Persons and even nations act as if they are independent from all others and Nature. This kind of thinking and acting represses the actual "roots" of persons and nations. Heidegger states:

> . . .we forget to ponder. . . .We forget to ask: What is the ground that enabled modern technology to discover and set free new energies in nature?[35]

As should be expected, the discourse pervading this atomistic model is alienating; it reiterates and reinforces dissociation. Ferrucio Rossi-Landi has developed the concept of linguistic alienation.[36] He shows the parallels between economic categories and language, arguing that linguistic 'money' becomes property of linguistic privilege which ultimately leads to linguistic alienation. This linguistic privilege is formed when one social group employs a restrictive usage of part of the lexicon. Rossi-Landi calls this restrictive use of language a "special sublanguage." This special sublanguage is possessed by only a few and is, therefore, a form of nonpublic discourse.

The special sublanguage sucks life from everyday language, taking away from the common masses both understanding and power.[37] Since such special sublanguages intentionally exclude a portion of the masses, when the "intentionally excluded party" hears or reads such privileged communication, it experiences linguistic alienation.[38] William Gay maintains that nuclear discourse is an example of such a special sublanguage. However, he further distinguishes two kinds of sublanguages: personal and private sublanguages. Examples of personal sublanguages, according to Gay, are "special terminologies developed by children in their play or lovers in their intimacy." [39] These sublanguages appropriately preserve personal privacy by establishing a separation. On the other hand, private sublanguages involve "special terminologies developed and exchanged by bureaucrats and strategists."[40] Private sublanguages inappropriately give power to a few and tend to exclude the majority of the public, those who should not be excluded. Gay argues that nuclear discourse is a special sublanguage of the latter type. Going beyond Rossi-Landi and Gay, I wish to observe that alienating discourse is not restricted to private sublanguages; "common" discourse or terminology can be alienating as well. The discourse employed in the atomistic model is one example. A further and more specific example of such alienation can be found in the way those in power refer to Nature.

The discourse employed within the atomistic model is rule-oriented, dominating and autonomous. The terminologies it uses avoid those "traditionally feminine" notions of connectedness, emotion and care. Instead, it displays notions of power, conquest, and separateness. One of the most effective examples of such "power language" is offered by Huston Smith:

> When Mount Everest was scaled the phrase commonly used in the West to describe the feat was "the *conquest* of Everest." An Oriental whose writings have been deeply influenced by Taoism remarked, "We would have put the matter differently. We would speak of the *befriending* of Everest."[41]

Whereas Taoism seeks an "in-tuneness" with Nature, the West seeks to exert control over, to *master* Nature. A similar discourse is often used to describe a sexual encounter with a woman. Gray cites an excerpt from a book about sexual love, published in 1973. It advised that:

> Every sexual encounter must be a pitched battle between your sureness and her timidity. . . .What you want is automatically best for her. . . .Nothing is more pitiful, pathetic, and even contemptible than a man who yields his position of masculinity to his woman.[42]

Such discourse is very alienating, though in ways that Gay's notion of private sublanguages does not capture. It is alienating because it is reductionistic. It is reductionistic in a two-fold manner. First, the tendency is to reduce the situation to the level of competition. No matter how "tender," "special," or "at-one" a situation or experience may be, some are reduced to a power-struggle designed for the success or the dominance of the autonomous ego. Second, it reduces the Other to mere object, stripped of any intrinsic value.[43] In the terminology of the examples I have cited, Nature and women are depicted as mere means to further the ends of the ego.

It may be objected that my critique only depicts the male as being a power-seeker, as the dissociator/autonomous one. While my illustrations may give this impression, I am well aware that some women fit into the atomistic category. With so many women entering the business world and other professions, there is a great demand for conformity to the rules of "man"-made worlds. What happens when a woman pursues power? Will she replicate the behavior of the masculine perspective as in the reduplication of consciousness of the Master in the Slave and become alienated from her own complementary status to the masculine? Or, will she bring this complementary status with her into the competitive realm and seek to transform the traditional modes of interaction? Such questions need to be asked of anyone from a traditionally excluded group who begins to pursue power.

My critique suggests that the proper alternative to the masculine/atomistic model is found in feminism. Now I will address the feminist/web model of relations as a contrast and will note its strength. I will further expose shortcomings in various feminist approaches which prevent them from becoming an entirely adequate alternative to the predominant masculine model.

B. A Web of Relations: The Feminist Model

Unlike the atomistic/masculine model whose focus is on dissociation, the feminist model focuses on integration/interrelatedness. This sense

242

of relationship is formed in early childhood. Whereas the little boy seeks his gender identity apart from his mother, the little girl tends to stay associated with her mother; thus, her gender identification arises through this association. Gilligan's work indicates that many girls and women do not identify themselves as radically autonomous, separate egos, unlike many boys and men. Rather, they see themselves as bound up within an intricate network of personal relationships, a "web." Thus, the "self" is identified in terms of this social nexus. Relationships for many females, then, are concrete and internal. As a result, according to Zimmerman, "If a relationship is removed or disrupted, the 'self' is inevitably affected."[44]

This model, generally, is characterized by care and "receptiveness." Traditionally women tend to exhibit "caring-concern" for others more so than men. Whereas the object mode tends to be self-centered, the feminist model, reflective of Deikman's receptive mode, tends to have a "world-centered" awareness. This is what has led feminism to perceive ecology as a feminist issue, and it is also a basis for making the quest for peace a feminist issue. Feminism recognizes the interrelatedness of humans with Nature, and many feminists see the oppression manifested against Nature as stemming from the masculine project. I am contending that the masculine project, atomism, lies behind not only sexism, racism, classism, and naturism, but also "nuclearism." The arms race is very much a masculine atomistic project and contains its ultimate means of perpetuation or destruction. Nevertheless, while peace is a women's issue, there are potential problems with the feminist model that come to light when one addresses issues of political transformation.

One objection to the "web" model is that, by overemphasizing interrelatedness, it tends to "lose the individual." Politically, totalitarian governments are also associated with the loss of the categories which preserve the individuality of persons and the significance of that individuality. While we need to recognize the various forms of interrelatedness, we also need to uphold the intrinsic value of the individual. Individuals in such a modified model may be portrayed as "internally related 'knots' within the fabric of reality."[45]

Another objection to the political viability of feminism might be that despite talk of unity and interrelatedness, the movement manifests several areas of dissent. Unlike the masculine/atomistic model which remains unified in its patriarchal perspective, feminism finds itself divided into at least two sections and, oftentimes, more. Joan Griscom places feminists in two camps: the "nature feminists," who derive their norms from nature, and the "social feminists," whose norms are derivative from history.[46] Ynestra King similarly identifies two feminist perspectives: radical feminism and socialist feminism, though she also posits a dialectical or ecological feminism as a means of transcending the impasse between the two.[47] Karen Warren identifies "four leading versions of feminism" and offers an eco-feminist's critique of each.[48] She then proposes a "transformative feminism." This brief listing shows that feminism is very divided. Moreover, the various versions are not compatible; in fact, they are often hostile toward each other.

Since a political solution to the arms race must involve men as well as women, the way in which the differences between men and women is handled is crucial. Zimmerman notes that "many feminists began to affirm those differences—and to conclude that woman is better than man."[49] However, many feminists argue that this move tends to reinforce the traditional dichotomy that women are "emotional" while men are "rational." Other feminists claim that these traits are essentially human, belonging to both sexes.[50] The attitude that "woman is better than man" is none other than the "flip-side" of "man is better than woman." This attitude only reinforces and encourages the dissociations it was trying to dispel. Even though such feminists may recognize the importance of their connectedness with Nature, they deny their connectedness with the male half of the species--in the *same* way that men have denied their interrelatedness with the female half of the species. Ynestra King states:

> [Mary] Daly believes that women should identify with nature *against* men, and that *whatever* we do, we should do it separately from men.[51]

How can this attitude of "against men" facilitate the achievement of feminist goals, namely, to reduce all forms of oppression?[52] It cannot. On the contrary, the dissociation between men and women only encourages sexist attitudes on both parts and prevents our working together to end sexism, racism, classism, and nuclearism. The two sexes are *complementarily differentiated.* They are differentiated aspects of the same species, that is, *intra*species, not *inter*species. To an extent, this point also applies to international politics. Instead of pursuing competition and war, nations need to recognize that their differences are at times complementary and that each system can learn from the other. We need a gender neutral term and discourse which displays the connectedness of all humans with each other and with the environment as a whole, so that humans recognize themselves as a part of the ecosphere and a global community.[53] I propose the term "autochthony."

I agree with the deep-ecologists that a new *ethos* is required if humans are to "dwell appropriately on Earth"[54] and that the basis of human domination of Nature is anthropocentrism or human-centeredness. Feminist critics of deep-ecology argue that their gender-neutral term, "anthropocentrism," ignores or denies the *real* basis for such domination which is *androcentrism.*[55] Similarly, they would criticize my gender-neutral term, "autochthony," and would charge that I am ignoring androcentrism. However, I recognize that the roots of much oppression is located in androcentrism, and this should be recognized by both men and women alike. I maintain that continually to reiterate such "blame" only intensifies linguistic alienation which reinforces dissociation between the sexes. Further, to focus only on the roots of the oppression is to maintain a "rearward-looking" vision. What is needed to accomplish the goals of diminishing and alienating oppression is a future vision, an *Aufhebung.* Granted, we are still reaping the *bitter fruits* of past metaphysical choices, but to maintain and perpetuate such a rearward-looking vision would be *fruitless.*

We live in an age of crisis. Every day the symptoms of the "disease" of dissociation worsen. Each day the problems of overpopulation, hunger, political exploitation, and the ecological crisis become slightly more real to us. Similarly, the *Angst* generated by the threat of the "unspeakable"—the possibility of planetary annihilation (ecocide)—has peaked with the escalation of the nuclear arms race.[56] The questions become: How are we responding to these issues? Are we so afraid to face these issues that we "shelve" them and practice denial? Or, are we so caught up in their imperativeness that we are lost in our own despair, wallowing in it? Both denial and despair, like blame, are stagnating. It is for this reason that we need to look beyond.

The call is to look forward, to develop a new ethos which transcends

(*Aufhebung*) the dissociation inherent within the present systems, an ethos which seeks to reduce the oppression of persons and Nature and to conserve and preserve the planetary ecosystem. The future vision, which reflects this ideal, is the autochthonic vision.

III. Toward An Autochthonic Perspective

Autochthony is rootedness. As humans, we have largely forgotten our rootedness. Instead, we have affirmed *autonomy* as the primary component of human ability and achievement. Granted, autonomy in a weak sense is good: it maintains individuality and preserves the individual as the "knot" in the web of reality. Nevertheless, historically, autonomy has been overstressed. This became very evident with the emergence of ego-consciousness stemming from the realm of patriarchy. Feminism, however, cannot be excluded from this discussion of excessive autonomy. Some feminist *positions* seek autonomy in the form of separation, or dissociation from the masculine. The autochthonic model is an appropriate blend of both the atomistic and feminist models. It recognizes our emergence from, and rootedness in, the Earth (Nature) and others, while promoting autonomy in the weak sense to preserve the individual and encourage individuality.

A program which takes a significant step toward what I have termed the "autochthonic model" is the Transformative Feminism proposed by Karen Warren. Her program, however, still retains the shadow of dissociation. Warren's proposal significantly seeks to initiate a movement to end all oppression, not only sexual oppression. Her program seeks to establish a theoretical place for the diversity of women's experiences. In terms of language, the discourse in the present patriarchal society is generally biased toward the masculine, as is effectively exhibited by Gilligan's account of psychology.[57] Warren suggests the rejection of the "logic of domination and the patriarchal conceptual framework that gives rise to it."[58] Such a rejection involves a rethinking of what it means to be human, which would involve a "restructuring of our attitudes and beliefs about ourselves and the world, including the non-human world." Further, it would "recast traditional ethical concerns to make a central place for values." Among the examples Warren offers are care, friendship, and reciprocity in relationships. Lastly, transformative feminism would challenge the technological biases of the patriarchal society so that they may be "brought into the service of preserving, rather than destroying, the Earth." This program has a lot of merit, and tends to reflect much of the move toward autochthony. However, the drawback to Warren's program is that it retains a feminist discourse which can be alienating, particularly to the other half of the human species.

Heidegger states:

> ...language is the flower of the mouth. In language the earth blossoms toward the bloom of the sky... body and mouth are part of the earth's flow and growth in which we mortals flourish, and from which we receive the soundness of our roots.[59]

To attain a language that respects the "earth's flow and growth," we need to speak in a nonoppressive and more public, rather than private, discourse. In order to achieve such a positive cycle of language and awareness which both grows and blooms, it is necessary to transcend sexual dissociation. Such an *Aufhebung* would negate the separateness/dissociation, while preserving sexual differentiation/complementariness. Wilber refers to such an *Aufhebung* as a form of higher mental androgyny, not a physical bisexuality which would be a regression to a prior level of human consciousness.[60]

Zimmerman sees the notion of androgyny as problematic since it maintains the dualism between male and female.[61] But I think that such "mental androgyny" does not necessarily reinforce dualism. Rather, it may recognize the *differentiation* that exists between men and women. Mental androgyny may recognize that the nature of the human species is present in both sexes. Because "mental androgyny" realizes this to be the case, it does not preclude the possibility of *differentiated* emphasis of a particular characteristic, or set of characteristics, by one sex more than the other. In fact in other species the characteristics of the species are often manifested differently between the sexes. Such a "mental androgyny" which recognizes differentiation, rather than dissociation, would facilitate an attitude of interrelatedness, since it would not perceive the other sex as radically different but rather as a complementary member of the species.

Conclusion: Visions of Global Autochthony

In this essay, I have outlined a serious metaphysical distortion termed "dissociation." Such a distorted metaphysics unfortunately has not only been perpetuated, but strengthened, in the West. The consequences of such a distorted and one-sided worldview—that each human being is a radically autonomous, unconnected creature—is manifested in the exploitation and oppression in sexism, racism, classism, naturism, and nuclearism. Moreover, even though these forms of oppression plague our Western societies, the East cannot be wholly excluded from the same disease. Nevertheless, we must look forward, we must maintain a future vision, and we must retain hope.

The future vision is that of a global community, "global" in its literal sense. A global community incorporates all of this globe we call Earth.[62] Such a global community would reflect the view of Earth from space. One would see no clear and distinct boundaries; nations would not be autonomous in the strong sense. Peoples and nations are like pieces in the grand and dynamic jigsaw puzzle of the world, where no piece is autonomous in the strong sense; rather, all pieces are connected, or rooted.[63] This recognition of our interrelatedness with others and with Nature and the cultivation of this autochthonic attitude is the key to effect the cure of the symptoms of oppression and to eradicate the disease called dissociation. Peoples and nations can be differentiated without being dissociated. We can recognize our differences as complementary rather than as alienating.

It might be objected that in this presentation of the autochthonic attitude, which allows for the reduction of oppression of persons and Nature, I have not provided a methodology which will turn this ideal into practice. Such a methodology is, at present, beyond the scope of this essay, but I can note that Heidegger suggests *Gelassenheit,* as the releasement toward things and the retention of an openness to the mystery, as the way in which "we should arrive at a path that will lead us to a new ground and foundation."[64] My concern at this point is not to decide a precise method but to elucidate the metaphysical origin of the negative and oppressive "-isms" which plague what would be a global community. It has also been the intent of this essay to show the need for a forward-looking vision in our pursuit of a better, less oppressive future. Such a vision incorporates hope in the struggle to overcome these "-isms" and the metaphysical tradition which sustains them.

While those pursuing world peace are far from achieving the type of global community I describe, they can find some hope and encouragement in recent developments in US/USSR relations. In particular, the concept of "glasnost" or openness, initiated by Yuri Andropov and enhanced by Mikhail Gorbachev, is a very significant and positive step.[65] It is bearing fruit not only in the Soviet Union but also between Soviet and American citizens. I will present just one case of a move from alienated dissociation to complementary differentiation in the political sphere. Recently, two journalists, Walter Anderson, the American editor of *Parade* magazine, and Vitaly Korotich, the Soviet editor of *Ogonyok*, visited each other's country in pursuit of the answer to the question, "Can We Wage Peace?"[66] The articles that each journalist wrote appeared side-by-side in both the American and Soviet newspaper magazines. Not too many years ago such an exchange would have been unheard of. Today, communication between the Soviets and the Americans is expanding. Now, we are beginning to see the Soviet people as *people,* not as some abstract object entity. Similarly, under glasnost, the Soviets are gaining better glimpses of Americans as *people* like themselves. Indeed, such increased openness and communication between the two superpowers *can* facilitate a nonoppressive, nonalienating discourse which reduces the tension created by the longstanding, alienated dissociation between these two countries. While glasnost is not the solution to all of the negative symptoms caused by dissociation, it is a step in the right direction. Each instance of alienated dissociation that is overcome brings increased awareness of our connectedness and lessens the grip of one of the oppressive "-isms." In struggling against these "-isms," we are struggling against a deeper, metaphysical crisis. There is at least a faint hope that we may rediscover our rootedness and live together in a non-oppressive, peaceful, global community. The words of Johannes Peter Hebel effectively express the needed autochthonic perspective:

> We are the plants which—whether we like to admit it to ourselves or not—must with our roots rise out of the earth in order to bloom in the ether and to bear fruit.[67]

Tulane University

Notes

[1] Ruth Leger Sivard, *World Military and Social Expenditures* (Washington, D. C.: World Priorities, Inc., 1985) 50.

[2] Sivard, 50.

[3] Sivard, 5.

[4] Sivard (1986) 5.

[5] Robert Lifton coins the term "nuclearism" for "the exaggerated dependency upon, and even worship of nuclear weapons." See Robert J. Lifton, "Imagining the Real: Beyond the Nuclear 'End'," *The Long. Darkness: Psychological and Moral Perspectives on Nuclear Winter,* ed., Lester Grinspoon (New Haven: Yale University Press, 1986) esp. 96-98.

[6] See Joan L. Griscom, "On Healing the Nature/History Split in Feminist Thought" *Heresies* 4.1 (1981) 4-9.

[7] For a complete discussion of the emergence of dualism with the evolution of ego-consciousness, see Ken Wilber, *Up From Eden: A Transpersonal View of Human Evolution* (Boulder: Shambhala, 1983).

[8] Wilber, 182.

[9] Wilber, 204.

[10] Wilber, 187.

[11] Wilber, 228.

[12] Wilber, 228

[13] Wilber, 229-30.

[14] Wilber, 232.

[15] Charles Ferguson, as cited in *Green Paradise Lost* Elizabeth Dodson Gray, (Wellesley, MA: Roundtable Press, 1981) 51.

[16] Karen Horney, as cited in Gray 50-51.

[17] David Riesman, as cited in Gray 50.

[18] See Hubert L. Dreyfus and Paul Rabinow, *Michel Foucault: Beyond Structuralism and Hermeneutics*, (Chicago: The University of Chicago Press, 1982, 2nd ed.), 134-35.

[19] Ferguson, as cited in Gray 51.

[20] For a discussion of these four forms of oppression, see Joan L. Griscom.

[21] Lewis Mumford, *Technics and Civilization* (New York: Harcourt, Brace, and World, Inc., 1934) 85.

[22] Mumford, 92.

[23] Mumford, 96.

[24] Carol Gilligan, *In a Different Voice: Psychological Theory and Women's Development* (Cambridge: Harvard University Press, 1982) 2.

[25] Arthur J. Deikman, *The Observing Self: Mysticism and Psychotherapy* (Boston: Beacon Press, 1982) 70-71.

[26] Deikman, 71.

[27] Deikman, 71.

[28] I wish to thank Michael Zimmerman for bringing this distinction to my attention.

[29] Nancy Chodorow, as presented in Gilligan, and in Michael Zimmerman, "Feminism, Deep Ecology, and Environmental Ethics" *Environmental Ethics*, 9 (1987).

[30] Gilligan, 8.

[31] Zimmerman, 31.

[32] Zimmerman, 31.

[33] Deikman, 73.

[34] Martin Heidegger, *Discourse on Thinking*, trans., John M. Anderson and E. Hans Freund (New York: Harper & Row, 1966), 50.

[35] Heidegger, 50.

[36] Ferrucio Rossi-Landi, "On Linguistic Money," trans., Heli Hernandez and Robert E. Innis, *Philosophy and Social Criticism* 7 (1980), 305.

[37] Rossi-Landi, 305.

[38] William C. Gay, "Nuclear Discourse and Linguistic Alienation," *Journal of Social Philosophy*, 18.2 (1987),42-49.

[39] Gay.

[40] Gay.

[41] Huston Smith, *The Religions of Man* (New York: Harper & Row), 209. Emphasis added.

[42] Gray, 48.

[43] I follow J. Baird Caldicott in his use of "intrinsic value." See his essay: "Intrinsic Value, Quantum Theory, and Environmental Ethics," *Environmental Ethics* 7 (1985), 257-75.

[44] Zimmerman, 31-32.

[45] Zimmerman, 35.

[46] Griscom, 5.

[47] See Ynestra King, "Feminism and Revolt" *Heresies* 4.1 (1981) 12-16.

[48] See Karen Warren, "Feminism and Ecology: Making Connections" *Environmental Ethics* 9 (1987) 4-20.

[49] Zimmerman, 34.

[50] Zimmerman, 34-35.

[51] King, 12. (first emphasis added)

[52] Karen Warren calls this effort to reduce all forms of oppression "Transformative Feminism."

[53] I use the term "ecosphere" because it shows no bias toward organic or organic matter but, rather, displays the significance of both.

[54] Zimmerman, 37.

[55] Zimmerman, 37.

[56] See Michael Heim, "A Philosophy of Comparison: Heidegger and Lao Tzu" *Journal of Chinese Philosophy* 11 (1984) 307-35.

[57] See Gilligan.

[58] See Warren, 18-20.

[59] Martin Heidegger, *On the Way to Language,* trans. Peter D. Hertz (New York: Harper & Row, 1971) 99 & 98, respectively.

[60] Wilber, 229.

[61] Zimmerman, 35.

[62] It should be noted that I am neither attempting overtly or covertly to exclude the universe which sustains the planet Earth in my use of the term "global community"; however, for the purposes of this essay, my discussion is restricted to the planet Earth.

[63] Special thanks to Michael Zimmerman for this metaphor.

[64] Heidegger, *Discourse* 56-57.

[65] Walter Anderson, "Can We Wage Peace?: How Different Are We?" *Parade* (Sunday, June 21, 1987) 6.

[66] Anderson, 1.

[67] Johannes Peter Hebel, as cited in Heidegger, *Discourse* 47.

R. Paul Churchill

Former president Richard Nixon is reported sometimes to have had a very cavalier attitude about the use of nuclear weapons under his control. On one occasion he said, "I can go into my office and pick up the telephone and in twenty-five minutes seventy million people will be dead."[1] During a radio test on August 11, 1984 President Reagan jokingly said that he had signed legislation that "outlaws Russia," and added, "We begin bombing in five minutes"—a juvenile attempt at humor that may have caused a partial Soviet alert.[2] These chilling anecdotes forcefully remind us that, in the nuclear age, the president and a small number of advisors can exercise the powers of absolute dictators in determining whether we die almost instantly or continue to enjoy life. Moreover, this power of life and death is a regular feature of the chief executive's prerogative to make weapons policies in pursuing the objectives of foreign affairs. Desmond Ball notes that there have been some twenty documented threats to use atomic or nuclear weapons since the annihilation of Hiroshima and Nagasaki.[3] But is any of this awesome power to risk the survival of American lives based on authority which the people of the United States have delegated to the president?

Although philosophers have been much concerned with nuclear weapons for over a decade, they have focused almost exclusively on the moral assessment of alternative nuclear deterrence strategies or on the logical and conceptual issues related to deterrence theory. Philosophers have given relatively little attention to the process by which nuclear weapons policies are made or to the justification of the president's authority to direct the policy process. This paper is an attempt to stimulate debate over assumptions about this critical policy process. It is motivated by concern over two popular, influential, and wholly unexamined assumptions about the connection between the quality of our nuclear weapons policies and the extent to which these policies are made in a democratic and representative manner.

As the nuclear freeze movement has demonstrated, many opponents of "nuclearism" simply assume that a policy process that is more responsive to public concern and more open to democratic participation will produce nuclear weapons policies of greater rationality and morality than those imposed upon us by governing elites.[4] For their part, officials in the national security establishment and their supporters either ignore the undemocratic tendencies of national security policy or assume that the higher quality of present weapons policies, which are made in a secretive and nonaccountable manner by an exclusive nuclear elite, justifies the semi-autocracy of the national security state. But as far as I can tell, no one has presented a persuasive argument for believing either that secretive and autocratic decision making is necessary for national security or that democratizing the security state apparatus would lead to saner and more ethical policies in a dangerous world.

Because we rightly share the presumption that governmental departures from democratic practices stand in need of justification, the burden of proof must be borne by those who believe that our national security is best promoted by limiting democratic control of nuclear weapons policies. Thus, if the policy process does not conform to accepted practices of democratic and constitutional control, then this process can be justified only if we agree that it produces security benefits which outweigh the corresponding losses of democratic control. Are nuclear weapons policies presently made in a manner inconsistent with fundamental principles of democratic and constitutional government?

While some elements of politics and institutional design restrict the policy options of the president and his national security advisers, the chief executive's freedom to make the most important policy decisions, I believe, is virtually unrestrained. The appearance of popular participation and democratic control is largely illusory; nuclear weapons policies are made in a largely autocratic manner by the president and a small number of cabinet officials and national security advisers who are accountable only to the president.[5] This is a condition I shall call "nuclear autocracy," and I shall not repeat here the arguments that this condition presently exists in the United States.[6] Instead, my present purpose is to identify and to assess the arguments for nuclear autocracy which can be extracted from the literature on nuclear deterrence and national security. There appear to be only three basic arguments which reoccur in many variations. I shall briefly characterize the three arguments and outline reasons why each fails. While this will not fully satisfy the need for a reasoned assessment of these positions, I hope it will be enough to stimulate debate on this neglected topic.

The first argument, which I shall call the argument from tacit consent, maintains that, however autocratically these weapons policies are made, they generally receive the consent of the people. According to this view, because citizens accept the outcome or final product of the policy process, they also consent, at least *tacitly,* to the undemocratic arrangements by which these policy "benefits" are acquired. Now, before proceeding further, it must be noted that this argument assumes that the weapons policies made by national security elites are generally superior to the policies which would result from a more open, democratic process. Thus the argument from tacit consent relies upon the conclusion of a further argument—the argument for guardianship which will be the second argument I examine in this paper. At present, however, I want to focus on what lies at the core of the argument from tacit consent, namely, a view of the relationship between the people and the leadership elite which has been described by C.B. MacPherson as the "pluralist elitist equilibrium model" and by Andrew Belsey as "minipart democracy."[7]

The "minipart" model of democracy depends heavily upon analogies with the market model of classical economics. Citizens are seen as passive consumers of political goods who rationally seek to maximize satisfactions while minimizing effort. Parties and political elites put their policies before voters in a competitive political "market" and exchange them for votes. The political party that can respond most effectively to "what the people want" will obtain political power, just as the businessman who responds most effectively to public demand will increase his profits.[8]

What must be the case if citizens can truthfully be said to *consent* to an autocratic arrangement that provides security "goods"? It must be true, at a minimum, that citizens freely choose these policies rather than others and that citizens have access to the information needed to decide that these policies really do serve their best interests. In terms of the market analogy, this means, at a minimum, that the basic conditions for a fair "market exchange" must be met. Potential "buyers" must be fully informed about what political "goods" are for "sale," with what "quality," and for what "price." Furthermore, there must be assurances that the goods promised will be delivered, and there must be reasonable alternative "products" competing for the "consumer's" vote. Of course, everyone knows that market models fulfilling these conditions do not correspond to anything in the real world.

However, as Belsey has noted, if this market model is far too simple to fit even the economic world, it fits the political world less well, and the realm of national security still less. The exclusivity and secrecy of defense planning prevents voters from obtaining the information they need to make rational choices; the nonaccountability of the president and his national security advisers, combined with their broad discretionary powers and the effects of politico-bureaucratic bargaining, deny voters any guarantee that the "goods" ordered will be delivered as promised; finally, the continuation of the arms race and the development of countervailing strategy, under Democratic as well as Republican administrations, gives the lie to the notion that there is any real competition in the national security "market."

It might be argued that part of the costs of national security, which voters must figure into the "bargain," are high levels of secrecy, nonaccountability, and self-dealing among elites, and that these costs limit drastically the information voters can acquire about security "goods" and relieve elites of the need to offer services on a competitive basis or even to be accountable for their decisions. In effect, in order to avoid confronting their anxiety over the nuclear peril, voters must grant national security elites the ability to maneuver carte blanche. It is almost as if, in cutting this "deal," elites said to voters: "We promise to provide you the maximum amount of security possible, but only according to our conception and estimate of your security needs, with no restraints on the means used to meet these needs, no guarantees that any security will be provided, and at the constant risk of catastrophic failure, the probability of which, however, must remain unknown to you."

If this account comes even close to hitting the mark, a major problem arises in connection with the way nuclear weapons policies are made. These arrangements approximate the conditions under which coerced bargaining occurs. For to acquire the security "goods" in question, voters are required to divest themselves of the means of voluntarily making "contracts." But certain rights or goods, such as access to the information needed for informed choice, and alternatives required to make choice meaningful, cannot be treated as commodities that are also subject to the "market economy." Like voting itself, these are goods citizens must possess if they are to be able to participate freely in even a minipart democracy.

It appears, therefore, that, as an arrangement, nuclear autocracy is more *coercive* than freely chosen by citizens. Is this condition of coerced bargaining, or "nuclear paternalism," nevertheless justified? It is reasonable to presume that a majority of citizens would regard national security as an indispensable good. It is therefore also reasonable to assume that the same majority would regard the practice of basic deterrence, that is, the threat to retaliate with nuclear weapons after nuclear aggression against the United States or its allies, as justified in pursuit of national security. Thus the claim that "nuclear paternalism" is justified requires the argument that the present autocratic process is necessary to practice the strategy of basic deterrence. Are there then plausible reasons for believing that a democratic policy process would produce nuclear defense decisions that would imperil the United States's ability to practice basic deterrence?

This brings us to the second argument for nuclear autocracy, the argument for guardianship. Generally one finds two versions of this argument. The first maintains that democratic processes cannot give rise to sound national security policy either because it would be impossible to develop the necessary consensus such a policy would require or because rational planning would be subverted by the kind of lobbying and vote trading that traditionally occurs in congressional politics. The second version of the argument simply maintains that policy made more or less exclusively by knowledgeable "experts" just is, or almost always is, so superior to policy made democratically that the difference justifies the loss of democratic control.

Now, the first version of the argument for guardianship is highly speculative just because it depends upon analogies and extrapolations from the experience of political decision making in other contexts, mostly domestic, to the probable effects of increasing democratic participation in the formation of national security policy. After all, it is not at all clear that democratizing the policy process must lead to the same old "politics as usual" or that we would not be able to develop new procedures and institutions which would increase effective participation without sacrificing rational deliberation and reflection. And the second version, about the superiority of the so-called "experts," also depends on strained and questionable analogies between the kind of technical or instrumental knowledge experts possess and need to implement policy and the *wisdom* required for the choice of sound policy in the first place.

However, having briefly mentioned why I believe both versions of the argument for guardianship fail, I shall not give it further consideration here, for two reasons. First, because the argument does depend upon the interpretation of a large body of evidence too detailed to sort through in this paper. And, second, because I believe that Robert Dahl, in his new book, *Controlling Nuclear Weapons,* has done as good a job of refuting the argument for guardianship as anyone might expect.[9] What I would like to pursue is the claim that unveiling and opening up the policy process might make it impossible for the United States to implement an effective nuclear deterrence strategy, even one receiving overwhelming approval from a majority of citizens.

One long-standing and frequently heard objection to democratizing national security policy is the claim that, by giving effect to beliefs that some strategic objectives or military tactics are impermissible, a democratic process might "tie the hands" of government officials by significantly limiting options for dealing with aggression.[10] Some nuclear elites appear to fear that, if policy making is opened to wider participation, certain nuclear options will be ruled out. For example, it is very plausible to believe that citizens might decide that, on balance, whatever the advantages to be accrued through building up our nuclear forces to attain an "escalation dominance" and "war fighting" capability, they are not worth the greater instability in superpower relations that implementing these plans would cause. Well, suppose that the decision making process concerning certain basic priorities of atomic warfighting strategies were more democratized. Suppose, too, that the American people were to decide that certain targeting strategies, or proposed weapons systems, are impermissible? Is not this precisely the sort of restraint on the pursuit of interests that democratic principles justify?

But what if weapons policies unacceptable to American citizens, as the development of a "war-fighting" nuclear capability may be, are nevertheless necessary to continue basic deterrence—a policy presumably endorsed by a majority of citizens? In the first place, it is not at all certain that American citizens would reject a "war-fighting" capability, provided that reasonable arguments show that it is really necessary for a successful policy of basic deterrence, and that nuclear elites discharge their responsibilities in making this clearly known. More serious, however, is the elitist view that we cannot form the public consensus needed to democratically endorse such a policy because revealing and debating information about key features of our military capability would make nuclear deterrence impossible. This view introduces the third argument for nuclear autocracy, the argument from "structural necessities."

An elitist might argue that, if any nuclear weapons policy is justified, then basic deterrence, which protects the lives and liberties of Americans, is justified, but that basic deterrence will succeed only if strategy and nuclear weapons policies are made in an autocratic manner. According to this view, because of certain "structural necessities,"[11] deterrence would fail if greater access to information and a decentralization of policy making were allowed. Dennis Thompson has advanced this argument in a recent article in *Philosophy & Public Affairs*.[12] Thompson maintains that effective deterrence "denies citizens the knowledge they need to assess defense strategy," and in this sense, "deterrence imposes a moral cost on democracies that it does not impose on non-democracies."[13] Effective deterrence requires the denial of the knowledge which citizens would need to assess defense strategy, Thompson argues, because deterrence requires "universal uncertainty." Thompson defines "universal uncertainty" as "limitations that affect anyone making decisions with imperfect information," and he contrasts universal uncertainty with "differential uncertainty," a term that refers to the distribution of limitations to information.[14]

Differential uncertainty characterizes our position as civilians vis-a-vis the president, his closest advisers, and the military high chain of command. They know the circumstances under which nuclear retaliation would be ordered whereas ordinary citizens do not. In addition, American citizens presumably share with Soviet leaders the condition of differential uncertainty vis-a-vis American war- planning. The effect of this differential uncertainty is the production of that universal uncertainty about American strategic plans which prevents the Soviets from calculating that there may be circumstances in which aggression would be to their advantage. In other words, Thompson believes that differential uncertainty is necessary to produce the universal uncertainty that underwrites deterrence. American leaders cannot share information about the precise role of the various options in strategic planning, Thompson argues, for "if citizens acquired such knowledge, so would enemies, and with respect to some of this knowledge the deterrent effect would be lessened."[15]

It is obviously true that effective nuclear deterrence depends upon a balance between certainty and uncertainty. While any potential aggressor must be certain that the United States shall maintain sufficient nuclear power to inflict a devastating retaliation, even after a first strike against it, an adversary must not feel certain either that the United States would use these weapons first or would never use them.

Nevertheless, Thompson's argument suffers from two related defects: it misunderstands the causes and effects of the uncertainty underlying effective nuclear deterrence, and it mistakenly assumes that increases in the information needed democratically to control security policy would automatically imperil deterrence. In fact, however, increased information about proposed uses of nuclear weapons might contribute to stable deterrence whereas increases of only certain kinds of information would reduce the effectiveness of deterrence. Negative performance characteristics, vulnerabilities such as the degree of hardening of missile silos, "go codes" for launching weapons, the locations of nuclear missile submarines on patrol, design configurations of control and command systems, and the allocation of particular weapons to particular targets—this sort of information must remain secret if we are to keep potential aggressors from believing that a nuclear attack on the United States could succeed. But it is equally obvious that information about the type and number of delivery systems and the characteristics of weapons such as megatonnage, flight time, and hard-kill capacity need not be kept secret. This sort of information is in the open literature and it is to the advantage of the United States that potential aggressors know of these military capabilities.

Moreover, many decisions about the policies intended to guide targeting or to guide a decision to launch weapons probably do not need to be kept secret. This information would include the national emergencies or other circumstances in which the president and his advisers would consider the use of nuclear weapons, whether and how far authority to use nuclear weapons has been pre-delegated, and what sorts of targets have or have not been selected.[16] Specific examples of the sort of information that does not need to be kept secret include whether or not the commanders of nuclear missile submarines have pre-delegated authority to use nuclear weapons, the contingencies that could lead to action on this authority, and how these attack "options" may be related to overall strategic objectives.

The basic point is that secrecy does not need to extend back very far from the positioning and programming of actual weapons and the communication links needed to control them.[17] No secrecy is required for the choice of strategy, and no secrecy is needed for the choice of weapons. Moreover, in addition to increasing the opportunities of American citizens to influence policies which control their fate, a general decrease in universal uncertainty with respect to this kind of information might enhance crisis stability by leading to policy choices which reduce adversaries' perceptions that American leaders might believe there could be circumstances in which it would be rational to initiate nuclear aggression.

Now, Thompson might respond, as some advocates of countervailing strategy do, by arguing that opening the policy process to antinuclear and pacifistic tendencies would undermine the resolve of American leaders to threaten nuclear retaliation.[18] After all, it must be remembered that, according to traditional deterrence theory, a potential aggressor will not be deterred if he feels assured that the United States would not respond with nuclear weapons. This is an important point about the way perceptions of resolve affect uncertainty in deterrence relationships. But it does not follow that countervailing strategy or a nuclear "war-fighting" capability are necessary to project this resolve. Thus it is dubious that a decision by the United States to renounce countervailing strategy will greatly reduce a potential aggressor's uncertainty. Theorists such as McGeorge Bundy and Robert McNamara prefer the term "existential uncertainty"[19] to Thompson's "universal uncertainty" because it more accurately designates the real cause of the uncertainty that might keep an aggressor at bay: and this is, of course, the sheer uncertainty over what national leaders might do after suffering a direct attack, or upon perceiving that a nuclear strike is imminent, whatever else they might have said. Advocates of "minimum deterrence" plausibly maintain that a survivable second-strike capability just large enough to inflict unacceptable damage is all we will ever need to generate the necessary uncertainty.[20]

The conclusion to be drawn from this analysis, therefore, is that Thompson has not shown that there are structural necessities which require nuclear autocracy. Thus, if my judgments about the arguments outlined in this paper are correct, no satisfactory defense of nuclear autocracy has yet been made. The present ways in which nuclear weapons policies are made unjustifiably violate fundamental principles of democratic and constitutional government. If we take seriously our status as autonomous and rational individuals, then we must be vigilant in protecting our rights and liberties against external threats, and against the efforts of earnest but benighted fellow citizens to provide paternalistically for our security needs.

Of course, one cannot be sanguine about the probable quality of security policies that would result from a democratized policy process. Remembering the old platitude that "a people get the government they deserve" should rightly make us uncomfortable. Perhaps greater self-government will not lead to reliably better policies until we, as a people, make more extensive efforts to be ethically concerned and informed about our security problems. So far, I have found no sound reason for believing that greater self-government will lead to security policies significantly worse than the policies political elites presently provide for us. We ought to prefer policies legitimately made to any that might be marginally better but illegitimate. Thus, the challenge for us is twofold: first to shoulder the responsibility to make national security an issue of active and constant concern, and second, to devise new and creative mechanisms by which to increase democratic participation without undermining the requirements for real national security.

The George Washington University

Notes

[1] Quoted by R. Neild, *How To Make Up Your Mind About the Bomb* (London: Andre Deutsch, 1981) 135.

[2] Howard Kurtz, "Reagan Bombing Joke Is Said to Cause Partial Soviet Alert," *The Washington Post.* September 14, 1984.

[3] "U.S. Strategic Forces: How Would They Be Used?" *International Security.* 7 (1982/1983) 31.

[4] The term "nuclearism" was coined by Robert Jay Lifton and Richard Falk, *Indefensible Weapons: The Political and Psychological Case. Against Nuclearism* (New York: Basic Books, 1982) ix.

[5] See Richard Falk, "Nuclear Weapons and the Renewal of Democracy," *Nuclear Weapons and the Future of Humanity,* eds., Avner Cohen and Steven Lee (Totowa, NJ: Rowman & Allanheld, 1986) 437-56; Joel Kovel, *Against the State of Nuclear Terror* (Boston: South End Press, 1983) 3-139; Lifton and Falk, 128-207; Eric Markusen and John B. Harris, "Nuclearism and the Erosion of Democracy," *Nuclear Weapons and the Threat of Nuclear War,* eds., Eric Markusen and John B. Harris (New York: Harcourt, Brace, Jovanovich, 1986); Peter Pringle and James Spigelman, *The Nuclear. Barons* (New York: Holt, Rinehart, and Winston, 1981); and Harry Howe Ransom, *Can America Survive Cold War?* (Garden City, NY: Doubleday, 1963).

[6] See Churchill, "Nuclear Autocracy and Nuclear Paternalism," *Social Philosophy Today,* ed., James P. Sterba (Lewistown, NY: Edwin Mellen Press, forthcoming).

[7] C.B. MacPherson, *The Life and Times of Liberal Democracy* (New York: Oxford University Press, 1977), and Andrew Belsey, "Secrecy, Expertise and Democracy," *Objections to Nuclear Defence,* eds., Nigel Blake and Kay Pole (London: Routledge, Kegan, Paul, 1984), 168-181.

[8] Belsey, 170.

[9] Dahl, *Controlling Nuclear Weapons; Democracy Versus. Guardianship* (New Haven: Yale University Press, 1984).

[10] See for example Gordon A. Crain and Alexander L. George, *Force. and Statecraft* (Oxford: Oxford University Press, 1983) esp. 60-72.

[11] The term is borrowed from Lifton and Falk 262.

[12] D. Thompson, "Philosophy and Policy" *Philosophy & Public Affairs* (1985) 205-218.

[13] Thompson, 210.

[14] Thompson, 208-210.

[15] Thompson, 208.

[16] Dahl, 34.

[17] Michael Walzer, "Deterrence and Democracy" *The New Republic* 191 (July 2, 1984) 20-21

[18] See, for example, Colin S. Gray, *Nuclear Strategy and Strategic Planning* (Philadelphia: Foreign Policy Research Institute, 1984).

[19] McGeorge Bundy, "Existential Deterrence and Its Consequences" *The Security Gamble: Deterrence Dilemmas in the Nuclear Age,* ed., Douglas MacLean (Totowa, NJ: Rowman & Allanheld, 1984) 3-13.

[20] See Robert McNamara, *The Essence of Security* (New York, Harper and Row, 1968) 51-62, and Solly Zuckerman, *Nuclear Illusion and Reality* (New York: Viking Press, 1982).

Laurence Bove

The current debate in post-analytic circles about the future of philosophy offers us a opportunity to reflect on the study of nonviolence and its relationship to the mainstream of ethical and social philosophy.[1] Philosophy since the enlightenment, say members of this debate, excessively relies upon an imperious notion of reason and uses methods that achieve little more than personal or social edification.[2]

Examining nonviolence from perspectives other than that of traditional utilitarianism or deontology, I will study three contributions to the discussion. Stanley Hauerwas, while criticizing standard accounts of moral rationality, argues that stories and interpretive communities are the sources of ethics. Barbara Deming, while discovering the ways society oppressed her, tells us why she remained nonviolent. Bernard Lonergan, while going beyond the limitations of classical and modern methods, develops a generalized method for the natural and human sciences. Unknown to each other, each is involved in a conversation that further enables a pluralistic study of nonviolence.

Though only a small minority of philosophers espouse nonviolence, I hope to broaden the conversation between proponents of nonviolence and those who uphold the moral legitimacy of violence. My approach is exploratory, and I undertake the task to reestablish contact with ultimate human problems. Finally, I believe stories from outside society's mainstream enrich everyone, if we have a framework to understand them. This paper is a step toward supplying such a framework.

A. Hauerwas and the Narrative Structure of Ethics

Stanley Hauerwas, a noted Christian ethicist, is important to this study for two reasons: he criticizes the standard accounts of ethical rationality, and he advocates a philosophy that requires nonviolent resistance to evil.

In *Truthfulness and Tragedy*, Hauerwas and Burrell write, "The hallmark of contemporary ethical theory, whether in a Kantian or utilitarian mode, has been to free moral philosophers from the arbitrary and contingent nature of the agent's beliefs, dispositions and character."[3] His criticism of the standard Kantian or utilitarian accounts questions using an analogy that subjects moral theory to the canons of physical science. In the standard accounts, moral objectivity is attained in judgments freed from "peculiarities of agents caught in the limits of their particular histories." To Hauerwas, the ethical reductionism of these standard accounts limit truthfulness because they require the moral agent to make judgments that are nonegoistic and a-historical. For him, this mandate of scientific rationality is ultimately inadequate as a guide for human living.

Instead, Hauerwas focuses upon the character and history of the moral agent, and notes that "character and moral notions only take on meaning in a narrative," and that "moral disagreements involve rival histories of explanation." This emphasis on personal and social experience and history leads him to a notion of truthfulness rooted in history. In this context "narrative can function as a form of rationality." He argues that his analysis actually broadens the scope of moral rationality because the "objective" standard accounts mistakenly led some to choose arbitrary subjectivity after they abandoned the reductionist approach.

In contrast to the standard utilitarian or deontological accounts, Hauerwas stresses the role of narratives, while he develops an ethic of virtue or character. Drawing inspiration from Alasdair MacIntyre's *After Virtue*, Hauerwas holds in *A Community of Character* that

> . . .an ethic of virtue centers on the claim that an agent's being is prior to doing. Not that what we do is unimportant or even secondary, but rather what one does or does not do is dependent on possessing a "self" sufficient to take personal responsibility for one's action. What is significant about us morally is not what we do or do not do, but how we do what we do.[4]

Noting the lack of inherent conflict between virtue and duty, Hauerwas says that in an ethic of virtue "action must contribute to or fulfill" our moral character.[5]

To Hauerwas, the excellences of character (*arete*) necessary for being moral are "context-dependent." He states:

> The significance of this point from my perspective cannot be over-estimated, since I will make no attempt to develop an "ethic of virtue" satisfactory for any society. Rather, I will try to show how an analysis of virtue turns on an understanding of human nature as historical and why, therefore, any account of virtue involves the particular traditions and history of a society.[6]

As summarized in *The Peaceable Kingdom*, narratives are fundamental to an ethical scheme.[7] The task of ethics is to remain true to a common vision or story of life. Consequently, the solutions to ethical quandries depend upon the people who confront them and the way they construe the world through language, habit, and feeling.

Hauerwas echoes Kierkegaard when he says that how one exists precedes what one ought to do. Avoiding moral abstractionism, he maintains that situations are more important than the rules with which we try to bind them. He points out that, while moral agency is derived from trying to live well, the excellences of character (*arete*) needed to reach one's goal are rooted in a narrative account of what we could or ought to be. Though Aristotle could not imagine an ethical ideal other than that of the polis, we, on the other hand, are presented with many such models, and our pluralistic society demands that we choose from among them.

For philosophers studying the ethical nature of nonviolence, the narrative story of what we can or ought to be forms a practical basis for a nonviolent ethic because, as Hauerwas's work prompts us to reflect, stories, whether we agree with them or not, form the backdrop of our living, acting, and choosing. Stories promote, as well as limit, our struggle for personal, social, economic and political freedom. Shared across cultures, stories create universal social meaning from individual and group experiences. Shared only within the group, stories insulate us.

Hauerwas's emphasis on stories or narratives never blossoms into a full account of nonviolence because in *The Peaceable Kingdom* nonviolence is understood through a Christian narrative; he does not develop a narrative of nonviolence based on human experience alone. However, in pursuing an account of nonviolence along lines intimated by Hauerwas, two tasks lie before us: developing a narrative of nonviolence that relies upon human experience, and including our rational, personal and historical concerns in our method. For the first, we turn to the writings of Barbara Deming; for the second, to Bernard Lonergan.

B. Barbara Deming's Narrative of Nonviolence

Barbara Deming consistently justifies nonviolence as a worthy course of action. In contrast to Hauerwas, she creates a narrative of nonviolence without using a religious basis. As Deming writes about her path from militarism and domination she validates what she saw and felt so clearly. Exposing the moral, psychological, and practical prisons in which we find ourselves, she broke with some of American society's key illusions and kept her integrity and dignity throughout situations that could have defeated her. No stranger to pain and anger, she continually chose nonviolence as a viable option.

Through her life and writings she contributes an excellent example of a story taken from the margins of our society. Raised in a middle class environment, she gradually discovered how to live a life where all people are equal, where all people can be free. She affirms the American dream, yet discovers that the dream and reality do not coincide.

As we understand ourselves primarily through dominant cultural interpretations, the question of narratives or stories embroils us in questions of truth and liberation. Dominant social narratives maintain the status quo, prevent the dominant group from understanding the minority, and make the minority feel their subordinate status more acutely. The majority's cultural narrative hinders the acceptance of stories that do not fit dominant cultural forms. In the end, the repetition of similar stories obscures truth and limits the common good.

A radical activist, an American against war, racism, and sexism, a lesbian, Deming realized what oppressed her and strove to free herself from it. She develops two strains of thought directly related to the philosophical study of nonviolence: she elucidates nonviolence as a way of life and she explores nonviolence as a mass movement. This section focuses on nonviolence as a way of life. In contrast to overly intellectualized approaches, she writes about an interior illumination that is almost physical. Of the 1971 demonstrations in Washington, she says:

270

> What was it that we were acting out, and that did generate a very real power? Not a bullying force, not the power to make people afraid. The power to make them see new things as possible. I experienced it in a very physical way.[8]

She tells us in *Revolution and Equilibrium* that her story involved transferring loyalty from the state to "a loyalty simply to other people".[9] This task took her longer than expected. To form her narrative of nonviolence she had to stop habitually "looking to that state to change itself".[10]

After her 1960 trip to Cuba, she talks about experiencing the liberating shock of "discovering the gap that lay between what I had been told was happening there. . .and what I learned for myself was happening."[11] Her intensely personal and person-centered story explores how different situations create different worlds. In her early anti-war protests, she tells us that "as the police car drove by, and I turned away it struck me that here were two people living in quite different worlds, breathing an altogether different air".[12]

On a march from San Francisco to Moscow in 1961, she tells us how nonviolence contrasts itself with the dominant cultural narrative:

> In laying down one's arms one enters unchartered ground. (This would be so even if all nations were to lay down their arms together.) They (the walkers) dare to enter this new world; and this daring distinguishes them as yet from the majority.[13]

For Deming, symbolic physical acts often occasion her moral commitments. On the trip to Moscow she observes "one primary purpose the walk serves is to recruit serious workers for the peace movement. It is a way of committing themselves, and a way of determining just how deeply they feel the commitment."[14]

Another theme in her narrative of nonviolence is the interconnectedness of people. She tells us:

> Those who are walking are caught up in spite of themselves in our government's commitment to a policy of retaliation—should war come—against not merely "the enemy" but millions who would admittedly be innocent victims of the event.[15]

When exploring our need for independence, she places before us the practical experience of interconnectedness.

> My charge has been that we have lost our independence; but we shall certainly not regain it until we are willing to affirm, too, our round-the-world dependence, one upon the other. That should, in this age, be hard to deny any longer. We have become in a new and awesome sense "members of one another"—now that if violence anywhere in the world should flare into general violence, the death of one would literally mean the death of all or nearly all. Even those who are unable to feel any particular sentiment about the unity of mankind should be able to now at least to see that it is a practical fact.[16]

Deming's involvement with the civil rights movement opens a new chapter in her narrative of nonviolence. During the demonstrations in Birmingham, she affirms that we live in different worlds bounded by different experiences, insights and values. "What a queer feeling to be able to travel in a few minutes from this world into quite another world—as they cannot. The day I leave Birmingham, I simply drive out of it, in a taxicab."[17] Her interconnectedness with other people and willingness to enter into unchartered ground, caused her to say, "now I am a negro. Except that I can drive away from it."[18]

Throughout her life significant events communicate convictions and feelings of a nonviolent way of life to her. Even in Birmingham she says, "the people I move among give me their courage. There is a contagion to it; and I catch it; it is simple as that. I catch it through closeness. They make me one of them."[19] In this simple but eloquent passage she counters much of the abstraction and depersonalization that modern technology and society reinforce. She presents to us a narrative of nonviolence that her human experience verifies.

Deming wrote the last and most challenging chapter of her narrative of nonviolence when she adopted feminism and openly acknowledged herself a lesbian. In this part of her story, she demonstrates the deepening maturity of her nonviolence because for the first time she could not "simply drive away" from the different world she experienced. Though earlier she reveals bravery in entering "unchartered territory," one senses the voluntariness of it. Now, as a lesbian, she acknowledged a world that was hers. Like the negro in Birmingham, she was no longer able to escape the oppression society imposed on her. Deming once again reaffirms the themes of interconnectedness and nonviolence as a response to her newly acknowledged position. Though more personal, she continues her nonviolent narrative and applies it to resisting sexism, a form of oppression which she took a long time to recognize.

In *We Cannot Live Without Our Lives* Deming once again justifies nonviolence in feminism and the resistance to sexism. She tells us, when writing to a friend from the civil rights movement:

> . . .I am not black but because I am homosexual I know in my deepest being what it feels like to be despised—so I didn't walk out of some sense that it would be nice of me to help the downtrodden; I walked because I am a nigger too. And no one of us should be a nigger. And my soul protested it for all of us. And I went to Vietnam because you and I are gooks too. No one should be a Gook.[20]

This excerpt answers for me a concern Deming posed to us in Birmingham when she drove away from the demonstrations. We cannot "drive away" from the part of ourselves that is oppressed. Each of us must recognize where it is and confront it. To do this each of us must "break our silence" about this aspect of our lives. But that is exactly what many of our dominant cultural narratives keep us from doing.

Nonviolence as a way of life takes on a renewed significance and affirmation from her feminist position. In overcoming sexism, many subtle changes between human relationships take place. In overcoming women's lack of individuality she reaffirms the theme of interconnectedness:

> Let the mother teach her son, yes, we must give of ourselves; "we are members of one another," but this is not to be read to mean simply: we (women) are members of you (men). Let her teach both son and daughter equity, mutuality. Which is to say, nonviolence." [21]

For her nonviolence combines the best aspects of the masculine and the feminine. It is androgynous. The impulse of "self assertion and the impulse of sympathy are clearly joined: the very genius of nonviolence . . .is that it demonstrates them to be indivisible, and so restores human community."[22]

C. Lonergan's Generalized Empirical Method

Bernard Lonergan is important to philosophers studying nonviolence because his understanding of method provides a rich context within which to put Hauerwas's criticisms of the enlightenment and Deming's emphasis on the interpersonal. As Lonergan says, "the development that is the constitution of one's world is also the constitution of one's self."[23] In his view, contemporary science has shifted from causal necessity to probability. "The ideal has ceased to be definitive achievement; it has become ongoing advance."[24] The natural and human sciences have moved from the discovery of static essences to the articulation of intricate systems.

Lonergan recognizes what he calls a "second enlightenment" because the first enlightenment's reliance on static abstract reasoning does not provide an adequate understanding of history and the human sciences. The first enlightenment swept away the remnants of feudalism and proclaimed the triumph of Newton's mechanics which

> . . .led philosophers to desert rationalism and swell the ranks of empiricists. The enlightenment has lasted into our day and still enjoys a dominant position. But, as it were, from within it has developed an antithesis, no less massive though, as yet, it has not crystalized. To it, I refer when I speak of a second enlightenment.[25]

The main features of the "second enlightenment" involve shifts from Euclidian geometry to n-dimensional geometries, from Newton's mechanics to Einstein's relativity and Heisenberg's uncertainty principle, from economics as political economy to the Keynesian neglect of ironclad laws, from trying to fit people into universal essences to interpreting their cultures. In this second enlightenment statistics and probability take the place of honor. As Lonergan puts it, "a deductivist world of mechanistic determinism was making way for the probability schedules of a world in process from lower to higher species and eco-systems."[26]

Kant's middle ground between empiricism and rationalism was rejected. Philosophy, rather than develop a priori structures of judgment, emphasized autonomy and freedom within the works of Schopenhauer, Kierkegaard, Newman, Dilthey and Nietzsche. This affirmation in philosophy was matched in human studies by hermeneutics and history. To Lonergan this second enlightenment affects society because it "may find a role and task in offering hope and leadership to the masses alienated by large establishments under bureaucratic management."[27]

In his second lecture on religious knowledge, Lonergan (1985) summarizes his new method as a "normative pattern of related and recurrent operations that yield ongoing and cumulative results."[28] He asks how inner conviction relates to objective truth, and answers that in light of his analysis of the second enlightenment "we have come up with a science that yields, not objective truth, but the best available opinion of the day."[29]

The important advance in his understanding of method is that all data are accounted: natural science attends to sense data, and hermeneutical and historical studies "turn mainly to data that are expressions of meaning."[30] In short, his generalized empirical method

> . . .operates on a combination of both data of sense and the data of consciousness: it does not treat of objects without taking into account the corresponding operations of the subject; it does not treat of the subject's operations without taking into account the corresponding objects.[31]

Lonergan goes behind the "diversity that separates the experimental method of the natural sciences and the quite diverse procedures of hermeneutics and history" to discover their common relatedness and "prepare the way for their harmonious combination in human studies"[32] For natural science, the key is discovery of something new; for hermeneutics and history, it is understanding. Attending to the data given to sense or consciousness, gaining insights which lead to understanding, grasping intelligibility, presenting appropriate questions are normative patterns that yield results in both the natural and human sciences. Lonergan affirms that one operation leads to the other. Most importantly, carried out by responsible human beings, these activities create norms. His summary of the process is a most apt closing:

> It is time to conclude. We have been asking whether there is any connection between inner conviction and objective truth. By inner conviction we have not meant passion, not stubbornness, not willful blindness, but the very opposite; we have meant the fruit of selftranscendence, of being attentive, intelligent, reasonable, responsible; in brief, of being ruled by the inner norms that constitute

the exigencies for authenticity in the human person. But for objectivity we have distinguished two interpretations. There is the objectivity of the world of immediacy, of the already-out-there-now, of the earth that is firm-set only in the sense that at each moment it has happened to resist my treading feet and bear my weight. But there is also the objectivity of the world mediated by meaning; and that objectivity is the fruit of authentic subjectivity, of being attentive, intelligent, reasonable, responsible.

In my opinion, then, inner conviction is the conviction that the norms of attentiveness, intelligence, reasonableness, responsibility have been satisfied. And satisfying those norms is the highroad to the objectivity to be attained in the world mediated by meaning and motivated by values.[33]

C. Conclusion

Underlying this study is the premise that a paradigm change which supports the philosophical legitimacy of nonviolence and opens new avenues of reflection is occurring. In this study, I explored three such contributions that should have promise for the philosophical study of nonviolence. Hauerwas and Lonergan's development of new methods for ethics and the humanistic sciences describe key features of this emerging paradigm. Their explorations into post-enlightenment methodology illuminate the region where objective reason complements the complexity of human experience. Barbara Deming's life exemplifies the narrative quality of experience described in post-enlightenment thought. Her clear and consistent affirmation of nonviolence transcends limits of the enlightenment and allows insights leading to a more complete study of nonviolence. Though this study raises more questions than it answers, I trust it will be of service to those studying nonviolence and to those struggling with its promise.

Walsh College

Notes

[1] See K. Baynes, J. Bohman, & T. McCarthy, eds., *After Philosophy: End or Transformation?* (Cambridge, MA: MIT Press, 1987), and J. Rajchman, & C. West. eds., *Post-Analytic Philosophy* (New York: Columbia University Press, 1985).

[2] See R. Rorty, *Philosophy and the Mirror of Nature* (Princeton: Princeton University Press, 1979).

[3] S. Hauerwas, with R. Bondi and D. Burrell, *Truthfulness and Tragedy: Further Investigations in Christian Ethics* (Notre Dame, IN: University of Notre Dame Press, 1977) 16. The quotations in this and the following paragraph are taken from pages 15-16.

[4] S. Hauerwas, *A Community of Character: Toward a Constructive Social Ethic* (Notre Dame, IN: University of Notre Dame Press, 1981) 113. The completed reference to MacIntyre's *After Virtue* is: Notre Dame, IN: University of Notre Dame Press, 1981.

[5] Hauerwas, *A Community* 113.

[6] Hauerwas, *A Community* 112.

[7] S. Hauerwas, *The Peaceable Kingdom: A Primer in Christian Ethics* (Notre Dame, IN: University of Notre Dame Press, 1983).

[8] B. Deming, *We Cannot Live Without Our Lives* (New York: Grossman, 1974, 20.

[9] B. Deming, *Revolution and Equilibrium* (New York: Grossman, 1971) xv.

[10] B. Deming, *Revolution* xv.

[11] B. Deming, *Revolution* xiv-xv.

[12] Deming, *Revolution* 29.

[13] Deming, *Revolution* 58.

[14] Deming, *Revolution* 53.

[15] Deming, *Revolution* 54.

[16] Deming, *Revolution* 119.

[17] Deming, *Revolution* 153.

[18] Deming, *Revolution* 153.

[19] Deming, *Revolution* 160.

[20] Deming, *We Cannot Live* 130.

[21] Deming, *We Cannot Live* 66.

[22] Deming, *We Cannot Live* 66.

[23] B. Lonergan, "Method: Trend and Variations," *A Third Collection: Papers by Bernard J. F. Lonergan, S. J.,* ed., F. Crowe (New York: Paulist Press, 1985) 18.

[24] B. Lonergan, "Aquinas Today: Tradition and Innovation," in Crowe 43.

[25] B. Lonergan, "Prolegomena to the Study of the Emerging Religious Consciousness of Our Time," in Crowe 63.

[26] Lonergan, "Prolegomena" 64.

[27] Lonergan, "Prolegomena" 65.

[28] B. Lonergan, "Second Lecture: Religious Knowledge," in Crowe 140.

[29] Lonergan, "Second Lecture" 140.

[30] Lonergan, "Second Lecture" 141.

[31] Lonergan, "Second Lecture" 141.

[32] Lonergan, "Second Lecture" 143.

[33] Lonergan, "Second Lecture" 144.

General Bibliography of Cited and Selected Works

In the general bibliography the editors bring together works cited by the nineteen essay authors, as well as selected works bearing on the topics covered. This bibliography differs from the succeeding one compiled by William Gay in several respects. First, this general bibliography combines philosophical with political, historical, and scientific works, while Gay's bibliography focuses on the philosophical. Second, this bibliography is selective by the authors and the editors, while Gay's, based on an index search, is more inclusive. Third, this bibliography correlates with the broader topics discussed by the authors, while Gay concentrates on philosophical works pertaining to nuclear weapons, and to more restrictive issues of war and peace. Within these categories Gay covers a wide range of subtopics.

The editors have subdivided the general bibliography for easy access by the reader. The first three major sections—Roman numerals I, II, and III—parallel the three divisions of the book: superpower ideologies; ethical justifications for war; and critiquing war, promoting peace. Within each of these divisions references are gathered for one, and sometimes two related articles, following the order in which the articles appear in the text. The number of sources under individual topics adheres to the citations given by the authors, with some exceptions. The editors have added sources considered relevant, and excluded sources deemed minor or not readily accessible. The latter are still acknowledged in the notes at the end of the essays.

A fourth section—IV—has been added for works that fit into more than one topical subdivision, and works that have been cited by more than one author. This section has allowed the editors to eliminate duplication in citing references. So if a work cited in an article cannot be found in the appropriate subdivision of the bibliography, the reader is encouraged to look in section IV. Some works cited from anthologies are given abbreviated references in Sections I-III, with the anthology referenced in section IV; in such cases the article citation is followed by the notation "(See Pt. IV)." In section IV many works go beyond an explicit focus on issues of war and peace. Nevertheless these sources are relevant for comprehending the broader context within which issues on war and peace can be understood. Section IV is divided into philosophical works, and political, historical and scientific works.

I. SUPERPOWER IDEOLOGIES

A. Cuban Missile Crisis and Millennarian Thinking

Allison, Graham. *Essence of Decision.* Boston: Little, Brown, 1979.

Barkun, Michael. *Disaster and the Millennium.* New Haven: Yale University Press, 1974.

Bernstein, Barton. "The Cuban Missile Crisis." *Reflections on the Cold War.* Eds. Lynn Miller and Ronald Pruessen. Philadelphia: Temple University Press, 1974: 122-24.

Betts, Richard. *Nuclear Blackmail & Nuclear Balance.* Washington: Brookings Institution, 1987.

Bundy, McGeorge, transcriber, and James Blight, ed. "October 27, 1962: Transcripts of the Meetings of the ExComm." *International Security* 12.3 (1987-88): 30-92.

Chomsky, Noam. "Strategic Arms, the Cold War and the Third World." *Exterminism & Cold War.* Eds. New Left Review. London: Thetford Press, 1983.

Cohn, Normal. *The Pursuit of the Millennium.* Fairhaven: Essential Books, 1957.

Divine, Robert, ed. *The Cuban Missile Crisis.* Chicago: Quadrangle, 1971.

Ellsberg, Daniel. Introduction. "A Call to Mutiny." *Protest and Survive.* Ed. E.P. Thompson and D. Smith. New York and London: Monthly Review Press, 1981.

Hofstader, Richard. *The Paranoid Style in American Politics.* New York: Alfred A. Knopf, 1966.

Kaplan, Fred. *The Wizards of Armageddon.* New York: Simon & Schuster, 1983.

Kavka, Gregory. "Morality and Nuclear Politics: Lessons of the Missile Crisis." Cohen and Lee: 233-54. (See Pt. IV).

Kennedy, Robert. *Thirteen Days: A Memoir of the Cuban Missile Crisis.* New York: Norton, 1969.

Khrushchev, Nikita. *Khrushchev Remembers.* Trans. S. Talto. Boston: Little, Brown, 1974.

Lilienthal, David. *Change, Hope and the Bomb.* Princeton: Princeton University Press, 1963.

May, Henry. *The Enlightenment in America.* New York: Oxford University Press, 1976.

Olson, Theodore. *Millenialism, Utopianism, and Progress*. Toronto: University of Toronto Press, 1982.

Schlesinger, Arthur, Jr. *A Thousand Days: John F. Kennedy in the White House*. Boston: Houghton Mifflin, 1965.

Somerville, John. *The Crisis: True Story About How the World Almost Ended*. Privately printed.

Sorenson, Theodore. "Kennedy Vindicated." Divine.

Steele, Ronald. "Lessons on the Cuban Missile Crisis." Divine.

Stone, I.F. "What Price Prestige?" Divine.

Talmon, Jacob. *Political Messianism*. London: Mercury, 1960.

Tuchman, Barbara. *The March of Folly*. New York: Alfred A. Knopf, 1984.

---. *Practicing History*. New York: Ballantine, 1982.

Tuveson, Ernest. *Redeemer Nation*. Chicago: University of Chicago Press, 1968.

Walzer, Michael. *The Revolution of Saints: A Study in the Origins of Radical Politics*. Cambridge: Harvard University Press, 1965.

Welch, David and James Blight. "The Eleventh Hour of the Cuban Missile Crisis: An Introduction to the ExComm Transcripts." *International Security* 12.3 (1987-8): 5-29.

Wills, Garry. *The Kennedy Imprisonment*. Boston: Little, Brown, 1981.

B. Military Strategy: Marxist and Western Views

Arbatov, Georgi and Willem Oltmans. *The Soviet Viewpoint*. New York: Dodd, Mead, 1983.

Brodie, Bernard. Introduction. Clausewitz.

Clausewitz, Carl von. *On War*. Eds. and trans. Michael Howard and Peter Paret. Princeton, NJ: Princeton University Press, 1976.

Gallie, W.B. *Philosophers of Peace and War*. Cambridge: Cambridge University Press, 1978.

Gorbachev, Mikhail. *Perestroika: New Thinking for Our Country and the World*. New York: Harper and Row, 1987.

Grier, Philip. *Marxist Ethical Theory in the Soviet Union*. Dordrecht, Holland: D. Reidel, 1978.

Hampsch, George. *Preventing Nuclear Genocide: Essays on Peace and War*. New York: Peter Lang, 1988.

Kahn, Herman. *On Escalation*. New York: Frederick A. Praeger, 1965.

---. *On Thermonuclear War*. Princeton, NJ: Princeton University Press, 1960.

Kennan, George. *The Nuclear Delusion: Soviet-American Relations in the Atomic Age*. New York: Pantheon, 1982.

Scanlon, James. *Marxism in the USSR: A Critical Survey of Current Soviet Thought*. Ithaca, NY: Cornell University Press, 1985.

Somerville, John, ed. *Soviet Marxism and Nuclear War: An International Debate*. Westport, CT: Greenwood Press, 1981.

C. Sociobiology and Nuclear Weapons

Barash, David and Judith Eve Lipton. *The Caveman and the Bomb: Human Nature, Evolution, and Nuclear War*. New York: McGraw-Hill, 1985.

---. "Psychology: Thinking and Not Thinking About the Unthinkable." *Stop Nuclear War! A Handbook*. New York: Grove Press, 1982: 214-39.

Hume, David. "Of the Original Contract." *Hume's Moral and Political Philosophy*. Ed. Henry Aiken. New York: Hafner, 1948: 356-72.

Oldenquist, Andrew. "Loyalties." *The Journal of Philosophy* 79.4 (1982).

Schonsheck, Jonathan. "Constraints on *The Expanding Circle:* A Critique of Singer." *Inquiries into Values: The Inaugural Session of the International Society for Value Inquiry*. Ed. Sander Lee. Lewiston, NY: Edwin Mellen: 695-707.

---. "Wrongful Threats, Wrongful Intentions and Moral Judgements about Nuclear Weapons Policies." *The Monist* 70 (1987): 330-56.

Shaw, R. Paul and Yuwa Wong. "Ethnic Mobilization and the Seeds of Warfare: An Evolutionary Perspective." *International Studies Quarterly* 31 (1987): 4-12.

---. *Genetic Seeds of Warfare: Evolution, Nationalism, and Patriotism*. Winchester, MA: Unwin, Hyman, 1988.

Singer, Peter. *The Expanding Circle: Ethics and Sociology*. New York: New American Library, 1981.

Wilson, Edward. *On Human Nature*. New York: Bantam, 1978.

D. Libertarianism and War

Center for Defense Information. "Militarism in America." *The Defense Monitor* 15.3 (1986). Washington, D.C.

DeGrasse, Robert, Jr., Paul Murphy and William Ragen. *The Costs and Consequences of Reagan's Military Buildup.* New York: The Council on Economic Priorities, 1982.

Friedman, Milton. *Capitalism and Freedom.* Chicago: University of Chicago Press, 1962.

Friedman, Milton and Rose Friedman. *Free to Choose.* New York: Harcourt Brace Jovanovitch, 1980.

Gauthier, David. *Morals by Agreement.* Oxford: Clarendon Press, 1986.

Held, Virginia. *Rights and Goods.* New York: Macmillan, 1984.

Lappe, Frances Moore. *Diet for a Small Planet.* Revised. New York: Ballantine, 1982.

Lappe, Frances Moore, Joseph Collins, and D. Kinley. *Aid As Obstacle.* San Francisco: Institute for Food and Development Policy, 1980.

Machan, Tibor, ed. *The Main Debate: Communism Versus Capitalism.* New York: Random House, 1987.

Melman, Seymour. *Pentagon Capitalism: The Political Economy of War.* New York: McGraw-Hill, 1970.

---. *The Permanent War Economy.* New York: Simon and Schuster, 1974.

Novak, Michael. *Moral Clarity in the Nuclear Age.* Nashville: T. Nelson, 1983.

---. *The Spirit of Democratic Capitalism.* New York: Simon and Schuster, 1982.

Nozick, Robert. *Anarchy, State, and Utopia.* New York: Basic Books, 1974.

Osterfeld, David. "The Nature of Modern Warfare." *The Libertarian Alternative.* Ed. Tibor Machan. Chicago: Nelson-Hall, 1974: 350-56.

Rand, Ayn. *Atlas Shrugged.* New York: Random House, 1957.

---. *The Fountainhead.* New York: Bobbs-Merrill, 1943.

---. "The Roots of War." *Capitalism: The Unknown Ideal.* New York: New American Library, 1966: 28-36.

---. *The Virtue of Selfishness.* New York: New American Library, 1964.

II. ETHICAL JUSTIFICATIONS FOR WAR

A. Moral Sceptics to Political Realists on Violence and War

Aron, Raymond. *Peace and War: A Theory of International Relations.* Trans. Howard & Fox. Garden City: Doubleday, 1966.

Bronfenbrenner, Urie. "Why Do the Russians Plant Trees Along the Road?" *Saturday Review* 10 May 1963.

Cohen, Marshall. "Moral Scepticism and International Relations." *Philosophy and Public Affairs,* 13.4 (1984): 299-346.

Easlea, Brian. *Fathering the Unthinkable: Masculinity, Scientists and the Nuclear Arms Race.* London: Pluto Press, 1983.

Falk, Richard. *Revolutionaries and Functionaries: The Dual Face of Terrorism.* New York: Dutton, 1988.

Falk, Richard, Gabriel Kolka and Robert Jay Lifton, eds. *Crimes of War.* New York: Vintage, 1971.

Fisher, Ronald. "International Relations." *Social Psychology: An Applied Approach.* New York: St. Martin's, 1982.

Fox, Michael. "The Nuclear Mindset: Motivational Obstacles to Peace." Fox and Groarke: 113-29. (See Pt. IV).

Gardiner, Robert. *The Cool Arm of Destruction: Modern Weapons and Moral Insensitivity.* Philadelphia: Westminster, 1974.

Gauthier, David. "Deterrence, Maximization, and Rationality." *Ethics* 94.3 (1983/84): 474-95.

---. "An Appendix: Hobbes on International Relations." *The Logic of Leviathan.* Oxford: Clarendon Press, 1969: 207-12.

Gellman, Barton. *Contending with Kennan: Toward a Philosophy of American Power.* New York: Praeger, 1984.

Groarke, Leo. "Nuclear Arms Control: Eluding the Prisoner's Dilemma." Fox and Groarke: 181-94. (See Pt. IV).

---. "Protecting One's Own: Hobbes, Realism and Disarmament." *Public Affairs Quarterly.* 2.1 (1988): 89-107.

Heilbroner, Robert. *The Nature and Logic of Capitalism.* New York: Norton, 1985.

Hilgartner, Stephen, Richard Bell and Rory O'Connor. *Nukespeak: The Selling of Nuclear Technology in America.* Harmondsworth: Penguin, 1982.

Holmes, Robert. "On Pacifism." *The Monist* 57 (1973): 489-506.

Kavka, Greogory. "Nuclear Weapons and World Government." *The Monist* 70 (1987): 298-315.

Kennan, George. *American Diplomacy: 1900-1950.* New York: New American Library, 1951.

---. *Realities of American Foreign Policy.* Princeton: Princeton University Press, 1954.

Mackie, J.L. *Ethics: Inventing Right and Wrong.* London: Penguin, 1977.

Merleau-Ponty, Maurice. *Humanism and Terror.* Boston: Beacon, 1969.

Morgenthau, Hans. *Politics Among Nations: The Struggle for Power and Peace.* New York: Alfred A. Knopf, 1973.

Morris, Christopher. "A Contractarian Defense of Nuclear Deterrence." *Ethics* 95.3 (1984/5): 479-96.

Niebuhr, Reinhold. *Christian Realism and Political Problems.* New York: Charles Scribner's Sons, 1953.

Nielsen, Kai. "Doing the Morally Unthinkable." Fox and Groarke: 57-61. (See Pt. IV).

---. "Interest and Pretension in American Foreign Policy." *Reinhold Niebuhr on Politics.* Eds. Davis and Good. New York: Charles Scribner's Sons, 1960.

Noble, Cheryl. "Political Realism, International Morality, and Just War." *The Monist* 57 (1973): 595-606.

Rapoport, David and Yonah Alexander, eds. *The Morality of Terrorism: Religious and Secular Justifications.* New York: Pergamon, 1982.

Santoni, Ronald. "The Arms Race, Genocidal Intent and Individual Responsibility." *Philosophy and Social Criticism* 10.3/4 (1984): 9-18.

Scheer, Robert. *With Enough Shovels: Reagan, Bush and Nuclear War.* New York: Random House, 1982.

Sextus Empiricus. *Selections from the Major Writings on Scepticism, Man, & God.* Ed. Hallie. Trans. Etheridge. Indianapolis: Hackett, 1985.

---. *Sextus Empiricus.* Trans. Robert Bury. 4 Vols. Cambridge: Harvard University Press, 1933-1949.

Trotsky, Leon. *Terrorism and Communism.* Ann Arbor: University of Michigan Press, 1963.

White, Ralph. *Fearful Warriors: A Psychological Profile of U.S.-Soviet Relations.* New York: Free Press, 1984.

B. Moral Assessments of Nuclear Policy

Anscombe, Elizabeth. "War and Murder." Wasserstrom 42-53. (See Pt. IV).

Dworkin, Gerald. "Nuclear Intentions." *Ethics* 95.3 (1984/5): 445-60.

Hoekema, David. "The Just War Tradition and the Nuclear Debate." *Peace and Change: A Journal of Peace Research* 10.3/4 (1984): 145-54.

Holmes, Robert. *On War and Morality*. Princeton, NJ: Princeton University Press, 1989.

Kavka, Gregory. "Doubts about Unilateral Disarmament." *Philosophy and Public Affairs* 12 (1983): 255-60.

Kemp, Kenneth. "Nuclear Deterrence and the Morality of Intentions." *The Monist* 70 (1987): 276-97.

Kunkel, Joseph. "Right Intention, Deterrence, and Nuclear Alternatives." *Philosophy and Social Criticism* 10.3/4 (1984): 143-55.

Lackey, Douglas. "Ethics and Nuclear Deterrence." *Moral Problems*. 3rd ed. Ed. James Rachels. New York: Harper & Row, 1979.

---. "Missiles and Morals: A Utilitarian Look at Nuclear Deterrence." *Philosophy and Public Affairs* 11 (1982): 189-231.

Somerville, John. "Nuclear 'War' is Omnicide." Fox and Groarke: 3-9. (See Pt. IV).

Sterba, James, ed. *The Ethics of War and Nuclear Deterrence*. Belmont, CA: Wadsworth, 1985.

Volbrecht, Rose Mary. "Nuclear Deterrence: Moral Dilemmas and Risks. *Philosophy and Social Criticism* 10.3/4 (1984): 133-41.

Wasserstrom, Richard. "Noncombatants, Indiscriminate Killing, and the Immorality of Nuclear War." Fox and Groarke: 39-49. (See Pt. IV).

---. "War, Nuclear War, and Nuclear Deterrence: Some Conceptual and Moral Issues." *Ethics* 95.3 (1984/5): 424-444.

Werner, Richard. "The Immorality of Nuclear Deterrence." *Political Realism and International Morality*. Eds. Kenneth Kipnis and Diana Meyers. Boulder, CO: Westview, 1987.

---. "Nuclear Deterrence and the Limits of Moral Theory." *The Monist* 70.3 (1987): 357-76.

Williams, Bernard. *Ethics and the Limits of Philosophy*. Cambridge, MA: Harvard University Press, 1985.

Woodward, Beverly. "The Abolition of War." Fox and Groarke: 245-56. (See Pt. IV).

C. Strategic Defense Initiative

Bowman, Robert. *Star Wars: Defense or Death Star?* Chesapeake Beach, MD: Institute for Space and Security Studies, 1985.

Bundy, McGeorge, George Kennan, Robert McNamara, and Gerard Smith. "The President's Choice: Star Wars or Arms Control." *Foreign Affairs* 63.2 (1984/5): 277-92.

Center for Defense Information. "Star Wars: Vision and Reality." *The Defense Monitor* 15.2 (1986). Washington, D.C.

Council on Economic Priorities. *Star Wars: The Economic Fallout.* Cambridge, MA: Ballinger, 1987.

Graham, Daniel. *High Frontier: There is a Defense Against Nuclear War.* New York: Tom Doherty Associates, 1983.

Gray, Colin. "Strategic Defense, Deterrence, and the Prospects for Peace." *Ethics* 95.3 (1984/5): 659-72.

Graybosch, Anthony. "SDI: Tactics and Ethics." *Philosophy in Context* 15 (1986): 62-72.

Hoekema, David. "The Moral Status of Nuclear Deterrent Threats." *Social Philosophy and Policy* 3.1 (1985): 93-117.

Jastrow, Robert. *How to Make Nuclear Weapons Obsolete.* Boston: Little, Brown, 1985.

Kavka, Gregory. "Critique of Pure Defense." *Journal of Philosophy* 83.11 (1986): 625-33.

---. "Space War Ethics." *Ethics* 95.3 (1984/5): 673-91.

Lackey, Douglas, ed. *Ethics and Strategic Defense: American Philosophers Debate Star Wars and the Future of Nuclear Deterrence.* Belmont, CA: Wadsworth, 1989.

Parnas, David. "Software Aspects of Strategic Defense Systems." *American Scientist* 13 (1985): 432-44.

Reagan, Ronald. Speech in *The Star Wars Controversy: An International Security Reader.* Eds. Steven Miller and Stephen Van Evera. Princeton, NJ: Princeton University Press, 1986: 257-58.

Schonsheck, Jonathan. "Confusion and False Advertising of the Strategic 'Defense' Initiatives." *International Journal on World Peace* 3 (1988): 69-107.

---. "Philosophical Scrutiny of the Strategic 'Defense' Initiatives." *Journal of Applied Philosophy* 3.2 (1986): 151-66.

Smith, R. Jeffrey. "Star Wars Chief Takes Aim at Critics." *Science* 225.4662 (10 August 1984): 600-602.

Sterba, James. "Just War Theory and Nuclear Strategy." *Analyse & Kritik* (1987): 155-74.

---. "Legitimate Defense and Strategic Defense." *Public Affairs Quarterly* 2.4 (1988).

Teller, Edward. *Better a Shield than a Sword: Perspectives on Defense and Technology.* New York: Free Press, 1987.

Thompson, E.P. "Folly's Comet." *Star Wars: Science Fiction, Fantasy or Serious Probability.* Ed. Thompson. New York: Pantheon, 1985.

Tirman, John, ed. *Empty Promise: The Growing Case against Star Wars.* Boston: Beacon, 1986.

Zuckerman, Solly. *Star Wars in a Nuclear World.* London: William Kimber, 1986.

III. CRITIQUING WAR, PROMOTING PEACE

A. Environmental Concerns

Arkin, William, Frank von Hippel, and Barbara Levi. "The Consequences of a 'Limited' Nuclear War in East and West Germany." Peterson. *Aftermath.*

Colwell, Thomas, Jr. "Ecology and Philosophy." *Philosophical Issues.* Eds. James Rachels and Frank Tillman. New York: Harper & Row, 1972: 355-64.

Committee for the Compilation of Materials on Damage Caused by the Atomic Bombs in Hiroshima and Nagasaki. *Hiroshima and Nagasaki: The Physical, Medical and Social Effects of the Atomic Bombings.* Trans. Eisei Ishikawa and David Swain. New York: Basic Books, 1981.

Committee to Study the Long-Term Worldwide Effects of Multiple Nuclear-Weapons Detonations, Assembly of Mathematical and Physical Sciences, National Research Council. *Long-Term Worldwide Effects of Multiple Nuclear-Weapons Detonations.* Washington, DC: National Academy of Sciences, 1975.

Convey, Curt, Stephen Schneider and Starley Thompson. "Global Atmospheric Effects of Massive Smoke and Dust Injections From a Nuclear War." *Nature* 308.5754 (1 March 1984): 21-25.

Devall, Bill and George Sessions. *Deep Ecology: Living as if Nature Mattered.* Layton, UT: Gibbs M. Smith, 1985.

Ehrlich, Paul, et al. "Long-term Biological Consequences of Nuclear War." *Science* 222 (23 December 1983): 1293-1300.

Ehrlich, Paul, Carl Sagan, Donald Kennedy, and Walter Orr Roberts. *The Cold and the Dark.* New York: Norton, 1984.

Fox, Michael. "Commentary: The Unacceptable Gamble." Fox and Groarke: 107-09. (See Pt. IV).

Garrison, Jim. *The Plutonium Culture: From Hiroshima to Harrisburg.* New York: Continuum, 1981.

Gorz, Andre. *Ecology as Politics.* Trans. Patsy Vigderman and Jonathan Cloud. Boston, MA: South End Press, 1980.

Greene, Owen, Ian Percival, and Irene Ridge. *Nuclear Winter: The Evidence and the Risks.* Cambridge: Polity Press, 1985.

Grinspoon, Lester, ed. *The Long Darkness: Psychological and Moral Perspectives on Nuclear Winter.* New Haven: Yale University Press, 1986.

Harwell, Mark. *Nuclear Winter: The Human and Environmental Consequences of Nuclear War.* New York: Springer-Verlag, 1984.

Harwell, Mark and T.C. Hutchinson. *The Environmental Consequences of Nuclear War.* Vol. II. *Ecological and Agricultural Effects.* New York: John Wiley, 1986.

Heidegger, Martin. "Hebel—Friend of the House." Trans. Bruce Foltz and Michael Heim. *Contemporary German Philosophy.* Vol. 3. Eds. Darrell Christenson, et al. University Park, PA: Pennsylvania State University Press, 1983.

Lackey, Douglas. "The Moral Case for Unilateral Nuclear Disarmament." *Philosophy and Social Criticism* 10.3/4 (1984): 157-71.

London, Julius and Gilbert White, eds. *The Environmental Effects of Nuclear War.* Boulder, CO: Westview, 1984.

National Research Council. *The Effects on the Atmosphere of a Major Nuclear Exchange.* Washington, DC: National Academy Press, 1985.

Peterson, Jeannie, ed. *The Aftermath: The Human and Ecological Consequences of Nuclear War.* New York: Pantheon, 1983.

---. "Scientific Studies of the Unthinkable—The Physical and Biological Effects of Nuclear War." *Ambio* 15.2 (1986): 60-69.

Pittock, A., T. Ackerman, P. Crutzen, M. MacCracken, C. Shapiro, and R. Turco. *The Environmental Consequences of Nuclear War.* Vol. I. *Physical and Atmospheric Effects.* New York: John Wiley, 1985.

Sagan, Carl. "Nuclear War and Climatic Catastrophe." *Foreign Affairs* 62.2 (1983/4): 257-92.

Schweitzer, Albert. *Peace or Atomic War?* New York: Henry Holt, 1958.

Shrader-Frechette, Kristin. "Nuclear Arms and Nuclear Power: Philosophical Connections." Fox and Groarke: 85-100. (See Pt. IV).

Taylor, Paul. *Respect for Nature: A Theory of Environmental Ethics.* Princeton, NJ: Princeton University Press, 1986.

Thompson, Starley and Stephen Schneider. "Nuclear War Reappraised." *Foreign Affairs* 64.5 (1985/6): 981-1005.

Turco, R.P., et al. "Nuclear Winter: Global Consequences of Multiple Nuclear Explosions." *Science* 222 (23 December 1983): 1289-92.

United States Congress. House Committee on Science and Technology, Subcommittee on Investigations and Oversight. *The Consequences of Nuclear War.* New York: Pantheon, 1983.

Wade, Nicholas. *A World Beyond Healing: The Prologue and Aftermath of Nuclear War.* New York: Norton, 1987.

Wasserman, Harvey and Norman Solomon with Robert Alvarez and Eleanor Walters. *Killing Our Own: The Disaster of America's Experience With Atomic Radiation.* New York: Delacorte, 1982.

Zimmerman, Michael E. "Anthropocentric Humanism and the Arms Race." Fox and Groarke: 135-49.

B. Warism and Peacemaking: Philosophical Sources

Aristotle. *Politics.* Trans. Benjamin Jowett. *The Basic Works of Aristotle.* Ed. Richard McKeon. New York: Random House, 1941.

Cady, Duane. *From Warism to Pacifism: A Moral Continuum.* Philadelphia: Temple University Press, 1989.

Collingwood, R.G. *The New Leviathan; or Man, Society, Civilization and Barbarism.* Oxford: Clarendon Press, 1942.

Dewey, John. *Human Nature and Conduct.* New York: Henry Holt, 1922.

---. *Problems of Men.* New York: Philosophical Library, 1946.

Emerson, Ralph Waldo. "War." *The Works of Ralph Waldo Emerson.* 12 vols. Boston: Houghton, Mifflin: 11: 149-76.

Fichte, J.G. *The Science of Rights.* Philadelphia: Lippincott, 1969.

Ginsberg, Robert, ed. *The Critique of War.* Chicago: Henry Regnery, 1969.

Glossop, Ronald. *Confronting War.* Jefferson, NC: McFarland, 1983.

Hartmann, George. "The Strength and Weakness of the Pacifist Position as Seen by American Philosophers." *The Philosophical Review* 53 (1944): 125-44.

Hegel, G.W.F. *Hegel's Philosophy of Right.* Trans. T.M. Knox. Oxford: Clarendon Press, 1942.

Hocking, William. "The Spiritual Effect or Warlessness." *A Warless World.* Ed. Arthur Larson. New York: McGraw-Hill, 1963: 169-72.

Hobhouse, Leonard. *Social Development.* New York: Henry Holt, 1924.

Howie, John. "Our War Problem and the Peacemaker Attitude." *Dialectics and Humanism* 13.4 (1986): 69-77.

Jenkins, Iredell. "The Conditions of Peace." *The Monist* 57 (1973): 505-26.

Kunkel, Joseph. "Just-War Doctrine and Pacifism." *The Thomist* 47.4 (1983): 501-12.

Lentz, Theodore. *Humatriotism.* St. Louis: The Future Press, 1976.

---. *Towards a Science of Peace.* New York: Bookmans, 1961.

Merton, Thomas. "War and the Crisis of Language." Ginsberg.

Mill, John Stuart. "A Few Words on Non-Intervention." *Dissertations and Discussions.* London: John Parker, 1859-75.

Narveson, Jan. "Pacifism: A Philosophical Analysis." Wasserstrom: 63-77. (See Pt. IV).

Nietzsche, Friedrich. *Human, All-Too-Human.* Part I. Trans. Helen Zimmern. Vol. 6 of *The Complete Works of Friedrich Nietzsche.* Ed. Oscar Levy. 18 vols. 1909-1911. New York: Russell & Russell, 1964.

Popper, Karl. *Objective Knowledge.* Oxford: Clarendon Press, 1972.

Rousseau, Jean-Jacques. *The Social Contract.* Trans. Willmore Kendall. Chicago: Henry Regnery, 1954.

Steinkraus, Warren. "War and the Philosopher's Duty." Ginsberg.

Thomas Aquinas, St. *On Law, Morality, and Politics.* Eds. William Baumgarth and Richard Regan. Trans. English Dominican Fathers. Indianapolis: Hackett, 1988.

Wasserstrom, Richard. "On the Morality of War: A Preliminary Inquiry." Wasserstrom: 78-101. (See Pt. IV).

Wells, Donald. *The War Myth.* New York: Western, 1967.

C. Nuclearism and Sexism

Calicott, J. Baird. "Intrinsic Value, Quantum Theory, and Environmental Ethics." *Environmental Ethics*, 7 (Fall 1985): 257-75.

Deikman, Arthur. *The Observing Self: Mysticism and Psychotherapy*. Boston: Beacon, 1983.

Elshtain, Jean Bethke. "Critical Reflections on Realism, Just Wars, and Feminism in a Nuclear Age." Cohen and Lee: 255-72. (See Pt. IV).

Gilligan, Carol. *In A Different Voice: Psychological Theory and Women's Development*. Cambridge: Harvard University Press, 1982.

Gray, Elizabeth Dodson. *Green Paradise Lost*. Wellesley, MA: Roundtable, 1981.

Griscom, Joan. "On Healing the Nature/History Split in Feminist Thought." *Heresies* 4.1.13 (1981): 4-9.

Hartsock, Nancy. "Prologue to a Feminist Critique of War and Politics." Stiehm *Women's Views* 123-50.

Jagger, Alison. "Commentary: Gendered Thinking and Nuclear Politics." Fox and Groarke: 173-76. (See Pt. IV).

---. *Feminist Politics and Human Nature*. Totowa: NJ: Rowman & Allanheld, 1983.

King, Ynestra. "Feminism and Revolt." *Heresies* 4.1.13 (1981): 12-16.

Litke, Robert. "Consciousness, Gender, and Nuclear Politics." Fox and Groarke: 159-72. (See Pt. IV).

Merchant, Carolyn. *The Death of Nature: Women, Ecology and the Scientific Revolution*. New York: Harper and Row, 1980.

Reardon, Betty. *Sexism and the War System*. New York: Teachers College Press, 1985.

Rossi-Landi, Ferruccio. "On Linguistic Money." Trans. Heli Hernandez and Robert Innis. *Philosophy and Social Criticism* 7 (1980): 346-72.

Ruddick, Sara. "Preservative Love and Military Destruction: Some Reflections on Mothering and Peace." *Mothering: Essays in Feminist Theory*. Ed. Joyce Trebilcot. Totowa, NJ: Rowman & Allanheld, 1984: 231-62.

Stiehm, Judith, ed. *Women and Men's Wars*. New York: Pergamon, 1983.

---. *Women's Views of the Political World of Men.* Dobbs Ferry, NY: Transnational, 1984.

Warren, Karen. "Feminism and Ecology: Making Connections." *Environmental Ethics* 9 (Spring 1987): 4-20.

Wilber, Ken. *Up From Eden: A Transpersonal View of Human Evolution.* Boulder, CO: Shambhala, 1981.

Zimmerman, Michael E. "Feminism, Deep Ecology and Environmental Ethics." *Environmental Ethics* 9 (Spring 1987): 21-44.

D. Nuclear Weapons and Democracy

Ball, Desmond. "U.S. Strategic Forces: How Would They Be Used?" *International Security* 7 (1982/83): 31-60.

Belsey, Andrew. "Secrecy, Expertise and Democracy." *Objections to Nuclear Defence.* Eds. Nigel Blake and Kay Pole. London: Routledge, Kegan, Paul, 1984.

Bundy, McGeorge. "Existential Deterrence and Its Consequences." *The Security Gamble: Deterrence Dilemmas in the Nuclear Age.* Ed. Douglas MacLean. Totowa, NJ: Rowman & Allanheld, 1984.

Churchill, R. Paul. "Nuclear Autocracy and Nuclear Paternalism." *Social Philosophy Today.* Ed. James Sterba. New York: Edwin Mellen.

Crain, Gordon and Alexander George. *Force and Statecraft.* Oxford: Oxford University Press. 1983.

Dahl, Robert. *Controlling Nuclear Weapons: Democracy Versus Guardianship.* New Haven: Yale University Press, 1984.

Falk, Richard. "Nuclear Weapons and the Renewal of Democracy." Cohen and Lee: 437-56. (See Pt. IV).

McNamara, Robert. *The Essence of Security.* New York: Harper and Row, 1968.

MacPherson, Crawford. *The Life and Times of Liberal Democracy.* New York: Oxford University Press, 1977.

Markusen, Eric and John Harris. "Nuclearism and the Erosion of Democracy." *Nuclear Weapons and the Threat of Nuclear War.* Eds. Eric Markusen and John Harris. New York: Harcourt, Brace, Jovanovich, 1986.

Neild R. *How to Make Up Your Mind About the Bomb.* London: Andre Deutsch, 1981.

Pringle, Peter and James Spigelman. *The Nuclear Barons.* New York: Holt, Rinehart, and Winston, 1981.

Ransom, Harry Howe. *Can America Survive Cold War?* Garden City, NY: Doubleday, 1963.

Thompson, Dennis. "Philosophy and Policy." *Philosophy & Public Affairs* 14 (1985): 205-18.

Walzer, Michael. "Deterrence and Democracy." *The New Republic* 191 (2 July 1984): 20-21.

E. Nonviolence: Pluralist and Christian Perspectives

Baynes, Kenneth, James Bohman, and Thomas McCarthy, eds. *After Philosophy: End or Transformation?* Cambridge, MA: MIT Press, 1987.

Deming, Barbara. *Revolution and Equilibrium.* New York: Grossman, 1971.

---. *We Can Not Live Without Our Lives.* New York: Grossman, 1974.

Hauerwas, Stanley. *A Community of Character: Toward a Constructive Christian Social Ethic.* Notre Dame, IN: University of Notre Dame Press, 1981.

---. *The Peaceable Kingdom: A Primer in Christian Ethics.* Notre Dame, IN: University of Notre Dame Press, 1983.

Hauerwas, Stanley with Richard Bondi and David Burrell. *Truthfulness and Tragedy: Further Investigations in Christian Ethics.* Notre Dame: University of Notre Dame Press, 1977.

Lonergan, Bernard. *A Third Collection: Papers by Bernard J.F. Lonergan, S.J.* Ed. Frederick Crowe. New York: Paulist Press, 1985.

---. "Aquinas Today: Tradition and Innovation." Lonergan *Third:* 35-54.

---. "Method: Trend and Variations." Lonergan *Third:* 13-22.

---. "Prolegomena to the Study of the Emerging Religious Consciousness of our Time." Lonergan *Third:* 55-73.

---. "Second Lecture: Religious Knowledge." Lonergan *Third:* 129-45.

MacIntyre, Alasdair. *After Virtue.* Notre Dame, IN: University of Notre Dame Press, 1981.

Rajchman, John and Cornel West, eds. *Post-Analytic Philosophy.* New York: Columbia University Press, 1985.

IV. GENERAL WORKS

A. Philosophical Works

Armstrong, William. "The Challenge of Nehemiah." *Perspectives on Peacemaking: Biblical Options in the Nuclear Age.* Ed. John Birnbaum. Ventura, CA: Regal Books, 1984.

Brunk, Conrad. "Realism, Deterrence, and the Nuclear Arms Race." Fox and Groarke: 223-39.

Cady, Duane. "Backing into Pacifism." *Philosophy and Social Criticism* 10.3/4 (1984): 173-80.

Camus, Albert. *Neither Victims nor Executioners.* Trans. Dwight MacDonald. Chicago: World Without War Publications, 1972.

Cohen, Avner and Steven Lee, eds. *Nuclear Weapons and the Future of Humanity: The Fundamental Questions.* Totowa, NJ: Rowman and Allanheld, 1986.

Dewey, John. *Theory of the Moral Life.* New York: Holt, Rinehart and Winston, 1960.

Dreyfus, Herbert and Paul Rabinow. *Michael Foucault: Beyond Structuralism and Hermeneutics.* 2nd ed. Chicago: University of Chicago Press, 1983.

Ford, John C. "The Morality of Obliteration Bombing." Wasserstrom: 15-41.

Fox, Michael and Leo Groarke, eds. *Nuclear War: Philosophical Perspectives.* New York: Peter Lang, 1985.

Gay, William. "Nuclear Discourse and Linguistic Alienation." *Journal of Social Philosophy* 18.2 (Summer, 1987): 42-49.

---. "Nuclear War: Public and Governmental Misconceptions." Fox and Groarke: 11-25.

Gay, William and Michael Pearson. *The Nuclear Arms Race.* Chicago: American Library Association, 1987.

Grovier, Trudy. "Nuclear Illusion and Individual Obligations." *Canadian Journal of Philosophy* 13 (1983): 471-92.

Habermas, Jurgen. *Legitimate Crisis.* Trans. Thomas McCarthy. Boston, MA: Beacon, 1975.

Heidegger, Martin. *Being and Time.* Trans. John Macquarrie and Edward Robinson. New York: Harper & Row, 1962.

---. *Discourse on Thinking.* Trans. John Anderson and E. Hans Freund. New York: Harper & Row, 1966.

---. *On the Way to Language*. Trans. Peter Hertz. New York: Harper & Row, 1971.

Heim, Michael. "A Philosophy of Comparison: Heidegger and Lao Tzu." *Journal of Chinese Philosophy* 11 (1984): 307-35.

Hirschbein, Ron. *Newest Weapons/Oldest Psychology: The Dialectics of American Nuclear Strategy*. New York: Peter Lang, 1989.

Hoekema, David. *Rights and Wrongs: Coercion, Punishment and the State*. Susquehanna University Press, 1986.

Howie, John, ed. *Ethical Principles for Social Policy*. Carbondale, IL: Southern Illinois University Press, 1983.

Kant, Immanuel. *Perpetual Peace*. Trans. Campbell Smith. London: George Allen & Unwin, 1903.

Kavka, Gregory. *Moral Paradoxes of Nuclear Deterrence*. Cambridge: Cambridge University Press, 1987.

---. "Some Paradoxes of Deterrence." *The Journal of Philosophy* 75 (1978): 285-302.

Lackey, Douglas. *Moral Principles and Nuclear Weapons*. Totowa, NJ: Rowman & Allanheld, 1984.

Marcuse, Herbert. *One Dimensional Man*. Boston: Beacon, 1964.

Narveson, Jan. "Getting on the Road to Peace: A Modest Proposal." *Ethics* 95.3 (1984/85): 589-605. Reprinted in Fox and Groarke: 201-15.

National Council of Catholic Bishops. *The Challenge of Peace: God's Promise and Our Response*. Washington, DC: United States Catholic Conference, 1983.

Schell, Jonathan. *The Abolition*. New York: Alfred A. Knopf, 1984.

---. *The Fate of the Earth*. New York: Alfred A. Knopf, 1982.

Schweitzer, Albert. *On Nuclear War and Peace*. Ed. Homer Jack. Elgin, IL: Brethren, 1988.

Smith, Huston. *The Religions of Man*. New York: Harper & Row, 1958.

Sterba, James. "Moral Approaches to Nuclear Strategy." *Canadian Journal of Philosophy* (Supplementary) 12 (1986): 75-109.

Walzer, Michael. *Just and Unjust Wars: A Moral Argument with Historical Illustrations*. New York: Basic books, 1977.

---. "Moral Judgment in Time of War." *Philosophical Issues: A Contemporary Introduction*. Eds. James Rachels and Frank Tillman. New York: Harper & Row, 1972: 276-82.

Wasserstrom, Richard, ed. *War and Morality*. Belmont, CA: Wadsworth, 1970.

Werner, Richard. "Ethical Realism." *Ethics* 93.4 (1982/3): 653-97.

B. Political, Historical and Scientific Works

Caldicott, Helen. *Missile Envy: The Arms Race and Nuclear War.* New York: William Morrow, 1984.

Carnesale, Albert, et al. *Living with Nuclear Weapons.* New York: Bantam, 1983.

Catudal, H. *Nuclear Deterrence: Does it Deter?* Atlantic Highlands, NJ: Humanities Press International, 1986.

Center for Defense Information. "No Business Like War Business." *The Defense Monitor* 16.3 (1987). Washington, D.C.

Cockburn, Andrew. *The Threat: Inside the Soviet Military Machine.* New York: Random House, 1983.

Dyson, Freeman. *Weapons and Hope.* New York: Harper & Row, 1984.

Einstein, Albert. *Ideas and Opinions.* New York: Dell, 1973.

Freedman, Lawrence. *The Evolution of Nuclear Strategy.* New York: St. Martin's, 1981.

Glasstone, Samuel and Philip Dolan, eds. *The Effects of Nuclear Weapons.* 3rd ed. Washington, DC: Government Printing Office, 1977.

Gray, Colin. *Nuclear Strategy and Strategic Planning.* Philadelphia: Foreign Policy Research Institute, 1984.

Kovel, Joel. *Against the State of Nuclear Terror.* Boston, MA: South End Press, 1983.

Lewis, Kevin. "The Prompt and Delayed Effects of Nuclear War." *Scientific American* 241.1 (1979): 35-47.

Lifton, Robert. "Imagining the Real: Beyond the Nuclear 'End'." *The Long Darkness: Psychological and Moral Perspectives on Nuclear Winter.* Ed. Lester Grinspoon. New Haven: Yale University Press, 1986.

Lifton, Robert and Richard Falk. *Indefensible Weapons: The Political and Psychological Case Against Nuclearism.* New York: Basic Books, 1982.

Mandelbaum, Michael. *The Nuclear Question.* Cambridge: Cambridge University Press, 1979.

McNamara, Robert. *Blundering Toward Disaster.* New York: Pantheon, 1987.

Mumford, Lewis. *Technics and Civilization.* New York: Harcourt, Brace, and World, 1934.

Scoville, Herbert, Jr. *MX: Prescription for Disaster.* Cambridge: MIT Press, 1981.

Sharp, Gene. *Making Europe Unconquerable: The Potential of Civilian-Based Deterrence and Defence.* New York: Taylor and Francis, 1984.

---. *National Security Through Civilian Based Defense.* Omaha: Association for Transarmament Studies, 1985.

---. *Social Power and Political Freedom.* Boston, MA: Porter Sargent Publishers, 1980.

Sivard, Ruth Leger. *World Military and Social Expenditures.* Washington, DC: World Priorities, an annual.

United States Congress. Office of Technology Assessment. *The Effects of Nuclear War.* Washington, DC: Government Printing Office, 1979.

United States Congress. Senate Committee on Banking, Housing and Urban Affairs. *Economic and Social Consequences of Nuclear Attacks on the United States.* Washington, DC: Government Printing Office, 1979.

United States Congress. Senate Committee on Foreign Relations, Subcommittee on Arms Control, International Organizations, and Security Agreements. *Analyses of the Effects of Limited Nuclear War.* Washington, DC: Government Printing Office, 1975.

Watzlawick, Paul, John Weakland, and Richard Fisch. *Change: Principles of Problem Formation and Problem Resolution.* New York: Norton, 1974.

Weeramantry, C.G. *Nuclear Weapons and Scientific Responsibility.* Wolfeboro, NH: Longwood Academic, 1987.

York, Herbert. *Making Weapons/Talking Peace.* New York: Basic Books, 1987.

Zuckerman, Solly. *Nuclear Illusion and Reality.* New York: Viking, 1982.

Philosophical Bibliography on War and Peace in the Nuclear Age

William Gay

   This topical bibliography cites selected philosophical sources on war and peace published in English since the atomic bombing of Hiroshima on August 6, 1945—an event that symbolizes the inauguration of the nuclear age. The basic division in this bibliography is between the philosophical literature that specifically addresses nuclear weapons, and the philosophical literature on more general issues of war and peace. Each of the two parts also has the following sections: a. anthologies and special journal issues; b. books; and c. articles. The sections on articles are subdivided under particular topics as well, because of the large number of relevant sources. Throughout the bibliography, my aim has been to organize a wide range of texts so that the reader may easily locate specific types of sources.

   A few further observations regarding this bibliography are in order. First, with only a couple of exceptions, this bibliography excludes all philosophical sources published before 1945, many of which (such as Kant's *Perpetual Peace*) are quite important. However, references to these classical works are readily available in a variety of sources.[1] Second, a selective and topical philosophical bibliography on both nuclear weapons and other post-war writings on war and peace has been lacking.[2] This bibliography attempts to fill this gap. In citing representative samples of the post-war literature, I am fairly selective in the early decades and more thorough for the '80s. Third, this bibliography excludes several types of marginally related sources. For example, I have excluded, with a few exceptions, works on topics like conscientious objection and military service, works that approach issues of war and peace primarily in relation to religion, and works by non-philosophers. Fourth, with the exception of a few particularly noteworthy sources, and for purposes of economy, the sections on articles do not list the individual essays in anthologies and special journal issues. For this reason, the citations of anthologies and special journal issues are particularly important for locating in a single volume a collection of current and relevant essays. Finally, some pertinent sources may have been omitted, and some citations included may have errors. For any later additions and corrections, and especially for information on sources issued since this bibliography has gone to print, interested readers can consult *Concerned Philosophers for Peace Newsletter,* which publishes recent bibliography, as well as book reviews, brief essays, program announcements, and other related news.[3]

I. THE SPECIFIC PROBLEM OF NUCLEAR WEAPONS

A. Anthologies and Special Journal Issues

Blake, Nigel and Kay Pole, eds. *Danger of Deterrence: Philosophers on Nuclear Strategy.* London: Routledge and Kegan Paul, 1983.
---. *Objections to Nuclear Defense: Philosophers on Deterrence.* London: Routledge and Kegan Paul, 1984.
Cohen, Avner and Steven Lee, eds. *Nuclear Weapons and the Future of Humanity.* Totowa, NJ: Rowman and Allanheld, 1986.
Copp, David, ed. *Nuclear Weapons, Deterrence, and Disarmament.* Spec. issue of *Canadian Journal of Philosophy.* Supp. 12 (1986).
Ford, Harold P. and Francis X. Winters, eds. *Ethics and Nuclear Strategy.* Maryknoll, NY: Orbis Books, 1977.
Fox, Michael Allen and Leo Groarke, eds. *Nuclear War: Philosophical Perspectives.* New York: Peter Lang, 1985.
Gay, William C., ed. *Philosophy and the Debate on Nuclear Weapons Systems and Policies.* Spec. issue of *Philosophy and Social Criticism* 10.3-4 (1984).
Goodwin, Geoffrey, ed. *Ethics and Nuclear Deterrence.* New York: St. Martin's, 1982.
Hardin, Russell et al., eds. *Symposium on Ethics and Nuclear Deterrence.* Spec. issue of *Ethics* 95.3 (1985). Rpt. with additions in *Nuclear Deterrence: Ethics and Strategy.* Ed. Russell Hardin et al. Chicago: The University of Chicago Press, 1985.
Hospers, John and James Sterba, eds. *The Ethics of Nuclear Warfare.* Spec. issue of *The Monist* 70.3 (1987).
---. *Philosophical Problems of Space Exploration.* Spec. issue of *The Monist* 71.1 (1988).

Jones, John D. and Marc F. Griesbach, eds. *Just War Theory in the Nuclear Age.* Lantham, MD: University Press of America, 1985.

Lackey, Douglas P., ed. *Ethics and Strategic Defense: American Philosophers Debate Star Wars and the Future of Nuclear Deterrence.* Belmont, CA: Wadsworth, 1989.

Lawler, Philip F., ed. *Justice and War in the Nuclear Age.* Lanham, MD: University Press of America, 1983.

MacLean, Douglas, ed. *The Security Gamble: Deterrence Dilemmas in the Nuclear Age.* Totowa, NJ: Rowman and Allanheld, 1984.

Paul, Ellen Frankel, ed. *Nuclear Rights/Nuclear Wrongs.* Spec. issue of *Social Philosophy and Policy* 3.1 (1985).

Roth, John K., ed. *Nuclear Violence.* Spec. issue of *Journal of Social Philosophy* 18.2 (1987).

Somerville, John, ed. *Soviet Marxism and Nuclear War: An International Debate.* Westport, CT: Greenwood, 1981.

Sterba, James P., ed. *The Ethics of War and Nuclear Deterrence.* Belmont, CA: Wadsworth, 1985.

B. Books

Child, James. *Nuclear War: The Moral Dimension.* New Brunswick: Transaction Books, 1986.

Finnis, John, Joseph M. Boyle, Jr., and Germain Grisez. *Nuclear Deterrence, Morality, and Realism.* Oxford: Clarendon Press, 1987.

Fowler, Corbin. *The Logic of U.S. Nuclear Weapons Policy: A Philosophical Analysis.* Lewiston, NY: The Edwin Mellen Press, 1987.

Gay, William and Michael Pearson. *The Nuclear Arms Race.* Chicago: The American Library Association, 1987.

Green, Philip. *Deadly Logic: The Theory of Nuclear Deterrence.* Columbus Ohio: Ohio State University Press, 1966.

Hampsch, George H. *Preventing Nuclear Genocide.* New York: Peter Lang, 1988.

Hook, Sidney. *The Fail-Safe Fallacy.* New York: Stein and Day, 1963.

Jaspers, Karl. *The Future of Mankind.* Trans. E.B. Ashton. Chicago: The University of Chicago Press, 1961. Trans. of *Die Atombombe und die Zukunft des Menschen.* Munich: R. Piper & Co., 1958.

Kavka, Gregory. *Moral Paradoxes of Nuclear Deterrence.* Cambridge: Cambridge University Press, 1987.

Kenny, Anthony. *The Logic of Deterrence.* Chicago: The University of Chicago Press, 1985.

Lackey, Douglas. *Moral Principles and Nuclear Weapons.* Totowa, NJ: Rowman and Allanheld, 1984.

Nye, Joseph S. *Nuclear Ethics.* New York: Free Press, 1986.

O'Brien, William. *The Nuclear Dilemma and Just War Tradition.* Lexington, MA: Heath, 1986.

Ramsey, Paul. *The Limits of Nuclear War: Thinking About the Do-Able and the Un-Do-Able.* New York: Council on Religion and International Affairs, 1963.

Robinson, Daniel S. *The Pursuit of Conduct.* New York: Appleton-Century-Crofts, 1948. [Pages 161-93.]

Russell, Bertrand. *Common Sense and Nuclear Warfare.* London: Allen and Unwin, 1959.

---. *Has Man A Future?* New York: Simon and Schuster, 1962.

Schweitzer, Albert. *Peace or Atomic War?* New York: Henry Holt and Co., 1958.

Smith, T[homas] V[ernor]. *Atomic Power and Moral Faith.* Claremont, CA: Claremont College, 1946.

Teilhard de Chardin, Pierre. *The Future of Man.* Trans. Norman Denny. New York: Harper & Row, 1964. [Pages 140-54.]

Walters, Gregory J. *Karl Jaspers and the Role of "Conversion" in the Nuclear Age.* Lanham, MD: University Press of America, 1988.

Weinberger, David. *Nuclear Dialogues.* New York: Peter Lang, 1987.

C. Articles

1. Conceptual and Metaphysical Analyses

Coulborn, Rushton. "Survival of the Fittest in the Atomic Age." *Ethics* 57.4/Part I (1947): 235-58.

Dewey, John. "Dualism and the Split Atom: Science and Morals in the Atomic Age." *The New Leader* 28 (Nov. 1945): 1+. Rpt. in *Concerned Philosophers for Peace Newsletter* 7.1 (1987): 5-7.

Flew, Anthony. "The Rationality of Arms Races." *Journal of Applied Philosophy* 3 (Oct. 1986): 245-53.

Gay, William C. "Myths About Nuclear War: Misconceptions in Public Beliefs and Governmental Plans." *Philosophy and Social Criticism* 9.2 (1982): 115-44.

Gay, William C. and Marysia Lemmond. "A Bibliography on Philosophy and the Nuclear Debate." *Journal of Social Philosophy* 18.2 (1987): 50-60.

Glossop, Ronald J. "Teaching About Nuclear War." *Teaching Philosophy* 10.2 (1987): 141-86.

Goodin, Robert E. "Disarming Nuclear Apologists." *Inquiry* 28.2 (1985): 153-76.

Govier, Trudy. "Nuclear Hardware and Power: The War of Perceptions." *Canadian Journal of Philosophy* 17.4 (1987): 749-66.

---. "Nuclear Illusion and Individual Obligations." *Canadian Journal of Philosophy* 13.4 (1983): 471-92.

Heim, Michael. "Reason as a Response to Nuclear Terror." *Philosophy Today* 28.4/4 (1984): 300-07.

Lee, Steven. "A Course on the Morality of Nuclear Weapons." *Teaching Philosophy* 72 (1984): 115-28.

Santoni, Ronald E. "Nuclear Insanity and Multiple Genocide." *Toward the Understanding and Prevention of Genocide.* Ed. Israel W. Charny. Boulder, CO: Westview Press, 1984. 147-53.

Schilpp, Paul Arthur. "The Abdication of Philosophy." *Kant Studien* 46 [c. 1955]: 480-95.

Schorstein, Joseph. "The Metaphysics of the Atom Bomb." *Philosophical Journal* 5 [c. 1962]: 33-46.

Schroeder, Steven. "Metaphysics in the Dark: Thinking About War and What Will Suffice." *International Journal of Philosophy* 4 (Spr. 1988): 59-63.

Smithka, Paula. "Heidegger and Nuclear Weapons." *Concerned Philosophers for Peace Newsletter* 7.1 (1987): 8-10.

Sterba, James P. "Between MAD and Counterforce: In Search of a Morally and Strategically Sound Nuclear Defense Policy." *Social Theory and Practice* 12.2 (1986): 173-99.

Zimmerman, Michael. "Humanism, Ontology, and the Nuclear Arms Race." *Research in Philosophy and Technology.* Eds. Paul T. Durban and Carl Mitchan. Vol. 6. Greenwich, CT: Jai Press, 1983. 157-72.

2. Deterrence, Strategic Defense, and Related Themes

Benn, S.I. "Deterrence or Appeasement: Or, On Trying to Be Rational About Nuclear War." *Journal of Applied Philosophy* 1 (Mar. 1984): 5-20.

Cohen, Avner. "Lackey on Nuclear Deterrence: A Public Policy Critique on Applied Ethical Analysis." *Ethics* 97.2 (1987): 457-72.

Farrell, Daniel M. "Strategic Planning and Moral Norms: The Case of Deterrent Nuclear Threats." *Public Affairs Quarterly* 1.1 (1987): 61-77.

Gauthier, David. "Deterrence, Maximization, and Rationality." *Ethics* 94.3 (1984): 474-95.

Graybosch, Anthony. "SDI: Tactics and Ethics." *Philosophy in Context* 15 (1985): 62-72.

---. "Star Wars: Close Encounters of the Worst Kind." *Cogito* (Dec. 1985): 1-20.

Hardin, Russell. "Unilateral Versus Mutual Disarmament." *Philosophy and Public Affairs* 12.3 (1983): 236-54.

Hoekema, David A. "Intentions, Threats, and Nuclear Deterrence." *The Applied Turn in Contemporary Philosophy.* Eds. Michael Brodie, Thomas Attig, and Nicholas Rescher. Bowling Green: Bowling Green State University, 1983. 111-25.

Hughes, M.W. "Nuclear Deterrence and Moral Argument." *International Journal of Moral Social Studies* 2 (Sum. 1987): 119-46.

Kavka, Gregory S. "Deterrence, Utility and Rational Choice." *Theory and Decision* 12 (Mar. 1980): 41-60.

---. "Doubts About Unilateral Nuclear Disarmament." *Philosophy and Public Affairs* 12.3 (1983): 255-60.

---. "Some Paradoxes of Deterrence." *The Journal of Philosophy* 75.6 (1978): 285-302.

Lackey, Douglas P. "Disarmament Revisited: A Reply to Kavka and Hardin." *Philosophy and Public Affairs* 12.3 (1987): 261-65.

---. "Ethics and Nuclear Deterrence." *Moral Problems.* Ed. James Rachels. New York: Harper and Row, 1975. 332-45.

---. "Missiles and Morals: A Utilitarian Look at Nuclear Deterrence." *Philosophy and Public Affairs* 11.3 (1982): 189-231.

---. "Moral Principles and Strategic Defense." *Philosophical Forum* 18 (Fall 1986): 1-7.

---. "Taking Risks Seriously." *Journal of Philosophy* 83.11 (1986): 633-40.

Lee, Steven. "Moral Vision of Strategic Defense." *Philosophical Forum* 18 (Fall 1986): 15-20.

---. "Morality, the SDI, and Limited Nuclear War." *Philosophy and Public Affairs* 17.1 (1988): 15-43.

Morris, Christopher W. "The Ethics of Nuclear Deterrence: A Contractarian Account." *Ethics, Theory and Practice.* Eds. Manuel Velasquez and Cynthia C. Rostankowski. Englewood Cliffs, NJ: Prentice-Hall, 1985. 203-13.

Myers, David B. "Understanding and Evaluating Strategic Defense." *Public Affairs Quarterly* 1.1 (1987): 43-60.

Plous, S. "Modeling the Nuclear Arms Race as a Perceptual Dilemma." *Philosophy and Public Affairs* 17.1 (1988): 44-53.

Schonsheck, Jonathan. "Hostages or Shields: An Alternative Conception of Noncombatants and Its Implications as Regards the Morality of Nuclear Deterrence." *Public Affairs Quarterly* 1.1 (1987): 21-34.

---. "Philosophical Scrutiny of the Strategic 'Defense' Initiatives." *Journal of Applied Philosophy* 3.2 (1986): 151-66.

Shaw, William H. "Nuclear Deterrence and Deontology." *Ethics* 94.2 (1984): 248-60.

---. "On the Morality of Nuclear Deterrence." *Journal of Applied Philosophy* 2 (Mar. 1985): 41-52.

---. "Threatening the Irrational: The Puzzle of Nuclear Deterrence." *Cogito* 3 (Dec. 1985): 21-37.

Shue, Henry. "Morality of Offense Determines the Morality of Defense." *Philosophical Forum* 18 (Fall 1986): 8-14.

Stevenson, Leslie. "Is Nuclear Deterrence Ethical?" *Philosophy* 61.236 (1986): 193-214.

Wolff, Robert Paul. "Maximization of Expected Utility as a Criterion of Rationality in Military Strategy and Foreign Policy." *Social Theory and Practice* 1.1 (1970): 99-111.

3. Just-War Theory, Morality, and Social Responsibility

Camus, Albert. "After Hiroshima: Between Hell and Reason." Trans. by Ronald E. Santoni. *Concerned Philosophers for Peace Newsletter* 7.2 (1987): 4-5. Rpt. in *Philosophy Today* 32.1/4 (1988): 77-78. Trans. of Editorial *Combat* (8 August 1945). Rpt. Albert Camus. *Essais.*

Churchill, Robert P. "Nuclear Arms as a Philosophical and Moral Issue." *Annals, AAPSS* 469 (Sept. 1983): 46-57.

Dombrowski, Daniel. "Gandhi, Sainthood, and Nuclear Weapons." *Philosophy East and West* 33.4 (1983): 401-06.

Fox, Michael Allen. "Nuclear Weapons and the Ultimate Environmental Crisis." *Environmental Ethics* 9 (Sum. 1987): 157-79.

Gay, William C. and Ronald E. Santoni. "Philosophy and the Contemporary Faces of Genocide: Multiple Genocide and Nuclear Destruction." *Genocide: A Critical Bibliographical Review.* Ed. Israel W. Charny. London: Mansell Publishing Ltd., 1988. 172-90.

Geller, Ann and David Weinberger. "What Can Philosophers Do?" *PANDORA* (Sept. 1981): 1-2. [Redesignated as *Concerned Philosophers for Peace Newsletter* 1.1 (1981).]

Jameson, Andrew. "Toward a Post-Nuclear Ethos." *Concerned Philosophers* n. 5 (Aug. 1983): 1-2. [Redesignated as *Concerned Philosophers for Peace Newsletter* 3.1 (1983).]

Quirk, Michael J. "Just War Theory, Nuclear Deterrence, and Reason of State." *The International Journal of Applied Philosophy* 3 (Fall 1986): 51-59.

Robinson, Daniel S. "A Philosophy for the Atomic Age." *The Philosophical Review* 55 (July 1946): 377-403.

Roszak, Theodore. "A Just War Analysis of Two Types of Deterrence." *Ethics* 73.2 (1963): 100-09.

Santoni, Ronald E. "'Just War' and Nuclear Reality." *Philosophy Today* 29.3/4 (1985): 175-90.

---. "Philosophers and the Nuclear Threat: An Introduction to Camus' 'After Hiroshima: Between Hell and Reason'." *Philosophy Today* 32.1/4 (1988): 75-76.

Wells, Donald. "How Much Can 'The Just War' Justify?" *Journal of Philosophy* 66.23 (1969): 819-29.

4. Political Assessments

Benoit-Smullyan, Emile. "An American Foreign Policy for Survival." *Ethics* 56.4 (1946): 280-90.

Hook, Sidney. "Bertrand Russell Retreats." *The New Leader* 41 (July 7-14, 1958): 25-28.

---. "A Foreign Policy for Survival." *The New Leader* 41 (April 7, 1958): 8-12.

---. "A Free Man's Choice." *The New Leader* 41 (May 26, 1958): 10-12.

Lackey, Douglas P. "The Curse at the Cruise." *Concerned Philosophers for Peace* n. 12 (Dec. 1985): 1-2. [Redesignated as *Concerned Philosophers for Peace Newsletter* 5.2 (1985).]

---. "Russell's Contribution to the Study of Nuclear Weapons Policy." *Russell* 4 (Win. 1984): 243-52.

Myers, David B. "The Legalist Paradigm and MAD." *International Journal of Applied Philosophy* 2 (Spr. 1985): 19-32.

Narveson, Jan. "Why Doves Should Love the Cruise." *Concerned Philosophers for Peace* n. 11 (Apr. 1985): 1-3. [Redesignated as *Concerned Philosophers for Peace Newsletter* 5.1 (1985.]

Neyer, Joseph. "Is Atomic-Fission Control A Problem For Organizational Technique?" *Ethics* 57.4/Part I (1947): 289-96.

Russell, Bertrand. "Freedom to Survive." *The New Leader* 41 (July 7-14, 1958): 23-25.

---. "How to Avoid the Atomic War." *Common Sense* 14 (Oct. 1945): 3-5.

---. "Man's Peril From the Hydrogen Bomb." *The Listener* 32 (Dec. 30, 1954): 1135-36.

Seckel, Al. "Russell and the Cuban Missile Crisis." *Russell* 4 (Win. 1984): 253-61.

II. GENERAL ISSUES IN WAR AND PEACE

A. Anthologies and Special Journal Issues

Beck, Lewis White, ed. *Philosophy of War.* Spec. issue of *The Monist* 57.4 (1973).

Betz, Joseph, ed. *Deterring or Limiting War.* Spec. issue of *Journal of Social Philosophy* 19.1 (1988).

Cohen, Marshall, Thomas Nagel, and Thomas Scanlon, eds. *War and Moral Responsibility.* Princeton, NJ: Princeton University Press, 1974.

Dialectics and Humanism 9, 11, 12, 13 (Aut. 1982-Aut. 1986).

Ginsberg, Robert, ed. *The Critique of War: Contemporary Philosophical Explorations.* Chicago: Henry Regnery, 1969.

Held, Virginia, Sidney Morgenbesser, and Thomas Nagel, eds. *Philosophy, Morality, and International Relations.* London: Oxford University Press, 1974.

Kainz, Howard, ed. *Philosophical Perspectives on Peace: An Anthology of Classical and Modern Sources.* Athens: Ohio University Press, 1988.

Roberts, Adam, ed. *Civilian Resistance as a National Defense.* Baltimore: Penguin, 1969.

Shaffer, Jerome A., ed. *Violence: Award Winning Essays in the Council for Philosophical Studies Competition.* New York: David McKay, 1971.

Wakin, Walham M., ed. *War, Morality and the Military Profession.* 2nd ed. Boulder, CO: Westview Press, 1986.

Wasserstrom, Richard A., ed. *War and Morality.* Belmont, CA: Wadsworth, 1970.

Woods, Martin T. and Robert Buckenmeyer, eds. *The Morality of War and Peace.* Santa Barbara, CA: Intelman Books, 1974.

B. Books

Arendt, Hannah. *On Violence.* New York: Harcourt, Brace and World, 1969.

Aronson, Ronald. *The Dialectics of Disaster: A Preface to Hope.* London: Verso, 1983.

Bok, Sissela. *Strategy of Peace.* New York: Pantheon, 1989.

Bondurant, Joan. *Conquest of Violence: The Gandhian Philosophy of Conflict.* Rev. ed. Berkeley: University of California Press, 1965.

Borman, William. *Gandhi and Non-Violence.* Albany, NY: SUNY Press, 1986.

Brock, Peter. *Twentieth-Century Pacifism.* London: Van Nostrand-Rein, 1970.

Cady, Duane L. *From Warism to Pacifism: A Moral Continuum.* Philadelphia: Temple, 1989.

Camus, Albert. *Neither Victims nor Executioners.* Trans. Dwight MacDonald. New York: Continuum, 1980. Trans. of serial essays in *Combat* in Fall, 1946.

Cox, Gray. *The Ways of Peace: A Philosophy of Peace as Action.* New York: Paulist Press, 1986.

Cox, Richard H. *Locke on War and Peace*. Oxford: Clarendon Press, 1960.

Ewing, Alfred Cyril. *The Individual, the State, and World Government*. New York: Macmillan, 1947.

Friedrich, Carl Joachim. *Inevitable Peace*. Cambridge: Harvard University Press, 1948.

Gallie, W.B. *Philosophers of Peace and War: Kant, Clausewitz, Marx, Engels and Tolstoy*. London: Cambridge University Press, 1978.

Gandhi, M.K. *Non-Violent Resistance (Satyagraha)*. New York: Schocken, 1951.

Glossop, Ronald J. *Confronting War: An Examination of Humanity's Most Pressing Problem*. 2nd ed. Jefferson, NC: McFarland & Company, 1987.

Gray, J. Glenn. *The Warriors: Reflections on Men in Battle*. New York: Harper & Row, 1970.

Holmes, Robert L. *On War and Morality*. Princeton, NJ: Princeton University Press, 1989.

Horsburgh, H.J.N. *Non-Violence and Aggression: A Study of Gandhi's Moral Equivalent of War*. London: Oxford University Press, 1968.

Howlett, Charles F. *The Troubled Philosopher: John Dewey and the Struggle for World Peace*. Port Washington, NY: Kennikat Press, 1977.

Huxley, Aldous. *Science, Liberty and Peace*. London: Chatto & Windus, 1947.

Johnson, James Turner. *Can Modern War Be Just?* New Haven, CT: Yale University Press, 1984.

---. *Just War Tradition and the Restraint of War: A Moral and Historical Inquiry*. Princeton: Princeton University Press, 1981.

Lackey, Douglas P. *The Ethics of War and Peace*. Englewood Cliffs, NJ: Prentice Hall, 1989.

Naess, Arne. *Gandhi and the Nuclear Age*. Totowa, NJ: The Bedminster Press, 1965.

O'Brien, William V. *The Conduct of Just and Limited War*. New York: Praeger, 1981.

Paskins, Barrie, and Michael Dockrill. *The Ethics of War*. Minneapolis: Minnesota University Press, 1979.

Phillips, Robert. *War and Justice*. Norman, OK: University of Oklahoma Press, 1984.

Puri, Rashi-Sudha. *Gandhi On War and Peace.* New York: Praeger, 1986.

Ramsey, Paul. *The Just War: Force and Political Responsibility.* New York: Charles Scribner's Sons, 1968.

---. *War and the Christian Conscience: How Shall Modern War Be Conducted Justly?* Durham, NC: Duke University Press, 1961.

Russell, Bertrand. *War Crimes in Vietnam.* London: Allen & Unwin, 1967.

Sartre, Jean-Paul. *On Genocide: And a Summary of the Evidence and the Judgments of the International War Crimes Tribunal* (by Arlette El Kaim-Sartre). Boston: Beacon Press, 1968.

Shannon, Thomas A. *What Are They Saying About War and Peace?* New York: The Paulist Press, 1983.

Sharp, Gene. *Making the Abolition of War a Realistic Goal.* New York: Institute of World Order, 1980.

---. *The Politics of Non-Violent Action.* Boston: Sargent, 1973.

Somerville, John. *The Peace Revolution: Ethos and Social Process.* Westport, CT: Greenwood Press, 1975.

---. *The Philosophy of Peace.* 2nd ed. New York: Liberty Press, 1954.

Stevenson, William R., Jr. *Christian Love and Just War: Moral Paradox and Political Life in St. Augustine and His Modern Interpreters.* Macon, GA: Mercer University Press, 1987.

Teichman, Jenny. *Pacifism and the Just War.* New York: Blackwell, 1986.

Tucker, Robert Warren. *The Just War: A Study in Contemporary American Doctrine.* London: Oxford University Press, 1960.

Walzer, Michael. *Just and Unjust Wars.* New York: Basic Books, 1977.

Wells, Donald A. *War Crimes and Laws of War.* Washington, D.C.: University Press of America, 1984.

---. *The War Myth.* Indianapolis: Bobbs-Merrill, 1967.

Yoder, John. *When War Is Unjust: Being Honest in Just War Thinking.* Minneapolis, MN: Augsburg Press, 1984.

C. Articles

1. Ethics and the Role of Philosophy

Allen, Joseph L. "The Relation of Strategy and Morality." *Ethics* 73.2 (1963): 167-78.

Anscombe, Elizabeth. "War and Murder." *Nuclear Weapons: A Catholic Response.* Ed. Walter Stein. New York: Sheed and Ward Inc., 1961. 45-62.

Ginsberg, Robert. "Philosophical Activity and War." *Philosophy and Phenomenological Research* 33.2 (1972): 174-85.

Grisez, Germain G. "Moral Objectivity and the Cold War." *Ethics* 70.4 (1960): 291-305.

Klingberg, Frank L. "Human Dignity and Modern War." *Philosophical Forum (Dekalb)* 10 (Sum. 1971): 53-82.

Mavrodes, George I. "Conventions and the Morality of War." *Philosophy and Public Affairs* 4 (Win. 1975): 117-31.

Morrow, Glenn R. "The Distinctive Contributions of Philosophy to the Issues of Peace." *Ethics* 56.4 (1946): 273-79.

Nagel, Thomas. "War and Massacre." *Philosophy and Public Affairs* 1 (Win. 1972): 123-44.

Somerville, John. "Human Dignity, Human Rights, and War." *Philosophical Forum (Dekalb)* 10 (Sum. 1971): 1-30.

Supek, Ivan. "The Task of Philosophy Today." *Philosophy and Phenomenological Research* 24.1 (1963): 117-24.

Wasserstrom, Richard A. "Three Arguments Concerning the Morality of War." *The Journal of Philosophy* 65.19 (1968): 578-89.

2. Just War

Brown, Lucy. "Intentions in the Conduct of the Just War." *Intention and Intentionality.* Ed. Cora Diamond. Ithaca: Cornell University Press, 1979. 133-45.

Kunkel, Joseph C. "Just-War Doctrine and Pacifism." *The Thomist* 47.4 (1983): 501-12.

O'Brien, William. "Just War, Limited War and Vietnam." *Journal of Social Philosophy* 4.1 (1973): 16-18.

O'Connor, D. Thomas. "A Reappraisal of the Just-War Tradition." *Ethics* 84.2 (1974): 167-73.

Prangle, Thomas L. "A Note on the Theoretical Foundation of the Just War Doctrine." *The Thomist* 43.3 (1979): 464-473.

Purtill, Richard L. "On the Just War." *Social Theory and Practice* 1.3 (1971): 97-102.

Steinkraus, Warren. "Does It Make Any Sense to Talk About A 'Just War'?" *Journal of Social Philosophy* 5.1 (1974): 8-11.

---. "Wellbank, Wells and War Talk." *Journal of Social Philosophy* 8.2 (1977): 7-10.

Struckmeyer, Frederick R. "The 'Just War' and the Right of Self-Defense." *Ethics* 82.1 (1971): 48-55.

Wellbank, J[oseph] H. "It Makes Good Sense to Talk About a 'Just War'." *Journal of Social Philosophy* 6.3 (1975): 1-3.

---. "Why We May Still Talk About a Just War." *Journal of Social Philosophy* 8.2 (1977): 4-6.

Wells, Donald A. "'Just War' Talk and 'Good Sense'." *The Journal of Social Philosophy* 7.2 (1976): 5-8.

---. "Vietnam and the Calculation of Atrocities." *The Journal of Social Philosophy* 4.3 (1973): 13-16.

3. Law and the Rules of War

Alexander, Laurence A. "Self-Defense and the Killing of Non-Combatants: A Reply to Fullinwider's 'War and Innocence'." *Philosophy and Public Affairs* 5.4 (1976): 408-15.

Brandt, R.B. "Utilitarianism and the Rules of War." *Philosophy and Public Affairs* 1 (Win. 1972): 145-65.

Ford, John C., S.J. "The Morality of Obliteration Bombing." *Theological Studies* 5 (1944): 261-309.

Fullinwider, Robert K. "War and Innocence." *Philosophy and Public Affairs* 5.3 (1975): 90-97.

Gottlieb, Gidon. "The New International Law: Toward the Legitimation of War." *Ethics* 78.2 (1968): 144-47.

Hare, R.M. "Rules of War and Moral Responsibility." *Philosophy and Public Affairs* 1 (Win. 1972): 166-81.

Kilzer, Ernest. "Natural Law and Natural Rights." *Proceedings of the American Catholic Philosophical Association* 24 (1950): 156-60.

Levinson, Sanford. "Responsibility for Crimes of War." *Philosophy and Public Affairs* 2 (Spr. 1973): 244-73.

Rommen, Heinrich. "Natural Law and War-Crimes-Guilt." *Proceedings of the American Catholic Philosophical Association* 24 (1950): 40-57.

Schwartzenberger, Georg. "Functions and Foundations of the Laws of War." *Archiv fur Rechts und Sozialphilosophie* 44 (1958): 351-64.

Sharp, Malcolm. "Aggression: A Study of Values and Law." *Ethics* 57.4/Part II (1947): 1-39.

---. "The Limits of Law." *Ethics* 61.4 (1951): 270-283.

Wasserstrom, Richard. "The Laws of War." *The Monist* 56.1 (1972): 1-19.

4. Marxism

Burlatskii, F.N. "The Philosophy of Peace." *Soviet Studies in Philosophy* 22 (Sum. 1983): 3-25.

Dmitriev, A.P. "Knowledge of War and Peace as an Element of World View." *Soviet Studies in Philosophy* 17 (Win. 1978-79): 3-24.

Dobroselski, Marjan. "Philosophy and Peace." *Soviet Studies in Philosophy* 12 (Spr. 1974): 5-18.

Fedoseev, P.N. "Contemporary Sociological Theories Concerning War and Peace." *Soviet Studies in Philosophy* 1 (Win. 1962-3): 3-24.

Frolov, I.T. et al. "In the Struggle For Peace and Social Progress." *Soviet Studies in Philosophy* 14 (Fall 1975): 3-21 and 15 (Spr. 1977): 3-24.

Grzegorczyk, Andrzej. "The Moral Basis for Peace: The Absolute Value of the Human Individual." *Dialectics and Humanism* 1 (Win. 1974): 19-28.

Kondratkov, T.R. "Sociophilosophical Aspects of the Problem of War and Peace." *Soviet Studies in Philosophy* 14 (Win. 1975-76): 24-43.

Kovalev, A.M. "War and Revolution." *Soviet Studies in Philosophy* 4 (Fall 1965): 43-49.

Krasin, Iu A. "Peaceful Coexistence and International Cooperation." *Soviet Studies in Philosophy* 1 (Spr. 1963): 36-43.

Kuczynski, Janusz. "Philosophical Problems of War and Peace." *Dialectics and Humanism* 1 (Win. 1974): 29-46.

Parsons, Howard L. "Creative Exchange and Peaceful Coexistence Between States." *Revolutionary World* 4/5 (1973): 114-25.

---. "Some Human Roots of Inhuman War." *Revolutionary World* 4/5 (1973): 22-42.

Riepe, Dale. "Idealist Philosophy and the Blueprints for Peace." *Revolutionary World* 6 (1974): 1-19.

Sandhuhler, Hans. Jorg. "The Problem of Peace and the Tasks of Philosophy." *Soviet Studies in Philosophy* 21 (Spr. 1983): 77-101.

Sredin, G.V. "The Problems of War and Peace Today." *Soviet Studies in Philosophy* 21 (Win. 1982-83): 68-90.

5. Nonviolence, Pacifism and Peace

Benjamin, Martin. "Pacifism for Pragmatists." *Ethics* 83.3 (1973): 196-213.

Federman, Joel. "Toward a World Peace Movement." *Humanities in Society* 5 (Win.-Spr. 1985): 137-48.

Freund, Norm. "Peace: A Myriad of Meanings." *Personalist Forum* 4 (Spr. 1988): 7-12.

Garver, Newton. "What Violence Is." *The Nation* 209 (June 24, 1968): 817-22. Rpt. and rev. in *Philosophy for a New Generation*. Ed. A.K. Bierman and J.A. Gould. 4th ed. New York: Macmillan, 1981. 217-28.

Glossop, Ronald. "War, Peace, and Justice." *Journal of Social Philosophy* 11.1 (1980): 9-11.

Hart, Charles A. "Metaphysics of Man's Nature and Peace." *The New Scholasticism* 21 (July 1947): 229-42.

Horsburgh, H.J.N. "The Distinctiveness of Satyagraha." *Philosophy East and West* 19.2 (1969): 171-80.

Ihara, Craig K. "In Defense of a Version of Pacifism." *Ethics* 88.4 (1978): 369-374.

Knight, Kathy. "Cultural Roots of a Peace Paradigm." *Personalist Forum* 4 (Spr. 1988): 13-26.

Lefort, Claude. "The Idea of Peace and the Idea of Humanity." *Diogenes* 135 (Fall 1986): 11-28.

Long, Wilbur. "The Philosophical Bases of Peace." *The Personalist* 27.1 (1946): 16-28.

Margolis, Joseph. "The Concepts of War and Peace." *Social Theory and Practice* 6.2 (1980): 209-26.

Narveson, Jan. "Is Pacifism Consistent?" *Ethics* 78.2 (1968): 148-50.

---. "Pacifism: A Philosophical Analysis." *Ethics* 75.4 (1965): 259-71.

---. "Violence and War." *Matters of Life and Death.* Ed. Tom Regan. New York: Random House, 1980. 109-47.

Okolo, C.B. "Philosophy and Peace." *Indian Philosophical Quarterly* 12 (July-Sep. 1985): 287-95.

Regan, Tom. "A Defense of Pacifism." *Canadian Journal of Philosophy* 2.1 (1972): 73-86.

Ryan, Cheyney C. "Self-Defense, Pacifism, and the Possibility of Killing." *Ethics* 93.3 (1983): 508-24.

Scheler, Max. "The Idea of Peace and Pacifism, Part I." *The Journal of the British Society for Phenomenology* 7 (Oct. 1976): 154-56.

Searles, Herbert L. "Social Conditions of Peace." *The Personalist* 27.2 (1946): 153-64.

Smith, F.J. "Peace and Pacifism." *Max Scheler (1874-1928) Centennial Essays.* Ed. Manfred S. Frings. The Hague: Nijhoff, 1974. 85-100.

Tanase, Alexander. "Humanism and Philosophy of Peace in the Context of Modern Civilization." *Philosophie et Logique* 18 (1974): 85-93.

Thompson, Merritt Moore. "Educating For Peace." *The Personalist* 27.2 (1946): 141-52.

Weilgart, Wolfgang. "A Peace Philosophy." *The Personalist* 28.1 (1947): 21-26.

West, Ranyard. "Fixed Laws of the Mind and Their Control in the Interests of Peace." *Synthese* 6 (July-Aug. 1947): 176-81.

Whitman, M. Jay. "Is Pacifism Self-Contradictory?" *Ethics* 76.4 (1966): 307-08.

Wijesekera, O.H. DeA. "The Concept of Peace as the Central Notion of Buddhist Social Philosophy." *Archiv fur Rechts und Sozialphilosophie* 46 (1960): 493-501.

6. Philosophers on Specific Philosophers

Avineri, Shlomo. "The Problems of War in Hegel's Thought." *Journal of the History of Ideas* 22.4 (1961): 463-74.

Bertman, Martin A. "Nietzsche on the State: Paideia and War." *Systematics* 11 (June 1973): 54-59.

315

Christensen, William and John King-Farlow. "Aquinas and the Justification of War." *The Thomist* 35 (Jan. 1971): 95-112.

Cywar, Alan. "John Dewey: Toward Domestic Reconstruction, 1915-1920." *Journal of the History of Ideas* 30.3 (1969): 385-400.

Doppelt, Gerald. "Walzer's Theory of Morality in International Relations." *Philosophy and Public Affairs* 8.1 (1978): 3-26.

Gilbert, Alan. "Marx on Internationalism and War." *Philosophy and Public Affairs* 7.4 (1978): 346-69.

Hartmann, George W. "The Strength and Weaknesses of the Pacifist Position As Seen by American Philosophers." *The Philosophical Review* 53 (Mar. 1944): 125-44.

Miller, Kenneth E. "John Stuart Mill's Theory of International Relations." *Journal of the History of Ideas* 22.4 (1961): 493-514.

Monasterio, Xavier. "Camus and the Problem of Violence." *The New Scholasticism* 44.2 (1970): 199-222.

Renna, Thomas. "The Idea of Peace in the Augustinian Tradition: 400-1200." *Augustinian Studies* 10 (1979): 105-11.

Schwarz, Wolfgang. "Kant's Philosophy of Law and International Peace." *Philosophy and Phenomenological Research* 23.1 (1962): 71-80.

Smith, Constance I. "Hegel on War." *Journal of the History of Ideas* 26.2 (1965): 282-85.

Smith, Tony. "Idealism and People's War: Sartre on Algeria." *Political Theory* 1.4 (1973): 426-49.

Stern, Alfred. "Kant and Our Time." *Philosophy and Phenomenological Research* 16.4 (1956): 531-39.

Wolfe, Bertram D. "'War is the Womb of Revolution': Lenin 'Consults' Hegel." *Antioch Review* 16.2 (1956): 190-197.

7. Theoretical and General Analyses

Bernard, Jessie. "Prescriptions for Peace: Social-Science Chimera?" *Ethics* 59.4 (1949): 244-56.

Bunge, Mario. "A Decision Theoretic Model of the American War in Vietnam." *Theory and Decision* 3 (June 1973): 323-338.

Chagin, B.A. "The Role of the Subjective Factor in the Prevention of War." *Soviet Studies in Philosophy* 3 (Win. 1964-65): 3-8.

Delos, J.T. "The Dialectics of War and Peace." *The Thomist* 13 (July 1950): 305-24 and 13 (Oct. 1950): 528-66.

Durfee, Harold A. "War, Politics, and Radical Pluralism." *Philosophy and Phenomenological Research* 35.4 (1975): 549-58.

Eckstein, Harry. "On the Etiology of Internal Wars." *History and Theory* 4.2 (1965): 133-63.

Flew, Anthony. "Ideology and 'A New Machine of War'." *Philosophy* 51.198 (1976): 447-53.

Ghyka, Matila. "Philosophy—War and Peace." *The Personalist* 27.1 (1946): 29-40.

Ginsberg, Robert. "Five Problems in the Philosophy of War." *Journal of Social Philosophy* 9.3 (1978): 8-12.

Gowin, D., Bob and Debra Dyason. "Epistemology and Peace Studies: Is Peace Knowledge Possible?" *Proceedings of the Philosophy of Education Society* 41 (1985): 35-60.

Gray, J. Glenn. "We Must Love One Another Or Die." *The Personalist* 33.3 (1952): 266-72.

Greene, Maxine. "Is Peace Knowledge Possible?" *Proceedings of · the Philosophy of Education Society* 41 (1985): 477-80.

Hare, R.M. "Philosophy and Practice: Some Issues in War and Peace." *Philosophy* 18 (Supp. 1984): 1-16.

Horowitz, Irving Louis. "Unilateral Initiatives: A Strategy in Search of a Theory." *Diogenes* 50 (Sum. 1965): 112-27.

Romanell, P. "The Ways of Peace and War." *The Personalist* 26.4 (1945): 349-54.

Somerville, John. "Democracy and the Problem of War." *The Humanist* 27 (May-June 1967): 77-80.

---. "World Authority: Realities and Illusions." *Ethics* 76.1 (1965): 33-46.

Tahsin, Ud-Din M. "The Philosophy of War." *The Pakistan Philosophical Journal* 7 (1960): 263-74.

Tauber, Kurt P. "Nationalism and Self-Defense." *Ethics* 62.4 (1952): 275-81.

Notes

This work was supported in part by funds from the Foundation of the University of North Carolina at Charlotte and from the State of North Carolina.

[1]See, for example, F.S. Northedge, "Peace, War, and Philosophy," *The Encyclopedia of Philosophy,* ed. Paul Edwards. 8 Vols. (New York: Macmillan Publishing Co., Inc., 1967), 6: 63-66.

[2]A selective bibliography on post-war sources through the '60s, most of which are philosophical, can be found in Robert Ginsberg (see this bibliography, II, B). An attempt at a complete philosophical bibliography on the philosophical sources on nuclear weapons can be found in William C. Gay and Marysia Lemmond (see this bibliography, I, C, 1), and a selective annotated philosophical bibliography on nuclear weapons can be found in William C. Gay and Ronald E. Santoni (see this bibliography, I, C, 3). An attempt at a complete philosophical bibliography on general issues in war and peace since 1980 can be found in Reginald Raymer, "Recent Bibliography by Philosophers on Nuclear and Peace Issues" *Concerned Philosophers for Peace Newsletter* 7.2 to date (1987-).

[3]*Concerned Philosophers for Peace Newsletter* can currently be ordered at $10 per year (or $1 per year for students and low income persons) from Laurence Bove, Walsh College, 2020 Easton Street, NE, North Canton, OH 44720. Currently, copies of back issues are available at $2 per copy and can be ordered from me at the Dept. of Philosophy, University of North Carolina at Charlotte, Charlotte, NC 28223.

318

INDEX

Abdalla, Georges 121
Abrahamson, James A. 153
Acheson, Dean 41
aggressiveness 2, 62, 85, 159, 164, 221, 232
Allison, Graham 36, 42, 46, 47
Anderson, Walter 249
androgeny 231, 247
androcentrism 245
Andropov, Yuri 249
anthropocentrism 198, 204, 245
anthropocide 173, 182, 184
Anti-Appeasement Alliance 87, 90
apocalypse 38, 39, 41, 190, 191, 193
arete 268, 269
Aristotle 110, 174, 217, 226, 269
arms
  control 73, 101, 148, 149, 203,
    limitation 50, 54, 80, 230
    reduction 50, 53, 65, 73, 83
  race 5, 15, 18, 69, 85-87, 90, 97, 103-105, 107-108, 113, 136, 144, 175,
    200, 204, 230-231, 241-245, 258
Armstrong, Sen. William 161, 168
Aron, Raymond 103
Aspin, Les 84
Aufhebung 233, 239, 245, 246, 247
Augustine of Hippo 174, 217, 226
authentic living 199
autochthony 175, 231, 245, 246, 247, 248, 249
autonomy 133, 175, 209, 264, 274
  as dissociation of self from others, nature, etc. 230-249

B-1 5, 154
Ball, Desmond 255
Bay of Pigs 26, 38, 42
Bayle, Pierre 109, 110
Begin, Menachem 118
Belsey, Andrew 257-258, 265
Bettelheim, Bruno 234
bifurcator 62-65
Birks, John 190
biocide 189, 191

blockade 28, 35, 42, 43, 45, 47
Bloembergen, Nicholas 152
Bove, Laurence 9, 176-177, 267f
Brandt, Richard 138
Brezhnev, Leonid 85
Bronfenbrenner, Urie 105
Brunk, Conrad 103, 142, 145
budget 18, 83, 84, 85, 87, 90, 161, 224
  defense budget 18, 79, 84, 87, 224
  federal budget 79, 85
Buchsbaum, Solomon 151
Bundy, McGeorge 263, 266
Burrell, David 267-268, 277
Bush, George 83, 84, 92

Cady, Duane 9, 174, 176, 193, 202, 207ff, 214
Caldicott, Helen 106
Camus, Albert 3, 39, 47, 115, 180, 189
Capehart, Senator Homer E. 27
capital 85, 198
capitalism 5, 15, 17-18, 69-80, 81, 82
Carlucci, Frank 83
Carter, Jimmy 83
Castro, Fidel 41
Catholic Bishops, U.S. Conference of 1, 5, 17, 18, 69, 161, 168
Challenger 93, 195, 197
Chamberlain, Neville 36
change
  first-order change 138-140, 143-144
  second-order change 139-141, 143-144
Chernobyl 173, 195-197
Chodorow, Nancy 239, 251
Chomsky, Noam 36, 42, 46
Churchill, R. Paul 9, 175-176, 255ff
civil rights 212, 272, 273
civilians 98, 108, 119, 120, 125, 142, 218, 227, 261
classism 175, 231, 236, 243, 244, 248
Clausewitz, Carl von 52, 53, 54, 117
Cockburn, Andrew 105
Cohen, Marshall 103, 112
Collingwood, R.G. 220
Collins, Joseph 74, 81
Colwell, Thomas B., Jr. 194

combatants 106, 134, 183
Concerned Philosophers for Peace 2
consequentialism 7, 69, 72, 73, 74, 75, 97, 98, 133
conservative use of morality 99-100, 139, 140-141, 142-144
constitution 224, 256, 264, 274
constitutional government 176, 256
Copernican revolution 207
Cordier, Andrew 21, 22
Cromwell, Oliver 40
cruise missiles 5, 90, 105, 150, 154, 161
Crutzen, Paul 190
Cuba 13-14, 21-32, 35, 40-45, 223, 271
Cuban Missile Crisis 5, 13-14, 21-32, 35-36, 40-45, 47
Ex-Comm 25, 26, 28, 35, 36, 41, 42, 43, 45, 47

Dahl, Robert 260, 265, 266
Dahlke, Karl 151
Daly, Mary 244
defense budget 18, 79, 84, 87, 224
civilian-based defense 109
Strategic Defense Initiative 16, 55, 97, 100, 101, 105, 147, 149,
    150, 121, 153
umbrella defense 148, 149, 150, 153
point defense 148, 149, 153
defense strategies 148-156, 159-168, 261
Deikman, Arthur 238, 240, 243, 251, 252
DeLauer, Richard 150
delivery systems 6, 50, 150, 262
Deming, Barbara 176, 267, 270-273, 274, 276, 277, 278
democracy 2, 9, 15, 120, 136, 175, 176
under threat by possession of nuclear weapons 255-264
democratic 15, 80, 82, 104, 118, 137, 175, 176, 224,
    258, 261, 262, 264
  control 173, 256, 259
  principle 260
  process 259, 260
deontology 7, 51, 97, 98, 129, 134, 135, 176, 267, 268
determinism 4, 5, 15, 104, 274
deterrence
  as a national nuclear policy 16-17, 55, 65-66, 159-67, 168, 169
  Marxist view 15, 49-54, 101
  literature on 8, 142, 145
  moral evaluation of 6-7, 99, 129-137, 140, 159-167, 169

  on democratic control of nuclear policy 255-266
Devall, Bill 197
Dewey, John 128, 138, 220, 212, 214
  dialectic 13, 15, 35, 36, 39, 40, 41, 226
  differential uncertainty 261, 262
  differentiation 232, 238, 239, 247, 249
Dilthey, Wilhelm 274
  disarmament 17, 19,49, 53, 65, 130, 131, 137, 142, 161, 164,
    167, 202
  discrimination 118, 134, 218
  dissociation 175, 231-237, 238, 248
Dobrynin, Anatoly 21
Dostoyevsky, Fyodor 179, 186
Dresden 106, 117, 119
Dürrenmatt, Friedrich 41
Dworkin, Gerald 133-134, 138

Easlea, Brian 104
ecocide 230, 236, 245
ecosystem 190, 198, 230, 236, 246
Einstein, Albert 141, 145, 274
El Salvador 223
Eliot, T.S. 229
Ellsberg, Daniel 45, 48
Emerson, Ralph Waldo 174, 219, 220, 225
environment
  as a concern of philosophy 173, 189, 194-200, 251, 252
  as exploiting nature (see naturism) 231
  contrasted with genetic effects on humans 56, 61, 63, 66, 134
  effects of Chernobyl 174, 195-196
  how the sexes view the environment 237-238
  potential damage from nuclear destruction 9, 190-91, 200, 201
ethics
  area of philosophy 1, 7-9, 97, 173
  applied to Cuban Missile Crisis 24, 29, 31
  applied to environmental philosophy 194-200
  applied to strategic defense 154-156, 159-168
  conservative and radical approaches to morality 139-144
  ethics and peacemaking 174, 204-213, 267
  subjective aspects 6, 97-98, 99, 104, 135-137
  narrative approach to 267-273
  toward transforming the world 17, 58-60, 246-249
  ethical theory 99, 129-136, 139-144, 268

deontological 7, 51, 97, 98, 129, 134, 135, 176,
just war 7, 97, 99, 100, 129, 134, 147, 155, 156, 157, 174,
  211, 214, 220, 268, 274
  utilitarian 51, 129, 130, 132, 133, 134, 135, 137,
  consequentialist 7, 69, 72, 73, 74, 75, 97, 98, 133
ethnocentric violence 61
evil empire 1, 19, 56, 58, 62, 63, 69, 88, 92, 202, 208, 231, 233, 250
evolution 4, 17, 56, 62, 63, 69, 88, 92, 112, 202, 208, 231, 233, 250
existential death 179ff
expanding circle 17, 58-60, 66

Falk, Richard A. 105, 108, 126, 265
falsifiability 19, 88, 89, 90, 91, 92, 93
falsification rule 88
fast-burn booster 153
feminism 175, 199, 212, 237-249, 250, 272-273
Ferguson, Charles 234, 235, 250
Feyerabend, Richard 104
Feynman, Richard 93
Fichte, J. G. 174, 219, 227
first strike 44, 129, 140, 154, 222, 226, 262
first use 45, 147, 228
Firth, Roderick 138
Fisher, Ronald 105
flak jacket 162
  teflon suit 163-165
Ford, Gerald 194, 195, 202, 230
Ford, John 194
Foucault, Michel 235, 251
Fox, Michael 105, 195, 203, 204
freedom 3, 4, 5, 16, 18, 19, 69, 71, 72, 75, 77, 81, 85, 86, 90, 91, 93,
  109,110,116, 125, 136, 167, 205, 209, 256, 269, 274
free trade 73, 75, 77, 80
Freud, Sigmund 38, 180, 234, 235
Friedman, Milton 18, 69, 72-78, 81
Friedman, Rose 73-78, 81
Fulbright, Senator William 27

Gandhi, Mahatma 125
Gardiner, Robert 105
Garrison, Jim 196, 203
Gauthier, David 102
Gay, William 9, 10, 173-174, 189ff, 200, 201, 204, 241, 242

gender 208, 211, 212
  female 233, 234, 235, 238, 243, 244, 247
  feminism 175, 199, 212, 237-249, 250, 272-273
  male 104, 233, 234, 235, 238, 239, 242 244, 253
  masculine 175, 233, 234, 235, 236, 239, 242, 243,
Gellman, Barton 108
genocide 51, 53, 119, 184, 230
Ghazali, Abu Humanid Muhammad 109
Gilligan, Carol 237, 238, 251
Ginsberg, Robert 9, 173
glasnost 4, 84, 86, 89, 249
global 17, 18, 18, 49, 60, 80, 85, 87, 130, 131, 142, 163 , 166,
  174, 175, 176, 191, 195, 198, 200, 225, 230, 245, 247, 248, 249, 253
Glossop, Ronald 221, 228
Gorbachev, Mikhail 4, 54, 83, 87, 88, 91, 295
Gorz, Andre 198, 203, 204
government
  aid 74, 75, 80
  and national security 26, 27, 167, 219, 271
  and power 37, 74, 78, 80, 117, 221, 243
  guarantor of individual freedom and personal security 167,209, 217
  principles of democracy 176, 256
  minimalist conception of 69ff, 76
  rights and obligations of 14, 80, 185, 208-209, 224, 264
  rival conceptions of 15, 92, 112
  records and officials 24, 195, 260
  relation to economic freedom 16, 18, 72, 79, 112
  source of institutionalized violence 115-125
  world governance 76-78, 142
Graham, Daniel O. 149, 157
Grant, George 109
Gray, Colin 169, 266
Gray, Elizabeth Dodson 234, 241, 250-252
Griscom, Joan 244
Groarke, Leo 6, 97-98, 99, 103ff, 195
gross national product 222
group selection 56, 61, 65
gulag 86

Habash, George 118
Habermas, Jurgen 198, 204
Hamilton, Alexander 144
Hampsch, George 5, 15, 49ff

Hardin, Garrett 80, 88, 137, 138
Hare, R. M. 138
Hartman, George W. 214
Hartz, Jerry 158
Harwell, Mark 190, 191, 200, 201
Hauerwas, Stanley 176, 267-270, 273, 276. 277
Hawatmeh, Nayef 118
Hebel, Johannes P. 249, 254
Hegel, G.F.W. 174, 219, 227
Heidegger, Martin 199, 204, 205, 240, 247, 248, 252, 253, 254
  House-Friend 199
Heilbronner, Robert 104
Held, Virginia 71, 81
Hilgartner, Stephen 105
Hiroshima 98, 117, 119, 173, 182, 201, 230, 255
  effects of the bombing 189-193
  comparison to Chernobyl 195-200
Hirschbein, Ron 5, 13, 35ff
Hitler, Adolph 125
Hobbes, Thomas 4, 5, 6, 71, 77, 103, 107, 109, 167, 168
Hobhouse, L.T. 220, 227
Hocking, W. E. 223, 228
Hoekema, David 6, 101, 159ff, 169
Holmes, Robert 6, 98, 115ff
holocaust 42, 49, 60, 119, 123, 222
Hook, Sidney 4
Horney, Karen 234-235, 251
Howie, John 9, 174-175, 217ff
humanicide 51, 53, 226, 228
humatriotism 226, 228
Hume, David 60, 69, 109

ICBMs 149, 150
ideology
  a function of philosophy 3-9, 13-20
  ideologies mitigated by skepticism 97, 103-113
  ideology as affecting ethical judgments 99, 129-137
  libertarian ideology 69-80
  Marxist ideology 49-54
  opening ideologies to falsification 91-93
impeachment 28, 29, 30, 43
in-group 60, 61, 62, 63
inclusive fitness 57, 62

individual selection 57, 58, 62
INF Treaty 8, 87, 90
informed choice 229
interconnectedness 2, 271, 272, 273
imperative 49, 123, 124, 133, 138, 222

James, Jesse 101, 164ff
Jaspers, Karl 4
Jesus Christ 39, 179
just cause 7, 147, 156
just means 147, 154, 155, 156
just war 7, 97, 99, 100, 129, 134, 147, 155, 156, 157, 174, 211, 214, 220, 268, 274
Kahn, Herman 54
Kaiser, the, William II 117
Kant, Immanuel 51, 123, 126, 129, 133, 134, 135, 138, 174, 199, 204, 219, 268, 274
Kavka, Gregory S. 54, 129, 130, 131, 133, 134, 137, 138, 168
Kendall, Henry 153
Kennan, George 103, 107, 108, 110, 113
Kennedy, John 13, 14, 21, 22, 23, 25, 26, 27, 28, 29, 31, 32, 35, 36, 37, 38, 40, 41, 42, 43, 44, 45, 47
Kennedy, Robert 14, 21, 22, 23, 25, 26, 27, 28, 29, 31, 32, 33, 35, 43, 45, 47
Khrushchev, Nikita 35, 41, 42, 43, 44, 45
Kierkegaard, Soren 269, 274
kin selection 57, 58, 62, 65
King, Martin Luther, Jr. 125
King, Ynestra 244, 252, 253
King David Hotel 118, 121, 123
Klein, Kenneth 1ff
Kohl, Helmut 148
Korotich, Vitaly 249
Kovel, Joel 197 198 199 204 205 265
Kremlin 35, 41, 43, 44
Kuhn, Thomas 104
Kunkel, Joseph 1ff, 5, 17-19, 69ff

Lackey, Douglas 66, 130, 131, 133, 134, 137, 138, 192, 193, 202
Lappé, Frances Moore 74, 81, 82
Lebanon 119, 124
Lewis, C. I. 138
Leviathan 77, 144, 167, 227

liberation 3, 4, 5, 118, 120, 125, 191, 270, 271
libertarian 2, 5, 9, 15, 17-19, 69, 70-80, 82, 199
liberty 4, 5, 70, 83, 86, 110, 111, 211. 212
Lifton, Robert Jay 105, 108, 126, 191, 201, 250, 265
Lilienthal, David 38, 46
Litke, Robert 6, 99-100, 113, 139ff
Locke, John 110
Lonergan, Bernard 176, 267, 270, 273-276, 278
loyalty 17, 64, 65, 219, 226, 271

Machan, Tibor 69
Mackie, J. L. 109
MacIntyre, Alasdair 267, 277
MacPherson, C. B. 257, 265
Marcuse, Herbert 37, 46
market model 257, 258
Marx, Karl 4
marxist 2, 4, 5, 7, 9, 15, 49-52, 61, 69, 79
McNamara, Robert 41, 42, 43, 263, 266
Melman, Seymour 115
Merleau-Ponty, Maurice 115, 126
military spending 223
Mill, John Stuart 110, 174, 219, 227
millenarian 13, 14, 16, 36, 38, 39, 40, 45, 46
missile silos 148, 149, 262
Montaigne, Michel 109, 110
Moore, G. E. 138
Morgenthau, Hans 103, 107, 108, 111, 113
Mumford, Lewis 236, 237, 251
Munich Olympics 118
MX 105, 154

Nagasaki 98, 117, 119, 192, 197, 202, 222, 255
comparison to Chernobyl 195-197
narrative 45, 267-273, 276
Narveson, Jan 80, 108, 137
national
  defense 92, 160
  security 25, 45, 47, 51, 84, 101, 154, 162, 168,
    257, 258, 259, 260, 264, 265
  security advisor 84
  security state 256
nationalism 174, 198, 204, 219, 221, 231

NATO 25, 26, 88
naturism 231, 236, 243, 248
Newman, John Henry 274
Nicaragua 98, 112, 120, 122, 223
Nicolas of Autrecourt 109
Niebuhr, Reinhold 103, 107
Nielsen, Kai 111, 113
Nietzsche, Friedrich 220, 227, 274
Nixon, Richard 31, 255
no-first-use 50, 53
noncombatants 106, 111, 133, 134, 138, 141, 145, 183, 198
nonviolence 98, 124-126, 142, 174, 176, 199, 209,
  226, 267-276
Novak, Michael 78, 82
Nozick, Robert 18, 69, 70, 71, 73, 76, 77, 80, 81
nuclear
  autocracy 175
  arguments for and against 257-264
  blackmail 32, 47, 129, 130
  deterrence (see deterrence)
  freeze 8, 50
  holocaust 42, 49, 222
  pacifism 50, 55
  retaliation 140, 159, 160, 261, 263
  tests 8, 88, 90, 196
  threat 105, 154, 198, 265
  war
    effects of nuclear war 189-192
    contrasting moral frameworks 139-144
    experiencing the death of humanity 179-187
    preparing to fight a nuclear war 4-6, 9, 14, 16, 41, 44, 82, 100, 111
    the view of environmental philosophy 194-200
  weapons
    criticizing them 3, 207-213
    deterrent 7, 15, 16-17, 55-56, 65-66, 129-137, 139-144
    form of oppression 229-231ff
    libertarian view 69, 77-80
    Marxist dilemma 49-54
    policy 16, 17, 55, 65, 66, 176, 255, 256, 264
    purpose of having them 5-8, 221-222
    strategic defense 147-156, 159-166
    threat to democratic procedures 255-264
    view of political realism 103-113

winter 173, 182, 189-200, 201
nuclearism 199, 229-249

Office of Technology Assessment 201, 203
Okamura, General 192
omnicide 13, 21, 28, 29, 32, 51, 53, 141, 145, 173, 230
out-group 17, 60, 61, 62, 63

pacifism 4, 6, 7, 97, 98, 160, 161, 197, 199, 202, 208, 209, 211,
    212, 214, 263
paradigm 28, 105, 129, 140, 276
Parnas, David L. 150, 151, 157
Partial Test Ban Treaty 8, 196
Partridge, Ernest 5, 19-20, 83ff
Patel, C. K. N. 152
patriarchy 175, 232, 233, 236, 239, 246
patriotism 28, 104, 221, 226
Pauling, Linus 196
peace
  an alternate to violence 124-126
  contrasting ethical approaches 129-137, 139-144
  criticizing war 207-214
  how would we know it 88-93
  feminist interrelationism 237-247
  global autochthony 247-249
  the peacemaker attitude 217-226
  peacemaking and nonviolence 267-276
peace studies 224
Pearson, Michael 200
perestroika 4, 84, 86, 89
Phillips, Howard 87
philosophy
  an existential approach to nuclear war 179-187
  environmental philosophy 194-200
  falsifying ideological claims 88-93
  generalized empirical method 273-276
  limits of moral theory 129-137
  metaphysical basis of nuclearism 229-237ff
  moral skepticism 108-113
  narrative structure of ethics 267-273
  philosophers' views of war 217-221ff
  three functions 2-10
  two views of the moral framework 139-144

329

Plato 110, 163, 213, 215, 217
Pluralism 3, 257, 267, 269
plutonium 1, 192, 197, 203
political realism 6, 7, 42, 46, 108, 138
Popper, Karl 213, 215
poverty 71, 124, 217
Powers, Gary 27
Powers, General Thomas 44
practical judgment 135
President
  Bush, George 83, 84, 92
  Carter, Jimmy 83
  Ford, Gerald 194, 195, 202, 230
  Kennedy, John 13, 14, 21, 22, 23, 25, 26, 27, 28, 29,
    36, 37, 38, 40, 41, 42, 43, 44, 45, 47
  Nixon, Richard 31, 255
  Reagan, Ronald 1, 19, 31, 41, 82, 83, 84, 85, 87, 90,
    118, 147, 149, 155, 156, 157, 159, 161, 165, 168, 255, 265
  Truman, Harry S. 191, 193
  Wilson, Woodrow 40
prisoner's dilemma 103
propaganda 19, 87, 89, 89, 92, 117, 190
proportionality, criterion of 134
public consensus 261
Pyrrhonean 109

racism 174, 175, 176, 199, 204, 212, 231, 236, 243, 244, 248, 270
radical use of morality 99-100, 139, 141-144
Rand, Ayn 18, 69, 71-72, 74-75, 78-80, 81, 82
Rawls, John 109, 138
Reagan, Ronald 1, 19, 31, 41, 82, 83, 84, 85, 87, 92, 92, 112,
  118, 147, 149, 155, 156, 157, 159, 161, 165, 168, 255, 265
realism, political 4-5, 6, 97-98, 103-113
Realpolitik 103, 105
receptiveness 243
Republic 163, 209, 213, 215
revolution 3, 40, 46, 76, 115, 116, 124, 131, 202, 207, 209,
  217, 223, 271, 277, 278
Reykjavik 165
Riesman, David 234-235, 251
rightful intention 217
rights 27, 31, 62, 63, 70, 78, 88, 90, 91, 93, 138, 209, 212, 227,
  259, 264, 272, 273

risk assessment 131, 132
rootedness 175, 176, 231, 232, 246, 249
Rossi-Landi, Ferrucio 240, 241, 252
Rousseau, J.J. 174, 218, 228
rules 7, 19, 137, 139, 199, 271, 242, 269
Rusk, Dean 21, 22, 23, 24, 26, 29, 30, 32, 44, 48
  Rusk's secret 29, 30, 48
Russell, Bertrand 4, 130

Sagan, Carl 190, 191, 194, 195, 200, 202
Sakharov, Andre 86
Sartre, Jean-Paul 3
satellite 6, 8
saturation bombing 106
Schell, Jonathan 56, 66
Schlesinger, Arthur 41
Schonsheck, Jonathan 5, 16, 55ff
Schopenhauer, Arthur 274
Schweitzer, Albert 196, 203
Scoville, Herbert 108
Scowcroft, Brent 84
Semipalitinsk 90
self-defense 5, 18, 26, 70, 79, 131, 136, 140, 141,
Sessions, George 70, 197, 203
sexism 56, 173, 174, 175, 176, 204, 210, 231, 328, 238, 243,
  244, 248, 270, 272, 273
Sextus Empiricus 109
Shamir, Yitzhak 118
Sharp, Gene 108, 145, 198, 199, 204
Shaw, R. Paul 17, 61-62, 63
Shrader-Frechette, Kristin 195, 202
Singer, Peter 17, 58-65
Sivard, Ruth Leger 203, 228, 229, 250
skepticism 84, 87, 97, 103-113, 152, 162,
Smith, Adam 73
Smith, Huston 241, 252
Smithka, Paula 9, 104, 175, 204, 229ff
socialist 15, 18, 49, 50, 51, 52, 53, 54, 71, 76, 78, 79, 80, 198, 244
sociobiology 55-66
Socrates 2, 180
Somerville, John 5, 13, 14, 21ff, 44, 48, 141, 145
Sorensen, Theodore 21, 24, 31, 36
Soviet Union, 1, 3, 4, 8, 13, 14, 15, 16, 19, 25, 26, 49, 69, 74,

76, 78, 79, 85, 87, 90, 91, 92, 112, 117, 131, 132, 133, 148, 156, 739, 222, 223, 249
Spencer, Herbert 220
Stalin, Joseph 4, 79, 95, 117
statism 18, 78-80
Steele, Ronald 43, 47
Steinkraus, Warren 209-210, 214
Sterba, James 6, 8, 100-101, 140-141, 143, 144, 145, 147ff, 157, 265
Stevenson, Adlai 25, 41
stories 9, 176, 267, 269, 270
Strategic Defense Initiative 16, 55, 97, 100, 100, 105, 147-156, 159-168
Sumner, William Graham 83, 220

Talmon, Jacob 37, 46
Taoism 241
territory 27, 159, 219, 272
terrorism 6, 98, 115-126, 169
  state terrorism 116, 117
  terrorist and soldier compared 119-124
  terror-bombing 119-120
Test Ban Treaty 8, 90, 196
Thant, U. 22
Thatcher, Margaret 148
Thomas Aquinas 174, 217, 226, 278
Thomas, Norman 221
Thompson, Dennis 261-264, 266
Thoreau, Henry David 219
Tolstoy, Leo 180
total war 6, 15, 53
Tower, John 84, 90
treaties 8, 87, 90, 162, 196, 219
  Antarctic 8
  Anti-Ballistic Missile 8
  Antisatellite 8
  Comprehensive Test Ban 8
  INF 8, 87, 90
  Non-Proliferation 8
  Partial Test Ban 8, 196
  SALT I 8
  SALT II 8
  Seabed 8
  START 8

Threshold Test Ban 90
Trident submarines 105, 154
Trotsky, Leon 116, 126
Truman, Harry S. 192, 193
Tuchman, Barbara 37, 46, 47
Turkey 61, 223
  as a factor in the Cuban Missile Crisis 22-27, 32, 42-44

U-2 13, 35, 42
ultimatum 14, 21, 23, 26-32, 35, 43, 44
Unamuno y Jugo, Miguel de 180
UNESCO 224
Union of Concerned Scientists 152
United Nations 22, 30, 44, 83, 118, 224
United States 8, 13, 16, 17, 21, 49, 55, 74, 75, 78, 79, 80, 83,
   84, 85, 86, 90, 92, 101, 120, 131, 160, 166, 171, 173, 201, 204,
   222, 223, 224, 255, 256, 259, 260, 262, 263
United States Institute of Peace 224
utilitarian 51, 129, 130, 132, 133, 134, 135, 137, 176, 267, 268

veil of ignorance principle 143
Vietnam 31, 98, 121, 122, 125, 223, 273
Vigeurie, Richard 87
violence
  coupled with defensive capabilities 164-177
  arising from human nature 16ff, 61-65, 232
  linkage with terrorism 115-126
  versus the peacemaker attitude 213-226
  pluralistic account of nonviolence 267-276
virtue 56, 69, 71, 81, 89, 221, 235, 268, 269, 277

Walzer, Michael 3, 9, 46, 103, 192, 193, 202, 211, 214, 266
war
  conventional 53, 98, 136, 141, 168, 222
  as terrorism 115-126,
  criticizing warism 207-214
  nuclear (see nuclear war)
warism 207-214
Warren, Karen 244, 246-247, 253
wars
  World War I 77
  World War II 117, 120, 131 192, 195, 223
  World War III 15, 35, 53, 125

Warsaw Pact 87, 88,
Wasserstrom, Richard 137, 141, 145, 202, 218, 226, 227
Watzlawick, Paul 139, 144
weapons
  battlefield 52, 196
  strategic 6, 52, 195, 229
  tactical 5, 8, 140, 196, 229
  nuclear (see nuclear weapons)
web-model 242, 24
Webster, William H 118
Weinberger, Caspar 166, 169
Wells, Donald 220, 222, 227, 228
Werner, Richard 6, 98-99, 129ff, 138
Wheeler, John T. 122
White, Ralph 105
Whitehead, Alfred North 207
Wilber, Ken 231-234, 238, 250, 253
Will, George 88
Williams, Bernard 135, 138
Wills, Gary 41, 47
Wilson, E. O. 17, 62
Wilson, Woodrow 40
Wong, Yuwa 17, 61-62, 63
Woodward, Beverly 142, 143, 145
world
  government 18, 73, 76, 77, 80
  hunger 18, 226
  United Nations 22, 30, 44, 83, 118, 224

Zimmerman, Michael E. 204, 239-240, 243, 244, 247, 251
Zuckerman, Solly 157, 266
Zwicker, Barrie 105